Art Quilts Unfolding

50 YEARS OF INNOVATION

Sandra Sider, editor | With contributions by Nancy Bavor, Lisa Ellis, and Martha Sielman

Schiffer Publishing Ltd

4880 Lower Valley Road · Atglen, PA 19310

Other Schiffer Books on Related Subjects:

Art Quilts International: Abstract & Geometric, Martha Sielman, ISBN: 978-0-7643-5220-1

Japanese Contemporary Quilts and Quilters: The Story of an American Import, Teresa Duryea Wong, ISBN: 978-0-7643-4874-7

Dimensional Cloth: Sculpture by Contemporary Textile Artists, Andra F. Stanton, ISBN: 978-0-7643-5536-3

Photographs are courtesy of the artist unless otherwise noted.

Front cover image: *Swimmers,* Tim Harding,
Photo: Petronella Tysma.
Spine image: *Spin Cycle,* Miriam Nathan-Roberts,
Photo: James Dewrance.
Back cover image: (top) *Hall of Memory #10: Guard Bear,*
Nancy Erickson; (bottom) *View from Grand River Road,*
Sue Benner, Photo: Eric Neilsen.
Title page image: *Seedpods,* Laura Wasilowski.

"Schiffer," "Schiffer Publishing, Ltd.," and the pen and inkwell logo are registered trademarks of Schiffer Publishing, Ltd.

Designed by Brenda McCallum

Type set in Marlbel/GeoSlab/Times
ISBN: 978-0-7643-5626-1
Printed in China

Published by Schiffer Publishing, Ltd.
4880 Lower Valley Road
Atglen, PA 19310
Phone: (610) 593-1777; Fax: (610) 593-2002
E-mail: Info@schifferbooks.com
Web: www.schifferbooks.com

For our complete selection of fine books on this and related subjects, please visit our website at www.schifferbooks.com. You may also write for a free catalog.

Schiffer Publishing's titles are available at special discounts for bulk purchases for sales promotions or premiums. Special editions, including personalized covers, corporate imprints, and excerpts, can be created in large quantities for special needs. For more information, contact the publisher.

We are always looking for people to write books on new and related subjects. If you have an idea for a book, please contact us at proposals@schifferbooks.com.

Contents

Susan Shie. *Prayer for the Serpent Mound.*

Acknowledgments

The authors would like to thank Kelly Ellis for her ability to juggle and coordinate the myriad images and fifty years of data; Deidre Adams for photographs that display the glory of the older works and designing all the promotional materials; Cynthia Wenslow for traveling to Bowling Green, Ohio, to interview Penelope McMorris; and to all the museums and collectors who provided images, information, and advice. This book would not have been possible without all of you.

We would also like to thank the generous supporters who made this book and the accompanying exhibitions financially possible. Without you, this book would never have reached completion.

Lead Donors
Nancy Bavor
Helen Blumen
Lisa Ellis
Marvin Fletcher
Maureen Hendricks
Ralph James
Klein Two Bar Limited, LLP
(Frank Klein, General Partner)
Shirley Neary
Dorothy Raymond

Art Patrons
Karey Bresenhan
Eliza Brewster
Carol Churchill
Noriko Endo
John Lefelhocz
Hsin-Chen Lin
Sandra Sider
Jean Tutolo
Adrienne Yorinks

Sustainers
Anonymous
Ludmila Aristova
Teresa Barkley
Peggy Brown
Maryline Collioud-Robert
Linda Colsh
Jane Dunnewold
Nancy Erickson
Caryl Bryer Fallert-Gentry
Dianne Firth
Jim Hay
Harue Konishi
Kristin La Flamme
Judy Langille
Judith E. Martin
Therese May
Eleanor McCain
Alicia Merrett
Pam RuBert
Dinah Sargeant
Joan Schulze
Martha Sielman

Meiny Vermaas-van der Heide
Nancy Whittington
Charlotte Ziebarth

Friends
B. J. Adams
Pamela G. Allen
Tafi Brown
Fenella Davies
Heather Dubreuil
Linda Filby-Fisher
Gloria Hansen
Judy Hooworth
Patricia Kennedy-Zafred
Judith Larzelere
Linda MacDonald
Velda Newman
Alison Schwabe
Daphne Taylor
Nelda Warkentin
Carol Watkins
Hope Wilmarth

Preface

I learned about art quilts for the first time from Studio Art Quilt Associates (SAQA) about ten years ago at the Houston International Quilt Festival. When I saw the SAQA exhibition, I knew I had found "my people." I was a new quilter making original work, but I didn't understand the distinctions between traditional and art quilts. My own work was an expression of my soul, my thoughts, and my inspirations. My work was not at the level of artists in that exhibition, but theirs was the path I wished to follow and they were the people I wished to get to know. So I joined, and here I am today serving as president.

Founded in 1989 by an initial group of fifty artists, SAQA members now number more than 3,500 artists, teachers, collectors, gallery owners, museum curators, and corporate sponsors from around the world. Over the past twenty-nine years, SAQA has evolved into an active and dynamic organization that offers many services to our members as well as to the community at large.

SAQA creates professional development opportunities for the membership that continue to address the ever-changing needs of our artists. From basic studio management to mastering current technology both for business and artistic purposes, SAQA members have support for taking their artwork and career to the next level.

Furthermore, SAQA is dedicated to bringing beautiful, thought-provoking, cutting-edge artwork to venues across the United States and around the world. In addition to mounting museum-quality exhibitions that travel the globe, SAQA documents the Art Quilt Movement through exhibition catalogs and the publication *Art Quilt Quarterly*, available on newsstands. SAQA continues to be the authoritative resource for information on art quilts and the artists who create them.

In this book, we are presenting art quilts that tell a powerful story embodying SAQA's definition of the art quilt: *a creative visual work that is layered and stitched or that references this form of stitched layered structure.* The artists documented here explore the tactile property of their work, the complexity of layers, and the texture achieved through stitching. I hear quilt artists talk about their stitching as slow art, as meditative. Recently a friend said, "As a textile artist, I choose cloth as my medium. Working with cloth connects me to my roots and the needlewomen who came before me. When I touch fabric, I touch my history." Luke Haynes remarks, "Art transforms the comfortably familiar into the visually evocative," and that is what we see in the Art Quilt Movement. Throughout *Art Quilts Unfolding*, you will learn about the artists and their work in their own words, prompted via interviews by members of our selection committee.

The artwork shown in this book is indicative of the art quilts being made at a certain time in the movement's history. Most of the artists featured here made work before the piece(s) shown and afterward through to the present day. I would encourage everyone to go to the artists' websites in order to enjoy the other art quilts that they have created.

I wish to thank the other members of our SAQA committee who worked for many months to assemble the contents of this book: Nancy Bavor, director of the San Jose Museum of Quilts and Textiles; Sandra Sider, editor of *Art Quilt Quarterly* magazine and curator of the Texas Quilt Museum; and Martha Sielman, executive director of SAQA since 2004.

And finally, I would like to thank the generous donors that made this book possible.

—Lisa Ellis, SAQA president, 2016–2018

From the Bed to the Boardroom: Art Quilts

By Janet Koplos

A fifty-year anniversary is a moment to celebrate. The second half of the twentieth century saw an explosion of handmade crafts not only in America but also around the world, and quilts were a leading genre. Organizations, exhibitions, and publications have tracked the expansion of quilts from a functional domestic creative form to one whose ambitions and achievements deserve the distinction—and accolade—of *art* quilts. With the formal appeal of color, pattern, imagery, and tactility, plus association with historic values and with the rising recognition of women's identity and expression, quilts have much to offer. Let's consider both the complications and the accomplishments of the field.

Gaining Recognition

One might think that the quilt could easily find a place in art galleries. It is primarily two-dimensional and can be hung on the wall for solely visual appreciation.

But the object itself, long a domestic craft restricted to home use and a female expression of hand skills, comfort, and pleasure, has been entangled in status restrictions. Fabric occupied the woman's sphere, where it was given high appreciation by other makers but did not have the cultural cachet of paintings. This was at least in part an issue of gender biases, because one could argue that a quilt was always as much a visual choice as a painting, but it was not treated the same way. Tapestries, which *did* make their way into art museums long ago, tended to be designed by men and executed by women, but quilts as an all-woman product were rarely exemplars of wealth and power. When they were included in museums, they tended to be preserved as historical artifacts rather than as personal expression. The few men who have been important in contemporary art quilts are still the exceptions that prove the rule of female dominance of this textile art.

One might assume that this bias has changed or is changing. Let's consider as a talking point two important and widely appreciated exhibitions at the Whitney Museum

of American Art: the 1971 *Abstract Design in American Quilts* and *The Quilts of Gee's Bend* in 2003. It's disappointing that both shows essentially treated the quilts as historic, anonymous, or intuitive achievements rather than regarding them as intentional products of self-aware makers. Amish quilts, honored by the first exhibition, were not accompanied by a vocabulary of theory and boundary pushing, despite their exquisite and intelligent color play. African American quilts displayed in the latter exhibition were certainly recognized by art magazines, and the social history of the quilters in their isolated

Michael James *Moonshadow*. 1979. 100" x 80".
Private collection

southern community made a good human-interest story, but the jazzlike rhythms and complexity of the quilt designs, although praised, were treated as folk wisdom rather than artistic genius. Likewise, *Provocative Parallels*, a 1975 book by Jean Lipman, an expert in folk art and longtime editor of *Art in America* magazine, provided an eye-opening array of works—including quilts—from the nineteenth century that "anticipated the highly sophisticated works of many of the leading artists of the twentieth century." At best the author encouraged openness of consideration rather than hierarchical categories, but the status remained slow to change.

Even decades later, art quilts—meant for display, not utility—by contemporary women artists have tended to be restricted to local exposure in smaller museums, quilt museums, or community centers. They have drawn enthusiastic crowds with their color, engaging surfaces,

and visual themes but have never made the big time. This is a fault, and a flaw, of the art world, connected to its assigning importance to assertiveness and differentness above all else. Contemporary quilts ascribe importance to uniqueness but they also acknowledge traditions, skill, and the value and satisfactions of the artistic materials themselves. These preferences continue to distinguish the quilt field. But there is no logical reason that these characteristics would disqualify the work as art.

One might ask whether part of the reason quilts remain separated is the strong sense of community and identity of the field. That rewarding association pleases the craft world at large, and medium-specific groups in particular. Quilts are most often shown in juried and invitational exhibitions, the most popular of which are specific to the quilt genre. Thus they make their own world easily accessible, but only to those who choose to step inside.

Molly Upton (d.) *Watchtower.* 1975. 90" x 10".
Collection: Museum of Fine Arts, Boston, donation
of the artist's family. Photo: J. Gordon Upton

and did not continue her elements across the expanse. She grouped her fabrics, whether printed or solid, by warm and cold hues (red and blue were favored). She made her quilts jazzy, jarring.

The polarities offered by these two examples—imagery (usually via appliqué) and abstraction (usually via piecing)—have characterized art quilts to this day.

Quilts received a boost from the '70s feminist movement, which celebrated traditionally female arts. Patricia Mainardi published "Quilts: The Great American Art" in *Feminist Art Journal* in 1973. Exhibitions encouraged visual development and technical innovation rather than echoing traditional quilt patterns, however esteemed. Pioneers of the time include M. Joan Lintault and Katherine Westphal.

A Brief History

The emergence of art quilts can be traced to impulse and happenstance in the 1950s. Jean Ray Laury created a quilt as part of a master's degree in art at Stanford University in 1956. It is rectangular and the size of a full-size bed quilt, but otherwise unconventional. Titled *Tom's Quilt*, it consists of polygon blocks of various sizes, each centering on a simplified object or person: an ice cream cone, a telephone pole, a turtle, a girl roller skating, a shower head, a school bus, and a circus tent, to name a few. The colors are varied but not vivid. The irregularity of the blocks makes them look like pictures tacked to a bulletin board. Both the simplification and the subject matter suggest a child's quilt, and the title implies a personal relationship. Unexpectedly, this quilt was seen by the editor of a new magazine, *Woman's Day*, which led to Laury's secondary career as a writer of magazine articles and books that helped popularize quilting.

Radka Donnell, who had trained as a painter, started making quilts in 1965. She considered the activity healing. Like Laury, she focused on personal expression. Her works were entirely abstract. Her works of the mid-'70s, for example, were titled to honor people she knew. Each included a vertical rectangle with a neat edge, but rarely was that regularity constant. She did not work in patterns

Lintault had been exposed to ethnic textiles as a Peace Corps volunteer in Peru and had also lived in Hawaii, which has its own quilting tradition. She began collecting quilts, and her own work was extremely imaginative. She worked in big scale and with unexpected materials. Lintault's *American Graveyard*, included in an important 1976 quilt show at the Museum of Contemporary Crafts in New York (now the Museum of Arts & Design), centers on a rectangular field composed of rows of photo-transfer images of headstones, surrounded by a beige field embellished with hand stitching that includes funeral wreaths in the four corners. Surrounding the entire quilt are rounded tabs printed with skulls. The whole design is essentially monochrome and, one might say, morbid. *Heavenly Bodies* (1979) consists of twenty-five openwork blocks of Xerox transfer photos of naked women and babies. The stuffed blocks were cut out around the body forms, leaving the centers open. They were entirely original and laborious to make.

ABOVE

M. Joan Lintault *Alphabet Soup*. 1998. 98" x 74".
Photo: Dan Overturf

RIGHT

Nancy Crow *March Study*. 1979 ©Nancy Crow. 80" x 80".
Photo: J. Kevin Fitzsimons

Westphal, on the other hand, was particularly known for wearables and for textile printing (photographic transfer processes, especially photocopying). Her *Unveiling of the Statue of Liberty* (1964) incorporated batik, quilting, and embroidery.

These two leaders reflect the broader practice of the time: quilters consumed new materials and techniques voraciously. Novel dyeing methods, silkscreen, opaque pigments, and old photographic methods such as gum bichromate were embraced, and machine quilting became accepted (Donnell had introduced it, for speed and sturdiness). There were any number of innovations. For example, Helen Bitar, in *Mountain in the Morning*, adapted the block organization common to quilts in a manner more like a filmstrip. The '70s saw the same energetic outreach in the fine arts, so that ironically quilt making appeared in the work of mainstream artists such as Lucas Samaras (his series called Reconstructions consists of elaborate, glittery pieced works) and Miriam Schapiro, who pieced fabrics onto her paintings in a technique she called "femmage," and used quilted borders to refer to domestic crafts as a feminist statement.

Nancy Crow and Michael James were part of the second "generation" of quilt artists. Both were trained in another field, began quilting in the 1970s, and had achieved national prominence by the '80s. Crow gave up ceramics for the color possibilities of fabric, at first doing experiments in hue via the traditional Log Cabin pattern. She was also influenced by the texture patterns of tramp art, by Mexican motifs, and by African American improvisational quilts. She has always been known for her dazzling color, and she began to dye fabrics to obtain desired hues and shadings within a color patch that could create a dimensional illusion. In addition to color, Crow is also known for conveying emotion in her quilts. Her works have addressed such subjects as her mother's death, human rights violations she witnessed abroad, and discomfort with isolation. Such messages are conveyed by formal means—color, line, direction, openness or compaction, etc., as well as title suggestions and her own written narratives. She also continues to work with pattern and with purely formal qualities, usually powerfully graphic. Historic quilts were certainly not without sentiment—consider memorial quilts and wedding quilts, for example—yet Crow's expressionist intensity and her sophisticated visual mastery altered expectations of the field. Another of her impressive achievements was following the model of an African American quilter to work more improvisationally by joining sections of fabric without measuring.

James studied painting and printmaking in art school, but by the summer after he completed his MFA degree, he had shifted to quilt making. Unattached to the domestic identity of quilts (although he continues to call himself a quilter rather than evading the issue by using the more general term "artist"), he sewed by machine from the beginning, adopted strip-quilting, a Seminole practice also widespread in traditional African American quilts, and attached front, filler, and back by sewing in the seams of the pieced quilt top, so as to avoid purely decorative tactile lines of stitching. In the beginning James was interested in pattern, color transitions, and figure-ground relationships, all of which are considerations in quilts just as much as in paintings. He gradually grew impatient with grid organization and first tried subverting it with extensions beyond the conventional rectilinear perimeter, but he eventually hit upon shifts of scale, curved seams, and complex arrangements in which color constantly shifts and lines seem to undulate and to interweave illusionistically. These works are festive, active, and perplexing. Later in his career James made a dramatic shift to irregular blocks of imagery, many based on photos, coupled with repetitive patterns that he accomplishes through digital image making. The tone of the later works is sometimes melancholy, provoked by the loss of his wife to early-onset dementia.

A third leading figure of the time who, like Crow and James, continues to be active in the field is Joan Schulze. Her distinguishing features have been a collage aesthetic (applied in various mediums) and an interest in language or other means of storytelling. She is also a published poet and began including text on her quilts in 1968. Among her innovations have been alternative photographic processes including Xerox transfer, two-sided quilts, and drawings using toner on silk. Her collage approach has yielded a practice of layering, and she may break through surfaces for effect. Her use of photography, imperfectly cut blocks, and jumbled or overlapped piecing gives the effect of an overfilled scrapbook. Colors are as elusive as memories.

All three artists have been featured in major solo exhibitions, an important step both in the development of an artist's aesthetic and in the public understanding of the seriousness of the art quilt as a form of expression.

Arturo Alonzo Sandoval *Ground Zero No. 10: Target Babylon IV.* 1989. 96" x 156". Collection: Museum of Arts and Design, New York. Photo: Mary S. Rezny Photography

Expansion of the Field

The boom in quilt making, with the establishment of institutions and publications from coast to coast, included historical research on African American quilt makers. Cuesta Benberry was well known for her expertise on the subject. In 1985 Carolyn Mazloomi founded the Women of Color Quilters Network. This was a movement of trained or self-taught quilters. Among the most admirable quilters of color at the time was Rosie Lee Tompkins, the child of sharecroppers who was working as a maid in San Francisco when her quilting came to the attention of collector Eli Leon. He organized a 1987 exhibition at the San Francisco Craft & Folk Art Museum titled *Who'd a Thought It: Improvisation in African-American Quiltmaking*, drawn from his collection, which traveled for several years. It made an argument for a much looser constructive approach, sprawling or energetic rather than neat and orderly. He said that these makers saw a quilt block as an invitation to variation. Tompkins was included in that exhibition, and subsequently her work was shown in art galleries, presented as a solo exhibition with a catalog at the Berkeley Art Museum, and included in a biennial exhibition at the Whitney Museum of American Art in New York City.

Tompkins's quilts were not scrap fabric constructions. She purchased velvets and other fabrics for depth of color or inviting texture, and synthetics for their sparkle. She seems to have worked improvisationally, with a freedom seldom seen in quilts, taking a block format but allowing it to grow or shrink as colors propel the viewer's vision across the surface. The whole is alive with movement. Her work resembles yet exceeds the Gee's Bend Quilts and is especially important because it was a lone effort that has to be credited to the artist's individual creative imagination.

By 1989, when Yvonne Porcella founded Studio Art Quilt Associates, a limitless range of art quilts was being created. But still, as noted earlier, quilts seemed to propound values other than those of the art world: craft (i.e., skill) remained a difference. While many painters or other artists used the imagery or the notion of a quilt in nonquilt works, where they were most thoroughly engaged, as in Faith Ringgold's early *Story Quilts*, precision and control were not significant parts of the message. She would use pattern (the best-known historical motif) as a frame but would tell her story by painted blocks providing a narrative (even

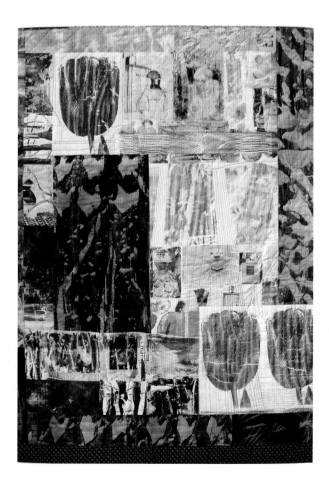

LEFT
Joan Schulze *Aroma*. 1997. 70" x 53".

ABOVE
Nancy Erickson *The Last Dance of Fall*. 1979-1980. 108" x 114". Private collection.
Photo: Jon Schulman

cinematic) sequence. Despite the fact that there had recently been such precision-seeking art movements as photorealism, it seemed as if the quilt was acceptable as a subject or a format, but not so much as a craft process. And perhaps that's still the primary differentiation. Or perhaps the distinction has been more about "tone," with quilts acceptable to the art world being critical, harsh, aggressive, even unpleasant. That's essentially what the art world validates.

The quilt world is rarely so aggressive. Perhaps fabric itself has such associations of comfort that it subdues painful messages. So even when Nancy Erickson is depicting animal images at large scale with environmental allusions, the message is nuanced rather than strident. And far more often the most dazzling achievements are optical, such as Joy Saville's fluttering, impressionistic color expanses, as in *Spring Moss*, or Marilyn Henrion's cubist complication of urban facades. Or they simply embrace beauty, such as Velda Newman's *Hydrangea*. Or they're playful, such as Barbara Watler's *Catch a Falling Star*—with pop imagery, a theatrically framed take on Venus rising from the sea.

Art quilts, whether historical or contemporary, embrace an aesthetic of their own rather than pursue the manner of painting or other mediums. Ideally they strike a chord (familiarity) and take the viewer somewhere unexpected. In Susan Shie's *American Pie: 6 of Potholders*, as in Teresa Barkely's *Midtown Direct*, one sees the accumulation of detail inherent to art quilts. Here it's pictorial, but it can also be abstract, as in Patricia Malarcher's *Ommatidia* or Arturo Sandoval's *Cityscape No. 1*.

Today it's almost hard to say what an art quilt is. It may be fabric or plastic or other materials. It will most likely engage stitching in some way and involve repetition in some way. It may be large or small, rectangular or eccentrically shaped. It typically exploits the color capabilities of its material nature. It may comment on popular culture—as in the Pixeladies' *American Still Life*—or examine its own constituent qualities. It may adopt extraneous objects. But no matter where it's heading, it never dismisses where it has come from. And securely rooted in that tradition, it should be seen in a painting context where its scale and manipulation of color and surface serve the personal conceptions of the maker.

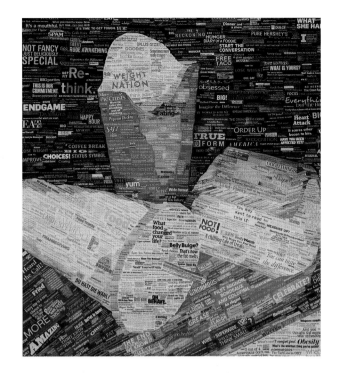

ABOVE
Pixeladies *American Still Life: The Weight of the Nation*. 2012. 60" x 60". Photo: Glenn Marshall

BELOW
Joy Saville *Seminole Study III: Gravity & Grace*. 1982. 92" x 68". Collection: Museum of Arts and Design, New York. Photo: William Taylor

CHAPTER ONE
1960s–1970s: Emergence of the Movement

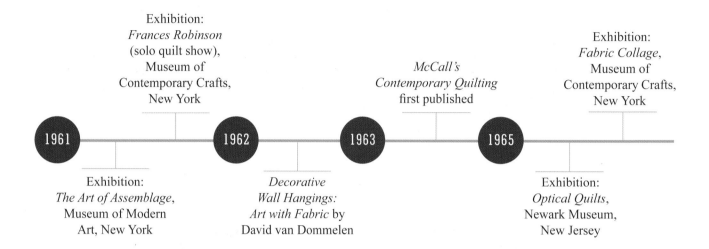

Exhibition:
Frances Robinson
(solo quilt show),
Museum of
Contemporary Crafts,
New York

Exhibition:
Fabric Collage,
Museum of
Contemporary Crafts,
New York

McCall's
Contemporary Quilting
first published

1961   1962   1963   1965

Exhibition:
The Art of Assemblage,
Museum of Modern
Art, New York

Decorative
Wall Hangings:
Art with Fabric by
David van Dommelen

Exhibition:
Optical Quilts,
Newark Museum,
New Jersey

Every contemporary art movement has originated from the efforts of key participants blazing a trail of inspiration and innovation. A core group of approximately sixty artists developed quilts in the studio as a form of fine art during the second half of the twentieth century. Their exhibitions, publications, and studio workshops helped create a groundswell of enthusiasm for contemporary quilt art by the early 1990s, when collectors were becoming aware of their talents and began acquiring art quilts for private and corporate collections. Several authors championed quilt artists and contributed to their reputations, notably Penelope "Penny" McMorris and Robert Shaw. The Houston International Quilt Festival began exhibiting art quilts in the mid-1970s, offering collectors an opportunity to view a plethora of new pieces each year, and beginning in 1979 the biennial juried *Quilt National* exhibitions have showcased the best in contemporary quilt art.

Quilts have long been recognized as outstanding examples of folk art and fine craft, but only during the last few decades have studio quilts been categorized as fine art, partly because the very definition of "art" has been in flux since the 1960s. The mainstream art world in the twentieth century challenged the notion of what could be considered art and what materials could be used to make art. The artists who began making art quilts were often university trained, where craft and "fine art" media were taught side by side.

One goal both of radical feminism and racial politics during the 1970s was to change the character of art, and quilts as art have successfully entered this arena. For example, the quilt was elevated to an art form in the early 1970s through the exhibition *Abstract Design in American Quilts* at the Whitney Museum of American Art, through feminists declaring quilting to be the Great American Art, and through the bicentennial celebration making quilts a very collectible art commodity. Also in the 1970s, Molly Upton was exhibiting her quilts in a Boston gallery alongside works by Christo. And in 1983, Faith Ringgold created her first *Story Quilt*, narrating her viewpoint of the African American experience in an ongoing series that continues today.

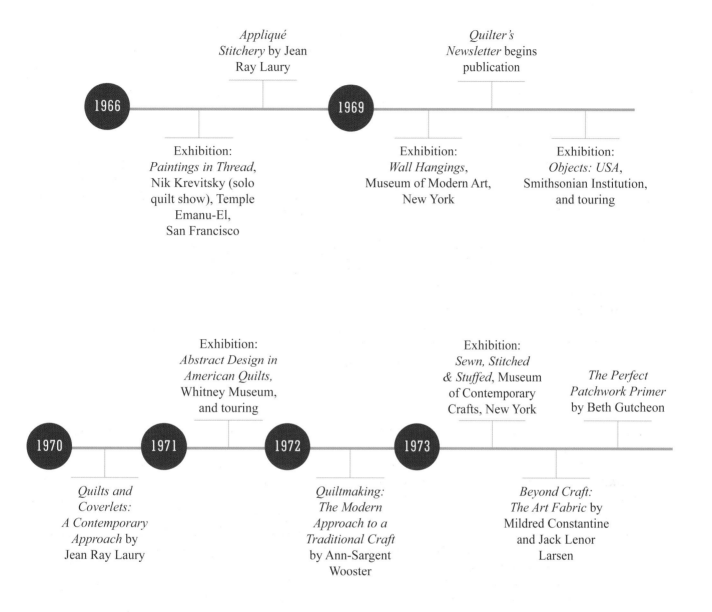

Appliqué Stitchery by Jean Ray Laury

Quilter's Newsletter begins publication

1966

1969

Exhibition: *Paintings in Thread*, Nik Krevitsky (solo quilt show), Temple Emanu-El, San Francisco

Exhibition: *Wall Hangings*, Museum of Modern Art, New York

Exhibition: *Objects: USA*, Smithsonian Institution, and touring

Exhibition: *Abstract Design in American Quilts,* Whitney Museum, and touring

Exhibition: *Sewn, Stitched & Stuffed*, Museum of Contemporary Crafts, New York

The Perfect Patchwork Primer by Beth Gutcheon

1970

1971

1972

1973

Quilts and Coverlets: A Contemporary Approach by Jean Ray Laury

Quiltmaking: The Modern Approach to a Traditional Craft by Ann-Sargent Wooster

Beyond Craft: The Art Fabric by Mildred Constantine and Jack Lenor Larsen

During the 1960s and 1970s, artists who began making quilts as contemporary art came from three directions: the world of stitchery and traditional quilt making; the academy of fine art; and, the alternative academy of fine crafts, especially fibers and ceramics. For many artists, these areas overlapped in productive ways. Moreover, the training in basic design undertaken by artists studying both crafts and art proliferated in the Art Quilt Movement as some of them became workshop teachers. Quilt making in the United States began to acquire a new sophistication.

Several institutions promoting art quilts were founded in the latter 1970s and mid-1980s, including the American Museum of Quilts and Related Arts (today's San Jose Museum of Quilts & Textiles) in 1977, Quilt San Diego (today's Quilt Visions) in 1985, and New England Quilt Museum in Lowell, Massachusetts, in 1987. Two nonprofit professional organizations helped bring momentum and innovation to the movement. Founded in 1977, the Surface Design Association (SDA) provided a platform for the exchange of ideas, methods, and materials in an expansive

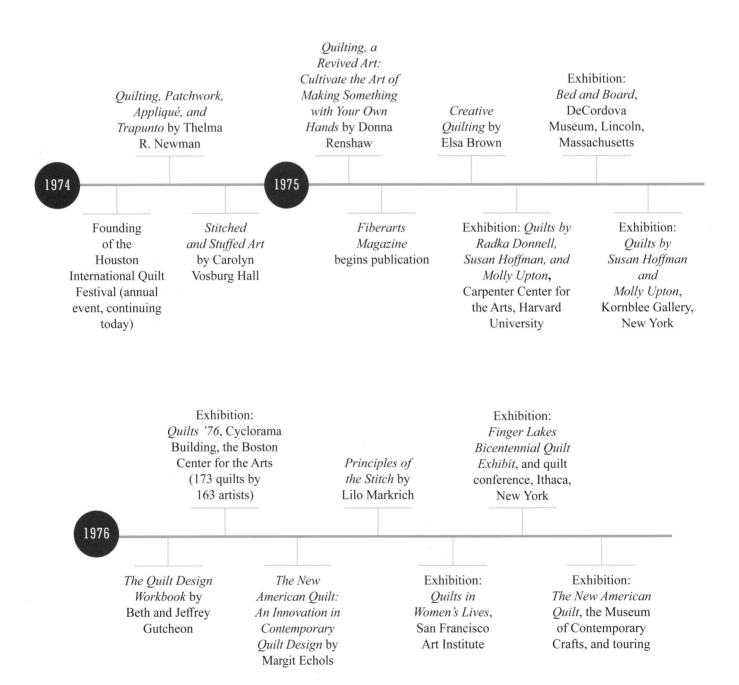

community working in textile media and fiber arts, which from the 1980s included art quilts. The SDA has also encouraged critical dialogues concerning fiber art and new directions in fiber and textiles, including performance and installation art. Founded in 1989, Studio Art Quilt Associates (SAQA) has supported the art quilt through education, numerous exhibitions, professional development, documentation, and publications. SAQA has become known around the world for juried touring exhibitions, accompanied by documentation in the form of gallery-

quality catalogs. By the 1980s, artists working in the quilt medium were exploring materials and processes beyond the commercial fabrics used by traditional makers, and networking to develop exhibition venues and markets for their new art form.

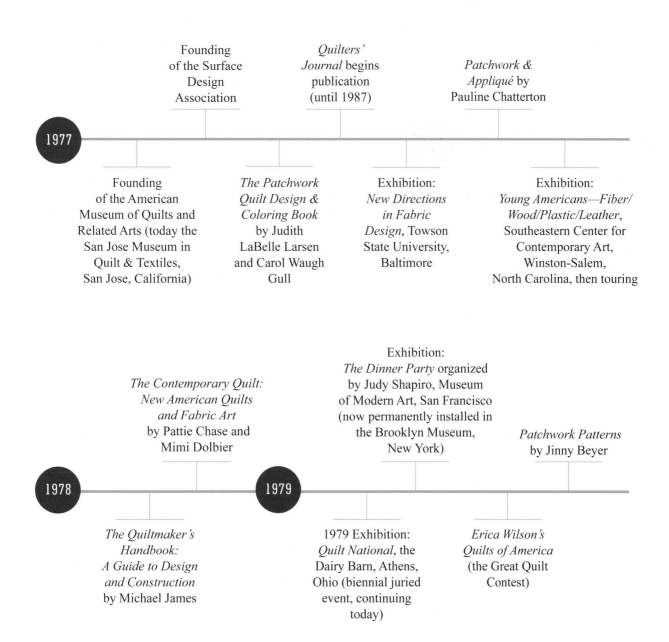

1977

Founding of the Surface Design Association

Quilters' Journal begins publication (until 1987)

Patchwork & Appliqué by Pauline Chatterton

Founding of the American Museum of Quilts and Related Arts (today the San Jose Museum in Quilt & Textiles, San Jose, California)

The Patchwork Quilt Design & Coloring Book by Judith LaBelle Larsen and Carol Waugh Gull

Exhibition: *New Directions in Fabric Design*, Towson State University, Baltimore

Exhibition: *Young Americans—Fiber/ Wood/Plastic/Leather*, Southeastern Center for Contemporary Art, Winston-Salem, North Carolina, then touring

Exhibition: *The Dinner Party* organized by Judy Shapiro, Museum of Modern Art, San Francisco (now permanently installed in the Brooklyn Museum, New York)

The Contemporary Quilt: New American Quilts and Fabric Art by Pattie Chase and Mimi Dolbier

Patchwork Patterns by Jinny Beyer

1978   **1979**

The Quiltmaker's Handbook: A Guide to Design and Construction by Michael James

1979 Exhibition: *Quilt National*, the Dairy Barn, Athens, Ohio (biennial juried event, continuing today)

Erica Wilson's Quilts of America (the Great Quilt Contest)

Jean Ray Laury | (d.) USA.

I was drawn to quilt making because it was the kind of work I could do at home with small children.* It didn't take a lot of space and it was immediate. I could do the work, and it would be accepted or not [to shows or magazines]. After a while, I was asked to do talks about my work. So whether I was writing, designing, or speaking, it was all about composition, how things were put together.

I almost never work out complete drawings or sketches of my work. I work directly with the fabric; I might just start laying fabric on a background, then tucking edges under or trimming. So the piece would grow; the fabric would grow. Sometimes, when illustrating a figure, I will do lots of doodles and drawings to see how best to get what I want.

Early in my career, I saw an exhibit of [Rufino] Tamayo's work; I loved his use of color. I loved all the Mexican muralists and their bright colors: [Diego] Rivera, [José Clemente] Orozco, but particularly Tamayo. Also, I was in Los Angeles and saw a [Henri] Matisse exhibit that included some of his large cut-paper pieces. That style of working opened up a whole new world for me.

I like to use humor in my art to make a point. Sometimes people think that if it is humorous, it must be trivial, or if there are recognizable images, it must be for children. For me, the work is worth doing if one person in a hundred sees the humor and gets what point I am trying to make; it's worth doing for that.

The best piece of advice I got was from my mother. "Don't do what everyone else is doing; do what YOU most want to do." I have also had some advice I didn't follow, which was to concentrate on one thing rather than spread my energies working on too many things. That advice didn't work for me. I want to work in a variety of media—cloth, paper, wood. I want to make art, write, teach, and lecture. www.jeanraylaury.com

*Based on a November 20, 2009, interview with Nancy Bavor. Jean Ray Laury, who died in 2011, was a pioneer in the Art Quilt Movement.

www.jeanraylaury.com

OPPOSITE
Boxed Illusions. 1981. 71" x 71".
Cotton. Machine pieced and quilted.
Collection: International Quilt Study Center & Museum,
University of Nebraska–Lincoln
Photo: International Quilt Study Center & Museum

I Do I Do. 2004. 67" x 21".
Cotton. Painted, machine appliquéd and quilted.
Collection: International Quilt Study Center & Museum,
University of Nebraska–Lincoln
Photo: International Quilt Study Center & Museum

Barefoot and Pregnant. 1987. 47" x 46".
Cotton. Painted, machine pieced.
Collection: International Quilt Study Center & Museum,
University of Nebraska–Lincoln
Photo: International Quilt Study Center & Museum

Listen to Your Mother. ca. 1990. 45" x 45".
Cotton, paint, marker. Machine pieced, silk-screened,
machine quilted.
Collection: Lizabeth Laury
Photo: James Dewrance

Nancy Crow | BALTIMORE, OHIO, USA

I am a quilt maker. I am an artist. I am an artist who makes quilts. I feel no need to be apologetic, nor do I need to make excuses as to whether my quilts are art or not. The phrase "art quilt" does not make a quilt a work of art.

I have always been good at mathematics and I love engineering structures, so my early work was very planned and geometric. After several years, I became bored by being so literal, often rigid. I needed to surprise myself in order to want to continue making quilts. I wanted my work to be more fluid. And in order for this to happen, I had to learn to cut out shapes and lines without using a ruler. I wanted my cut edge to be more like drawing.

I love finding the results from this improvisational journey. All of my work has an underlying emotion driven by a lifetime of experiences. I choose not to state any of this explicitly but rather hope that my works exude beauty and strength.

I am often asked why I love quilt making and, in particular, machine piecing. First of all, I love fabric, and I mean I love fabric! The feel of it, running my fingers through the folds, the colors of it, seeing the possibilities. This intense love is intuitive. I don't have to think about it, I just know it. I feel it. I also love my sewing machine—an old Bernina 930. The 930 hums along quietly but furiously as I sew what I cut out. We work harmoniously together.

On my tables are piles of two-yard cuts of fabrics I have dyed twice and sometimes three times for a saturation level that satisfies my love of intense coloration. I study my piles of colors and intuitively choose those colors I like together while trying for more unusual groupings that challenge me. Just cutting pure shape out of pure color is extremely exciting to me, as is putting these shapes up on my work wall, seeing how they interact with what else is pinned on the wall. I love shapes, lines. I love composition. Using color is a joy!

How did I come to start *Quilt National*? I was asked to teach a workshop in quilt making in 1977 by a very influential woman in Athens, Ohio, whose name was Harriet Anderson. Harriet was a painter who loved textiles and who wanted to revive more interest locally in the arts. I told her that although I was willing to teach, the need was not for more workshops but rather for a wonderful space in which to show contemporary quilts. Harriet said, "Let's do it. Let's figure out how to find a space in which to exhibit contemporary quilts."

www.nancycrow.com

OPPOSITE
Constructions #45. 2001 ©Nancy Crow. 64" x 63".
Photo: J. Kevin Fitzsimons

Constructions #10. 1997 ©Nancy Crow. 81" x 31".
Photo: J. Kevin Fitzsimons

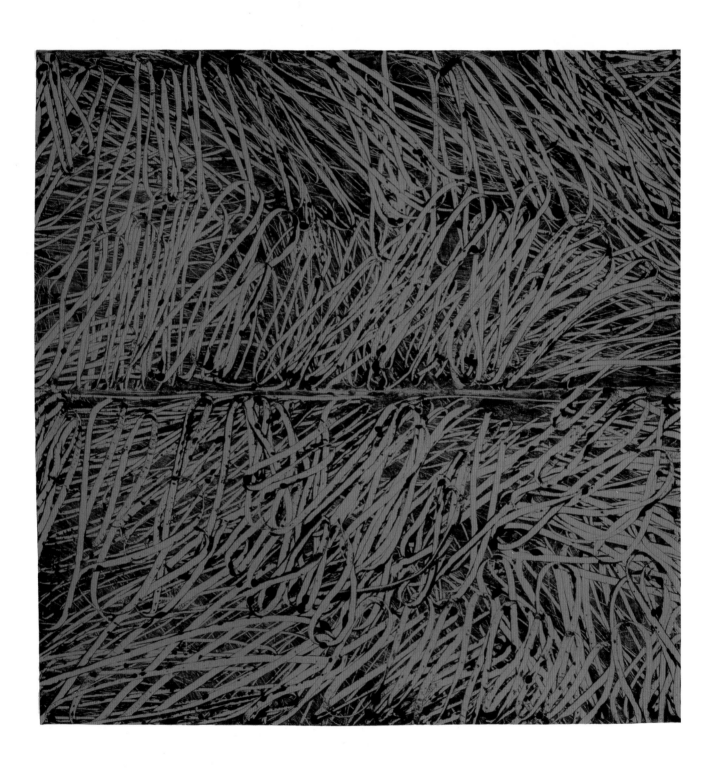

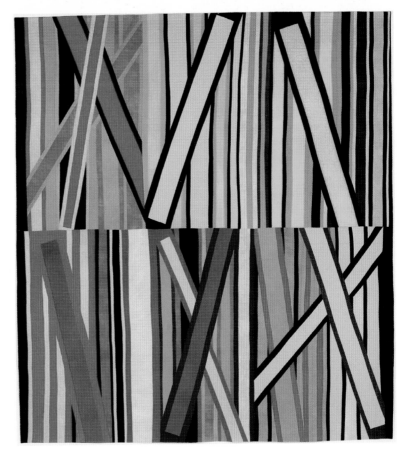

OPPOSITE
*Self-Portrait: Focus Mono-Prints
#21/#22 (red)*. 2012–2014
©Nancy Crow. 79.5" x 79".
Photo: J. Kevin Fitzsimons

ABOVE
*Self-Portrait: Focus Mono-Prints
#21/#22 (red)* (detail).

Constructions #82: Breaking Control!
2006 ©Nancy Crow. 83" x 75".
Photo: J. Kevin Fitzsimons

Chris Wolf Edmonds | BERRYTON, KANSAS, USA

I can't remember a time when I didn't want to be an artist. As a child, I filled notebooks with stories and drawings. As an adult, after trying my hand at printmaking, pot throwing, and weaving, I decided to focus on a form whose techniques I had learned from my mother and grandmothers, who were all fine seamstresses though not quilt makers.

In the 1970s I created a series of pictorial appliqué quilts, of which *Cherokee Trail of Tears* was later named one of the best 100 quilts of the 20th century. This early work led to exhibiting, lecturing, and teaching internationally, which led in turn to lasting friendships with other artists

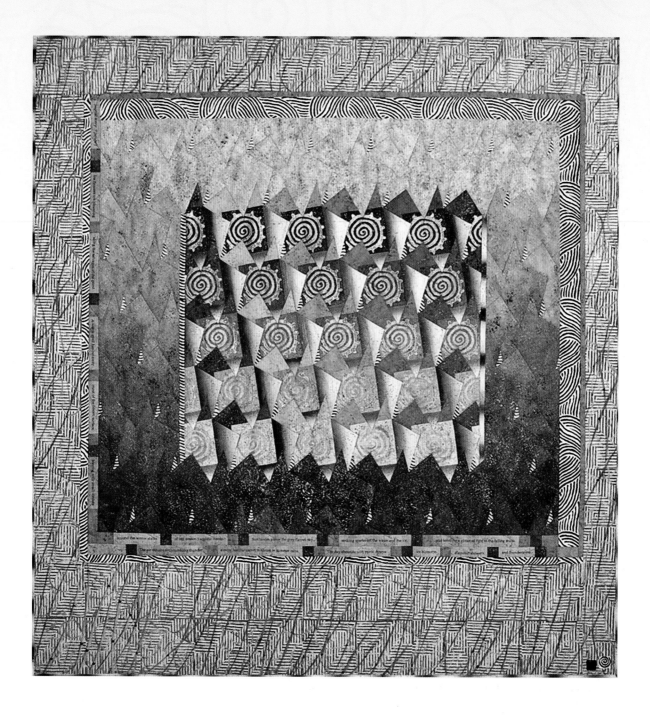

and with my students, whom I encouraged to extend the art form, not merely repeat it—to respect the tradition by advancing it.

I began dyeing, painting, and printing my own fabric in the 1980s. A piece from my Night Rainbow series of fourteen quilts was chosen as the poster design announcing the *Quilt National '83* show opening at the American Craft Museum in New York City. I served as a juror for *Quilt National '88* alongside my dear friend and SAQA founder, Yvonne Porcella.

Inspiration for my work in the 1990s was drawn from the colors of nature. In 1997 I brought together the visual and written aspects of my artistic life in a gallery show that combined twelve abstract color-study quilts with a book titled *Once around the Sun* (an edition of thirty-six copies sewn and bound by hand, with hand-painted cover cloth from the quilts).

In the new millennium, I have turned more directly still to the patterns of nature by collecting images with a camera, creating designs on a computer, and printing fabric on an inkjet printer. I am inspired by the world around me and believe that it is the nature of artists to manipulate the art of nature.

www.chrisedmondsstudioquilts.com

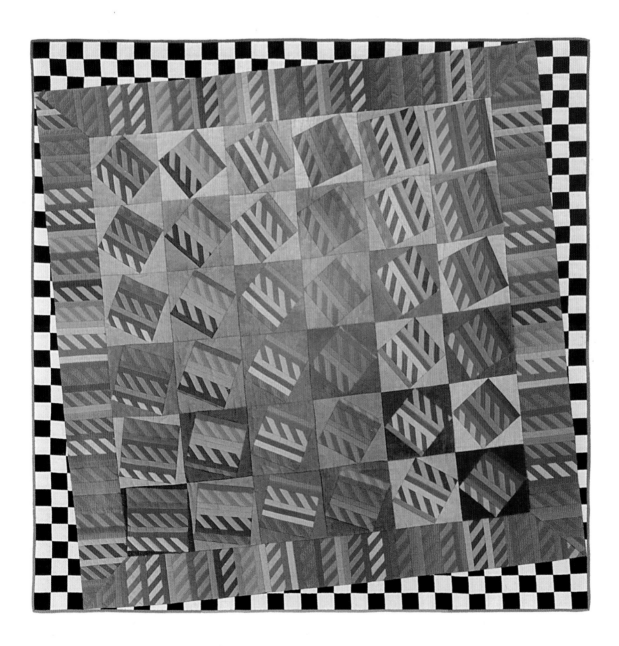

OPPOSITE
Tessellations: Ice Flowers. 1997. 55" x 53". Hand-painted cotton. Hand carved, woodblock printed, machine pieced and quilted.

Left-Handed Compliments. 1988. 50" x 50". Hand-dyed cotton. Machine pieced and quilted.

Nancy Erickson | MISSOULA, MONTANA, USA

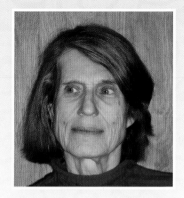

What draws me to using paint, oil paint sticks, and fabric? The immediacy of oil paint sticks and the fact that they can be drawn over in a few hours really appeals to me. My drawings are copied from the 30,000-year-old drawings in the Chauvet Cave in France, so that the cave animals (and the humans) in my quilts are "wearing their past."

Many years ago I was exploring the idea of layering in my compositions. Fabric appeals to me because a piece can be arranged and rearranged on the wall, painted or not, yet one does not have to make a final decision until later, while considering the result. This stage of the quilt-making process allows for flexibility without permanence. In the next stage, I glue the fabric pieces and stitch them onto the background. Sewing with thread

adds a new element, more lines to the composition, as well as adhering the pieces to the structural background. Thread becomes an essential part of the work, especially in the quilts of the last twenty years. The part I like best is the final stitching, and putting the large piece up on the wall to see how it works.

I've used animals as subject matter since the late 1960s, sometimes juxtaposed with the human figure, bombs, explosions, and the like. Although I love process and the way that the process has changed over the years, what really drives me is content. My content has always focused on animals, many of whom have lives as difficult and interesting as our own. We have evolved together over thousands of years and we continue to share space on an ever-more-crowded planet.

My parents were supportive of my work, giving me a full set of miniature oil paints as well as the linseed oil, brushes, and turpentine to go with them when I was only ten. The scent was heavenly, and I kept the wooden box forever. I completed an MFA in painting at the University of Montana, where the best piece of advice from a teacher was "Just do it."

www.nancyerickson.com

Pleistocene Memory (three parts). 2005. 78" x 74".
Velvet, paint, satin, cotton. Machine appliquéd and sewn.
Collection: Montana Museum of Arts and Culture

OPPOSITE
The Purple Lynx. 2014. 36" x 40".
Velvet, satin, paint. Machine appliquéd and sewn.

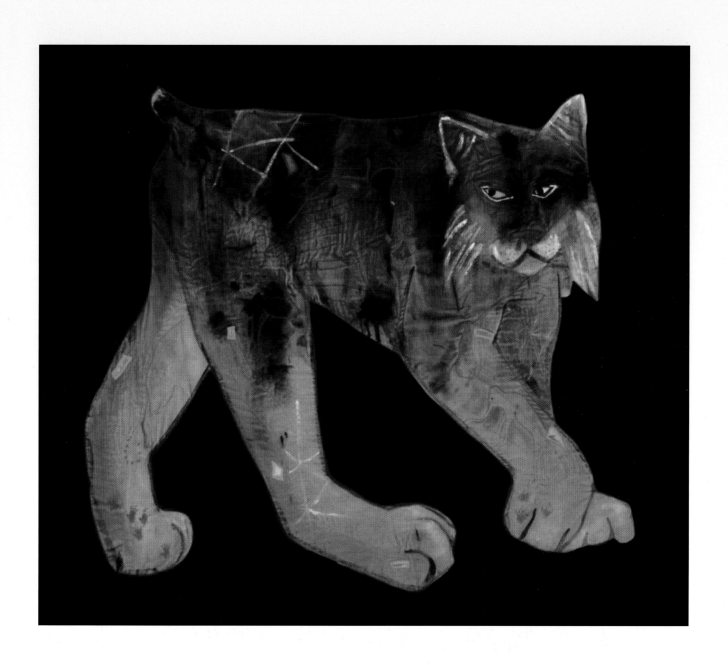

Leslie Gabriëlse | ROTTERDAM, NETHERLANDS

I was exposed to art at a very young age, as my grandfather and aunt were painters. As a student at the Academy of Art in Rotterdam, I was exposed to the traditional fine-arts media of drawing, painting, sculpture, and printmaking. It was the applied arts department that appealed to me. Needlework, silkscreen, and surface design were part of the curriculum.

I have always been interested in the range of motifs and textures of commercial fabrics. Rather than oil or acrylic paints on canvas, the variations of the tactile structure of fabric were more appealing. The opportunities to work in the commercial art world came through commissions from various architects to embellish their interior spaces.

Generally, I get my ideas by doodling, resulting in pencil sketches that are loose, simple contours with slight color suggestions. I constantly improvise when it comes to the final work, using swatches of fabric that give the composition an immediacy and spontaneity. I complete the work by using acrylic paint. A variety of hand stitches enhance the tactile surface.

I was not aware of the Art Quilt Movement for the first twenty years of my career. After visiting California in the 1980s, I was exposed to that world: I felt bonded! My subject matter became more varied, including more nonrepresentational works. Continued creativity comes by never giving up the desire to work!

www.gabrielse.com

OPPOSITE
Motorcycle with Sidecar. 1975. 70" x 102".
Commercial fabrics. Hand stitched.
Collection: Cees Van Stijgeren

Star. 2000. 48" x 48".
Commercial fabrics. Hand stitched.
Collection: San Jose Museum of Quilts & Textiles
Gift of Penny Nii and Edward Feigenbaum
Photo: James Dewrance

Michael James | LINCOLN, NEBRASKA, USA

I like that my creative processes are unpredictable, somewhat mysterious. That when I go into the studio, I'm faced with a very humbling enterprise: creating something from nothing in a sense. I may have some vague vision in my head but need to depend on the process to help me locate it, give it life in the materials. . . . It's always something of a struggle, and it requires persistence and patience. The older I get, the more I seem to have of both, so I no longer resist. Just go with it, wherever it seems to want to go.

One of the things that has been an underlying current in all of my work for the last fifteen or more years has been this idea of these emotional and psychological undercurrents of all of our lives—how do you represent that or how do you depict that? These are attempts to give visual form to these

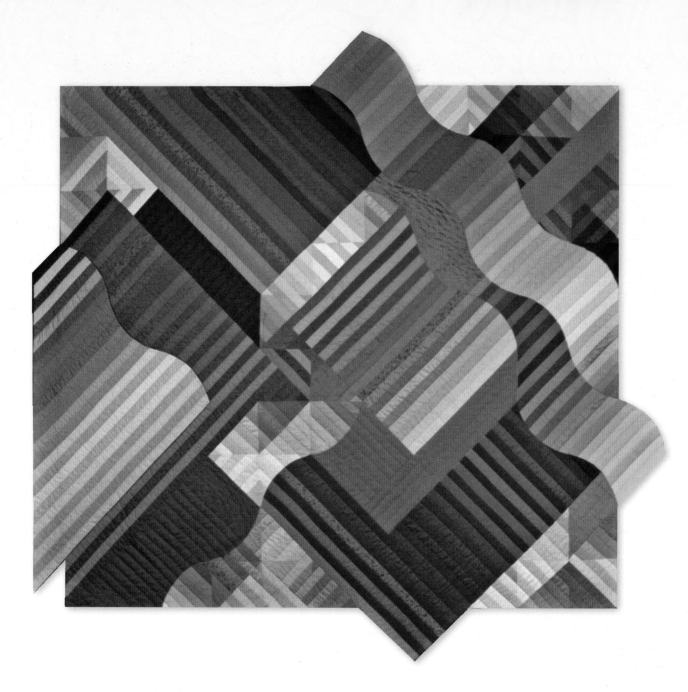

states of reality that are not the surface state but are the underlying conditions for an individual's personality or an atmosphere in a particular place.

My work builds very intuitively. I almost never do any kind of preliminary drawings. Once in a while I'll do a simple sketch to outline the organization. But for the most part, especially with this fabric I've been making digitally for the last fifteen years, I like to cut a section out of some printed yardage. These are not printed as repeat designs in any way. They're printed as panels that are photo based but have been enlarged and built on in multiple layers until I get something that I think is interesting and unique. Then I cut from parts of those fabrics to get the shapes that people actually see in these quilts. I pick that particular area because that area has the complexity of color, images, lights, darks, the balance of visual weight I need in the context. It gets put on the wall as a function of how that particular area is going to relate to what's around it. It will stay to the degree that it adds something to the conversation that's happening on the surface.

That's really important, the notion that when I'm putting pieces of fabric on the wall, I'm looking to get some direction from the piece. I'm waiting to hear what it's going to suggest I do. Do I want something that's aggressive here? Do I want something that cancels a particular area out or reduces its strength or its value? These kinds of questions are constant.

www.michaeljamesstudioquilts.com

OPPOSITE
Red Zinger. 1986. 67" x 69".
Cotton, silk. Machine pieced, machine and hand quilted.
Private collection
Photo: David Caras

Inside Out. 1999. 42.5" x 79".
Cotton. Hand-painted, machine pieced and quilted.
Private collection
Photo: Larry Gawel

The Concept of Qi. 2007. 50.5" x 52".
Cotton (digitally printed with reactive dyes).
Machine pieced and quilted.
Private collection
Photo: Larry Gawel

Allegory. 2016. 36" x 48.5".
Cotton, sateen, dye. Pieced, appliquéd,
digitally developed and printed fabrics.

Penelope McMorris

Portrait. Bowling Green, Ohio, USA
Photo: Cynthia Wenslow

"I got involved with art quilts because I felt that the artists needed someone to tell them that they had permission, that this was art, and that other people should see it as art, collect it, and exhibit it."

In 1976, supported by a grant from the National Endowment for the Arts, curator Penelope ("Penny") McMorris conceived a quilt competition and show composed of recent quilts by Ohio quilters. "When I saw quilts by Nancy Crow and Françoise Barnes, I knew then that the joy for me was in the looking. If I could see other people's quilts that were truly great works of art and champion those, then that's what I really wanted to do."

Along with managing and expanding the corporate art collection of Owens Corning, McMorris proposed a television series on quilting to the local Public Broadcasting System (PBS) station. Beginning in 1981, her three television series aired: *Quilting* (1981); *Quilting II* (1982); and, *The Great American Quilt* (1991).

In each part of her career, McMorris made important connections with curators, gallerists, quilters, quilt artists, and quilt historians across the United States. In 1986, she collaborated with Michael Kile on the groundbreaking exhibition *The Art Quilt* at the Los Angeles Municipal Art Gallery.

McMorris was instrumental in the development of the Ardis and Robert James Collection of Antique and Contemporary Quilts, and the John M. Walsh III Collection of Contemporary Art Quilts. In her continuing quest to champion excellence in quilting, McMorris served as a board member during the formation of the International Quilt Study Center & Museum (IQSCM) in Lincoln, Nebraska. Her research and television production materials now reside at the IQSCM. McMorris also served for six years on the Board of Studio Art Quilt Associates.

McMorris is the author of several books, including *Crazy Quilts* (1984), and *The Art Quilt* (1996), coauthored with Kile. Among her other accomplishments, McMorris founded the Electric Quilt software company with her husband, Dean Neumann.

"Today we don't need to tell anyone that this is art. SAQA is helping so many artists and the work is being exhibited and collected. It has a life. That was my goal."

*Based on an interview with Cynthia Wenslow in early 2017.

Beth Gutcheon

From the early 1970s, Beth Gutcheon and Jeffrey Gutcheon, her husband, had a fabric shop in Manhattan catering to quilters, and they both created quilts. The studio workshops at Gutcheon Patchworks gave many quilt artists their start, especially after *New York Times* columnist Rita Reif reviewed the store with positive press coverage. Beth Gutcheon's 1973 book, *The Perfect Patchwork Primer*, became a bible for many quilt makers. Today a

well-established novelist, Gutcheon was publishing articles and critical reviews concerning contemporary quilt art in the late 1970s, including "The Quilts of Molly Upton as Works of Art" in *Lady's Circle Patchwork Quilts*. She reviewed the first *Quilt National* for *Fiberarts Magazine*, noting that the exhibition "has turned out to be the stimulating and all-encompassing show one hoped for."

Gallery 1960s–1970s

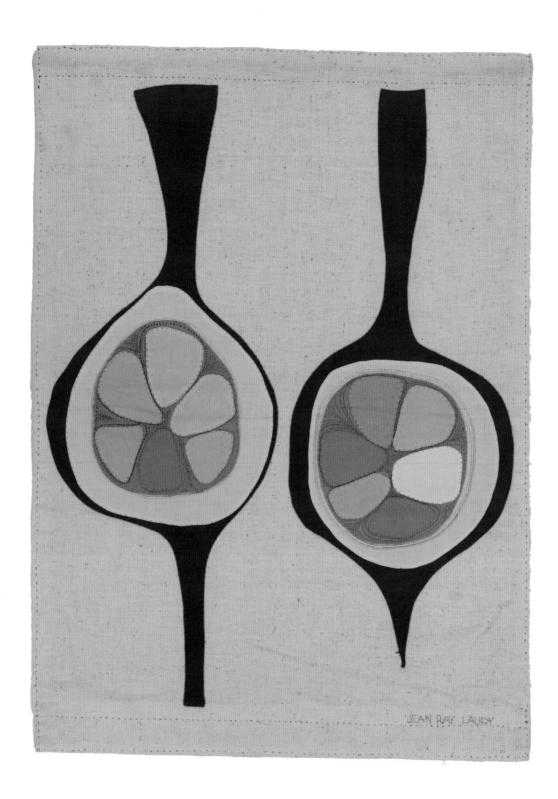

Jean Ray Laury (d.)

USA
Two Pods. 1959. 23" x 16".
Cotton. Hand appliquéd, embroidered.
Collection: International Quilt Study Center & Museum, University
of Nebraska–Lincoln
Photo: International Quilt Study Center & Museum

Chris Wolf Edmonds

Berryton, Kansas, USA
Cherokee Trail of Tears. 1979. 82" x 58".
Cotton. Machine pieced, hand appliquéd and quilted.

BELOW

Nancy Crow

Baltimore, Ohio, USA
March Study. 1979 ©Nancy Crow. 80" x 80".
Photo: J. Kevin Fitzsimons

Nancy Erickson

Missoula, Montana, USA
Red Rain #2: Rabbit Alone. 1978. 108" x 84".
Satin, cotton, mixed fibers. Machine appliquéd
and stitched.
Private collection
Photo: Jon Schulman

BELOW

Leslie Gabriëlse

Rotterdam, Netherlands
Girl Combing Her Hair. 1967. 70" x 96".
Commercial fabrics. Hand stitched.
Private collection
Photo: Eric Kievit

Michael James

Lincoln, Nebraska, USA
Moonshadow. 1979. 100" x 80".
Cotton, satin, velveteen. Hand pieced and quilted.
Private collection

BELOW

Deborah Ann

Yakima Washington, USA
Nude in Chair. 1977. 42" x 31".
Satin, crepe, embroidery floss. Hand appliquéd,
machine quilted.

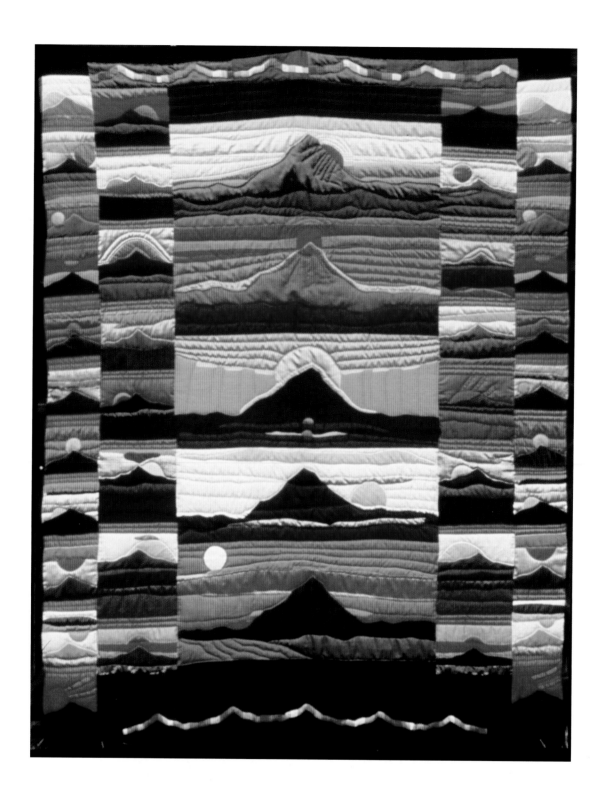

Helen Bitar

Sheridan, Oregon, USA
Mountain in the Morning. 1976.
106" x 83".
Satin, cotton. Appliquéd.

OPPOSITE TOP

Ros Cross

Los Angeles, California, USA
*Pancakes, Butter and Syrup Quilt with
Bacon Rug.* 1973. 106" x 96" x 2".
Quilt: Polycotton fabrics. Appliquéd.
Rug: Wool on canvas mesh. Needlepointed.
Collection: John M. Walsh III

BELOW

Ulva Ugerup

Malmö, Sweden
Sailing. Early 1970s. 20" x 30".
Cotton. Machine quilted,
machine pieced, appliquéd, hand
embroidered.

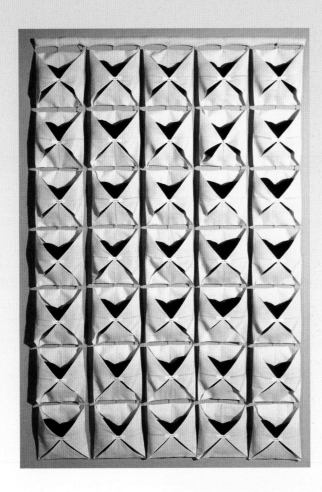

Sylvia H. Einstein

Belmont, Massachusetts, USA
Pattern of Least Regret. 1978. 65" x 45" x 2".
Fabric, socks converted to hearts. Fabric sewn into
pockets, ironed-on label, stuffed sock hearts.
Photo: Sam Sweezy

BELOW

Patricia Malarcher

Englewood, New Jersey, USA
Ommatidia. 1979. 48" x 48" x 2".
Mylar, fabric, thread.
Stitched by hand and machine.

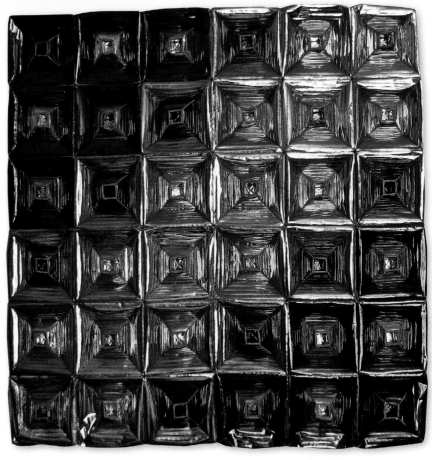

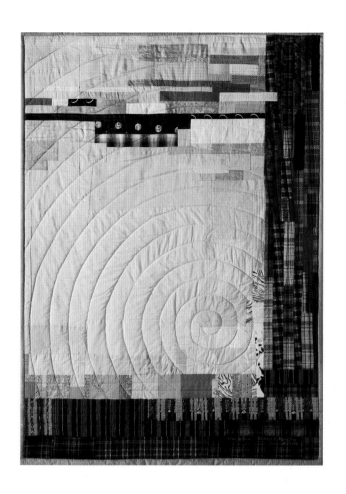

Susan Hoffman

Germantown, New York, USA
Mourning in Manhattan. 1977. 84" x 61".
Cotton, wool, polyester, linen, silk. Machine
and hand pieced, hand quilted.
Photo: George Bouret

BELOW

Molly Upton (d.)

USA
Watchtower. 1975. 90" x 110".
Cotton, silk, wool, synthetics. Hand and
machine pieced, hand quilted.
Collection: Museum of Fine Arts, Boston,
donation of the artist's family
Photo: J. Gordon Upton

Therese May

San Jose, California, USA
Bridget Quilt. 1968. 84" x 72".
Recycled wool. Machine appliquéd.
Collection: San Jose Museum of Quilts & Textiles
Gift of Therese May
Photo: James Dewrance

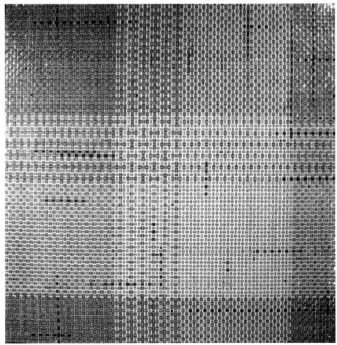

Wenda von Weise (d.)

USA
Old North Wharf. ca. 1978. 83" x 52".
Silk, cotton. Photo-screen printed, hand and
machine stitched.
Private collection

BELOW

Arturo Alonzo Sandoval

Lexington, Kentucky, USA
Cityscape No. 1. 1977. 84" x 84".
Laundry tag paper, 16 mm film, silver Lurex,
diffraction opalescent Mylar. Layered,
machine stitched, and interlaced.
Collection: Museum of Modern Art
Photo: Mary S. Rezny Photography

Katherine Westphal (d.)

USA
The Puzzle: Floating World #2.
1976. 85" x 68".
Cotton/poly. Transfer print,
quilted.

OPPOSITE

Charlotte Yde

Frederiksberg, Denmark
Steen's Quilt. 1979. 59" x 59".
Cotton, cotton chintz. Machine
pieced, hand quilted.
Photo: Steen Yde

BELOW

Nancy Whittington

Chapel Hill, North Carolina, USA
Seasons Quilt. 1978. 112" x 112".
Ultra suede, satin. Machine and
hand pieced, hand quilted.
Photo: Deidre Adams

Patricia Malarcher | ENGLEWOOD, NEW JERSEY, USA

Two of my aunts were artists, and I grew up surrounded by their paintings and drawings. They were the only adults whose activity looked enjoyable. Because of them, I always knew that "an artist" was a possible thing to be. But I held editorial jobs before committing myself to the study of art in my twenties.

Kenneth Noland, my first design teacher, influenced my approach to materials with his enigmatic statement, "Design is the way things are." Early on, I created pieced constructions from geometric units equivalent to quilt blocks. Metallized Mylar was a dominant material; I liked crisply cut edges that did not distort the geometry. Gradually I introduced color with thread, paint, or fabric. I also moved toward less rigid designs,

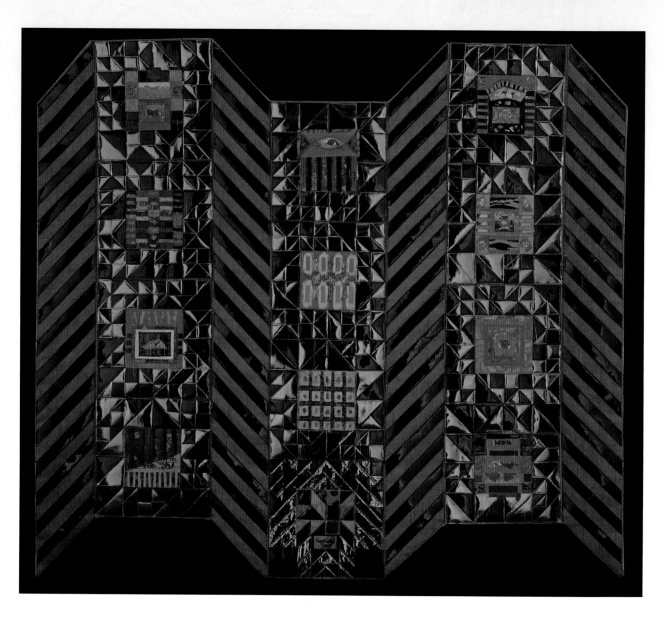

sometimes testing the extent to which a pattern could be interrupted and still retain its integrity. As I continued using Mylar with reflective surfaces that changed according to ambient light, I started seeing my work as iconic images of quilts rather than actual quilts. I also began to play with "fictional geometry" that resulted in the illusion of a fold or a third dimension. Over time, the work became more intuitive and playful, combining collage-type elements in mixed media with geometric areas.

What I love about piecework is the discovery of unexpected relationships between elements that were not originally meant to go together. This introduces continual surprise in the process of working and often an end result that could not have been predicted at the beginning.

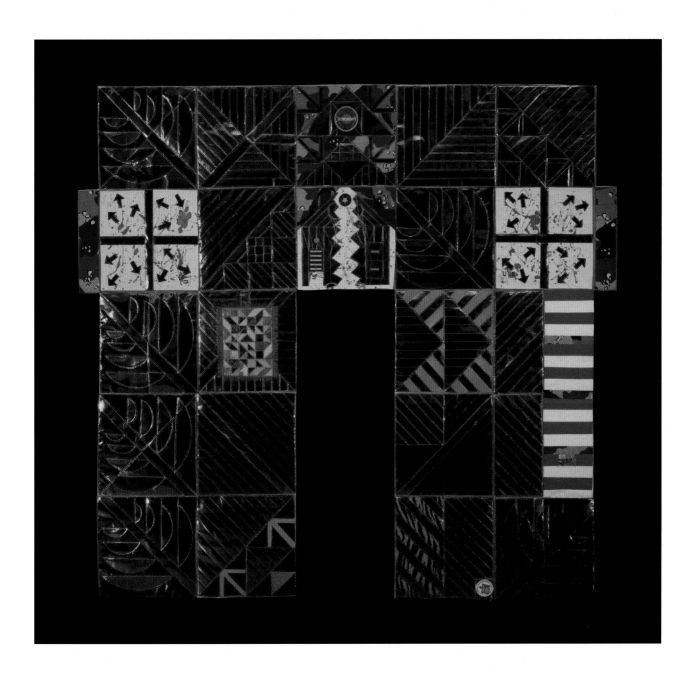

OPPOSITE

Iconostasis. 1996. 54" x 60".
Mylar, fabric, painted canvas. Stitched by hand and machine.
Photo: D. James Dee

Passage. 1991. 60" x 66".
Mylar, fabric, paint, ready-made textile elements. Machine appliquéd, hand-sewn construction.
Photo: D. James Dee

Therese May | SAN JOSE, CALIFORNIA, USA

Art quilts provide a vehicle that has given me a voice for many years and continues to be a medium of great meaning and connection with all kinds of people.

Drawing has always been my main talent, but I also enjoy sewing and the tactile quality of fabric and color. When I look back on this process, I see that my imagery comes from a very personal space and is my own.

In the beginning, partly because of my abstract expressionistic approach that I learned as a painter in art school, I used very loose appliqué techniques. Hanging threads and the imperfection of the quilt's surface got people's attention. Later, my work was noticed because I "dared to paint on the quilt" after all of the sewing and construction was complete. My quilts gave viewers permission to have a little fun.

A lot of creating happens in my head, but the ideas really evolve once I start making the work. No matter how much planning has taken place, the work has a life of its own. Surprises are so much fun!

My work has evolved from loose threads, recycled fabrics, drawing and painting, photo quilting, and appliquéd fantasy images with and without acrylic paint. I range from embracing imperfection to trying to have perfect techniques and neatly trimmed threads and back again. I like translating my drawings into appliqué images, printing these on fabric yardage, and creating mixed-media art quilts. I also now do longarm quilting, which changes the process in many ways.

In my youth, my parents, as well as just about everyone I came into contact with, encouraged me to identify as an artist. Although my German grandmother was not very talkative, watching her always creating something beautiful from whatever she had on hand still influences my work today. I'm very grateful to all of the artists who inspired me to look at my own ideas because they were expressing theirs in their own unique ways.

www.theresemay.com

OPPOSITE
Dairy Queen Salt and Pepper Shakers. 1981. 39" x 50".
Recycled fabric, buttons. Machine appliquéd.
Collection: San Jose Museum of Quilts & Textiles
Gift of Therese May
Photo: James Dewrance

Therese at the Kitchen Sink. 1977. 72" x 96".
Recycled fabric. Machine appliquéd.
Collection: San Jose Museum of Quilts & Textiles
Gift of Therese May
Photo: James Dewrance

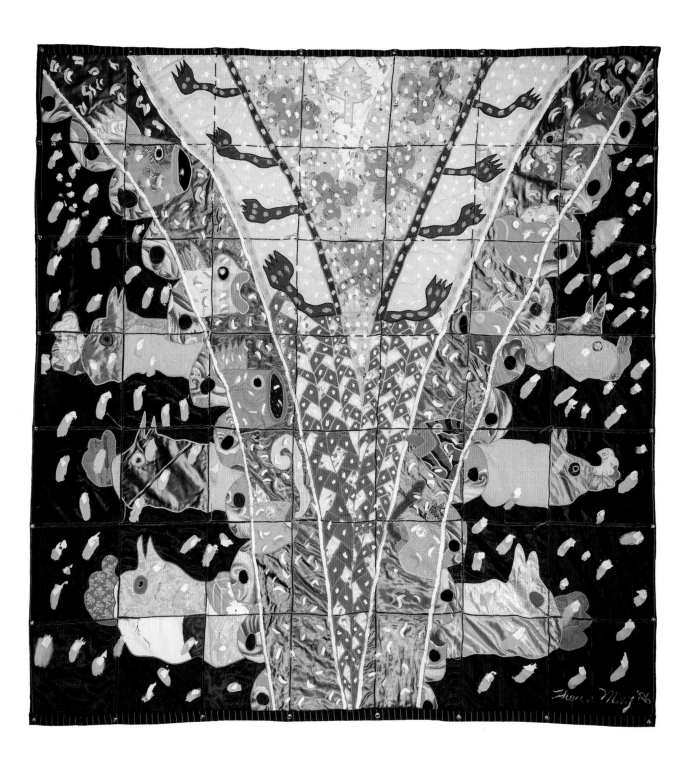

Fish & Chicks. 1984. 72" x 72".
Recycled fabric, paint. Machine appliquéd, painted.
Collection: San Jose Museum of Quilts & Textiles
Gift of Therese May
Photo: James Dewrance

Love of Money. 2002. 38" x 37.5".
Various fabrics. Machine appliquéd, embellished, machine quilted.
Collection: San Jose Museum of Quilts & Textiles
Gift of Therese May
Photo: James Dewrance

Katie Pasquini Masopust | FORTUNA, CALIFORNIA, USA

What excites me about making art quilts is designing an original piece, working on composition, and choosing the color scheme and the fabrics. I love the fabrics—their colors and textures. I am excited about choosing each piece of fabric and either piecing or turning the edges and appliquéing them in place. The quilting is one of my favorite parts as I get to draw all over the surface of the quilt with thread. Each step of quilt making excites me.

The first person to inspire me as an artist was my high school teacher, Jim Sullivan. I still thank him to this day for showing me how to be an artist and for encouraging me to explore my talent. Michael James inspired me to design my own quilts and is a great mentor to me.

Pizzicato. 2011. 46" x 72".
Cotton, blends, lamé, ultrasuede, painted canvas.
Machine appliquéd and quilted.
Private collection
Photo: Carolyn Wright

I developed my personal style by exploring what excites me about design and color and trying different things. I have changed my style every few years as I explore one idea to its conclusion for me. Then I come up with another design technique and work on that. I have gone from traditional quilts to mandala designs, to three-dimensional design and then to isometric perspective. More recently, I developed approaches that I call Fractured Landscapes, Ghost Layers, and Color Washes. Now I am creating abstract designs based on my paintings.

I still construct the same way that I have always done, but the designs and compositions change. I have always worked in series, working through one idea or technique until I am satisfied and ready to move on. I have always turned my edges when I appliqué and stitch down to a foundation.

Ideas come from doing, seeing, teaching, and playing with fabrics and paints. They come from taking long walks with my dogs and thinking of all the things that inspire me. An idea comes and becomes clearer when I am in my studio exploring the possibilities.

The best pieces of advice I have been given are "Don't be afraid to fail" and "Just do it."

www.katiepm.com

Rio Hondo. 1994. 54" x 80".
Cotton, blends. Machine appliquéd and quilted.
Collection: John M. Walsh III
Photo: Hawthorn Studio

Heavens Reach. 1981. 80" x 80".
Cotton, blends. Machine pieced and quilted.
Photo: Lindsay Olsen

Dimensional Portal. 1994. 83" x 83".
Cotton, blends, lamé, satin. Machine pieced, hand appliquéd and quilted.
Collection: International Quilt Study Center & Museum, University of
Nebraska–Lincoln
Bob Masopust Sr. Collection
Photo: Peter Stazione

Arturo Alonzo Sandoval | LEXINGTON, KENTUCKY, USA

My mother initially encouraged me in the arts by taking me as a child to Broadway traveling musicals, operettas, movies, and, especially, a summer art course in the seventh grade at a local high school. And Richard Devore told me in 1970, "Always make your art larger than you in height and width; it is more impressive and requires more thought."

Perhaps I am best known for creating art quilts from nonwoven industrial materials, stitching strips of materials by machine and then interlacing these vertical elements with similarly created horizontal elements to create "woven" art quilts. My preference is to take linear industrial materials and visualize how I might construct various interlaced surfaces with them. The compositional permutations are infinite and limited only by my imagination.

My personal style developed after I received my first National Endowment for the Arts (NEA) Crafts Fellowship in 1973. This award validated my innovation and research into my first art quilt ideas using modular and interlaced elements. The NEA recognition guided me to focus on distinguishing myself using these industrial materials and my machine-stitched, layered, and interlaced manner of constructing art quilts. These early investigations were shown through the Hadler-Rodriguez Gallery. In addition, New York's Museum of Modern Art purchased *Cityscape No. 1*, and noted designer Jack Lenor Larsen purchased *Sky Grid: Topaz*. Additional validation came with being juried into the seventh (1977) International Contemporary Tapestry competition in Lausanne, Switzerland, and being published in Edward Lucie Smith's book *Art in the Seventies*.

In 1981, my submissions to the exhibition *Filaments of the Imagination*, curated by Judith C. Brooks, were more subtractive in the use of processes. Polymer medium held the materials together and machine stitching was used only on the perimeter of the constructions to hold down the edges. Going into my fifth decade as an artist, I am embracing the commercial jacquard loom as my tool to create a new body of political work from digital images and appliqué. This may be the tool I use most after retirement from academia as I follow through with my teaching mantra, "Work produces results." First and foremost, I am inspired by the beauty of an idea, followed by being surprised by the materials used, and challenged by the scale of my art quilts.

www.arturoart.com

OPPOSITE
Flag for the Americas. 1992. 74" x 50".
USA flag, commercial and hand ikat-dyed and woven fabric, netting, paint, colored threads, braid, rayon fringe, fabric backed, Velcro. Layered, machine stitched, cutout stars.
Collection: Leepa-Rattner Museum of Art at St. Petersburg College, Tarpon Springs Campus, Tarpon Springs, Florida
Photo: Mary S. Rezny Photography

Ground Zero No. 10: Target Babylon IV.
1989. 96" x 156".
16 mm color film, 16 mm microfilm, Mylar, color acetate transparencies, color photographs, paint, netting, rag paper, color threads, braid, polymer medium, eyelets, fabric backed. Layered, interlaced, machine stitched and embroidered, pieced.
Collection: Museum of Arts and Design, New York
Photo: Mary S. Rezny Photography

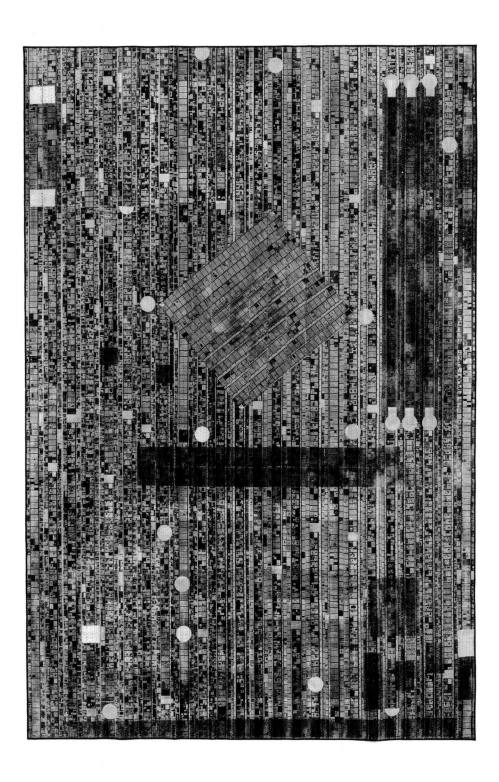

Pattern Fusion No. 14: Motherboard No. 5. 2016. 80.5" x 54".
Repurposed auto industry Mylar, recycled library 35 mm microfilm,
transparent polyester film, monofilament and multicolored threads,
plaited braid edging, holographic film, Pellon, polymer medium.
Layered, spliced, machine stitched, interlaced.
Photo: Walz Photography

OPPOSITE
State of the Union No. 15: Covert Affairs—
Two Futures Diptych. 2017. 63" x 83" each.
Netting, tulle, digital prints on fabric, monofilament
threads, various fringes, braid, paint. Jacquard woven,
machine stitched, fused appliqué.
Photo: Walz Photography

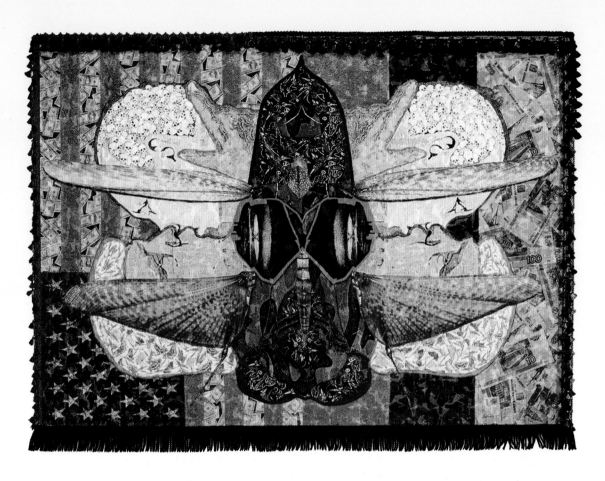

Joan Schulze | SUNNYVALE, CALIFORNIA, USA

Making things led to making art. I always used what I had available.

The family scrap bag was the source of material to make presents. In high school I started making my clothes. Scraps were saved and often interested me more than the clothes I made. Being an elementary-school teacher involved gathering recycled and easily obtained materials for classroom use. This form of creativity carried over into my studio work. Tools that I use were and still are ordinary and simple. My sewing machine from the 1960s was used for making my clothes and naturally transitioned into being an important tool in my art making. That first machine is still being used, although I have acquired others.

Materials and processes were often chosen because they were at hand. Art, thrift, and fabric stores were my go-to places for unusual art-making materials. When I began my art career, it was natural that fabric would be my material. Over time I included paper and plastic as "fabric" and have incorporated traditional art materials.

Early in my career I fit in studio work between the demands and needs of raising four children. Work had to be portable or it wouldn't get done. The offices of the doctor and dentist functioned as my floating studio, which also involved our Volkswagen van.

I acquired a dream studio in 1995. Until last year my San Francisco studio schedule was three days a week unless I was traveling. Family circumstances have necessitated moving my studio work back home. An expanded workspace in the garage now functions as my main studio. San Francisco functions as a gallery with daytime visits when possible.

Since time for actually creating work is now hit-or-miss, I relegate problem solving to when I sleep. The actual work gets done. If anything, growing older has increased my sense of urgency to be in the studio. I try to honor the gift of time.

My sourcebook of ideas is from living a life. Inspiration can attack at any time. I just need to pay attention and be receptive.

www.joan-of-arts.com

OPPOSITE
Aroma. 1997. 70" x 53".
Silk, cotton, paper. Monoprinted, blueprint process, photo transfers.

Thirteen Bowls. 2002. 21" x 24".
Silk, cotton, paper. Direct printed on silk by photocopy process, appliquéd, machine quilted.
Collection: Adobe Systems International, San Jose, California

Opus. 2017. 94" x 134".
Packing tape, paper, canvas. Tape strip collaged, glued,
stitched, mounted on canvas.

Where Dreams Are Born. 1976. 90" x 90".
Cotton, transparent overlays, velour, lace,
commercial fabrics. Machine pieced, hand quilted.
Collection: San Jose Museum of Quilts & Textiles
Gift of Joan Schulze
Photo: James Dewrance

Charlotte Yde | FREDERIKSBERG, DENMARK

I saw my first two quilts at a barn sale in Connecticut when I was visiting family at the age of sixteen. Those quilts made a big impression on me. I wanted to express myself artistically and had a strong interest in textiles, so when I found that I could combine my love for colors, shapes, and textural effects, I was sold.

I developed my personal style through hard work over the years. Being Danish meant that I didn't have access to quilt teachers and had to teach myself everything through books back in the 1970s. In the beginning I was young and insecure and thought that I needed to know every new technique. Sometimes I would be sidetracked by techniques that I thought

Dialogue 2. 2010. 55" x 74".
Cotton. Deconstructed screen printed, block printed. Digitally programmed and free machine embroidered, hand and machine quilted.

I ought to know in order to be a good teacher—I have been teaching for more than forty years. Now I am very selective in regard to techniques and surface design trends when it comes to my own work.

I have always wanted to say something with my quilts, but at the same time I also have been very cautious, trying not to throw the message too much in the face of the viewer—trying to do it so subtly that the work can be enjoyed for its aesthetic and visual qualities.

I love when the creative process becomes a dialogue between myself and the work. Most importantly: Does my work do the job and make it possible to say or show what I want?

www.yde.dk

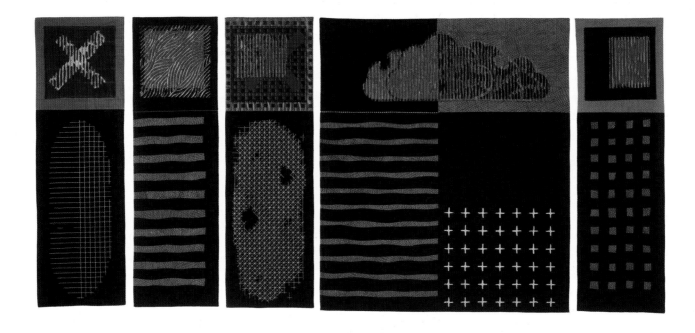

Kindred Spirits. 1999. 45" x 98.5".
Cotton, silk organza, metallic organza. Machine pieced and quilted.
Collection: Susan Denton

Dr. Carolyn L. Mazloomi

The Women of Color Quilters Network (WCQN) is a nonprofit organization founded in 1985 by Dr. Carolyn L. Mazloomi, a nationally acclaimed quilt artist and lecturer, to foster and preserve the art of quilt making among women of color. WCQN supports its membership through presentations, providing venues for sharing technical information, grant writing, and other services. The organization offers quilts and fiber art to museums for exhibition, and it researches and documents African American quilt making. In recent years, WCQN has showcased the work of its members before national and international audiences. An important component of the network's activity is its use of quilt making in social and economic development projects. Educational projects and workshops foster exposure to the arts, creative development, and improved self-esteem. These programs present the benefits of quilting to audiences of all ages, income levels, ethnic backgrounds, and learning abilities.

www.wcqn.org

Organized in Ohio by Nancy Crow, Françoise Barnes, and Virginia Randles, the first *Quilt National* (QN) in 1979 was a watershed event for art quilts. These talented women and other artists across the country were creating original, innovative designs in fabric that were pieced, layered, stitched, and stuffed—quilts meant to be displayed on the wall. The only exhibition opportunities in the Midwest for these artists were in mixed-media fiber shows alongside baskets and weavings, or in general craft shows. *Quilt National* founders recognized the need for an appropriate showcase for what are now known as "art quilts."

Fortunately, this need coincided with the efforts of local artists and art lovers to preserve and renovate an abandoned dairy barn, the venue for *QN* since 1979. *Quilt National* was founded to publicize and promote the transformations taking place in the world of quilting. Its purpose was then, and still is, to carry the definition of quilting far beyond its traditional parameters.

This international juried exhibition's driving force for many years was Hilary M. Fletcher (d. 2006), executive director beginning in 1982. *Quilt National* celebrated its twentieth biennial exhibition in 2017, featuring eight-five artists from eight countries. Selections from each *QN* exhibition tour for several years, bringing museum visitors here and abroad the best in contemporary quilt art. Full-color catalogues from the exhibitions serve as important documents of the Art Quilt Movement.

http://dairybarn.org/quilt-national/

THE
DAIRY BARN
ARTS
CENTER

CHAPTER TWO
1980s: Art Quilts Go National in Publications and Exhibitions

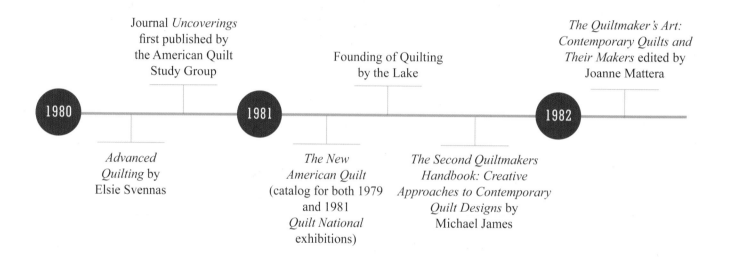

Journal *Uncoverings* first published by the American Quilt Study Group

Founding of Quilting by the Lake

The Quiltmaker's Art: Contemporary Quilts and Their Makers edited by Joanne Mattera

1980

1981

1982

Advanced Quilting by Elsie Svennas

The New American Quilt (catalog for both 1979 and 1981 *Quilt National* exhibitions)

The Second Quiltmakers Handbook: Creative Approaches to Contemporary Quilt Designs by Michael James

Art quilts achieved national prominence during the 1980s due to several touring exhibitions accompanied by illustrated catalogues, with reviews in *American Craft*, *Art News*, *Craft Horizons*, *Fiberarts Magazine*, and other publications with thousands of subscribers.

Robert Shaw explains the impact of the most noteworthy touring exhibition: "In the 1980s the art quilt was also given a tremendous boost by the late San Francisco quilt dealer Michael Kile, the cofounder [with Roderick Kiracofe] of the highly influential journal the *Quilt Digest*. . . . Soon after launching the *Quilt Digest* in 1983, Kile teamed with curator and writer Penny McMorris to organize *The Art Quilt*, a catalogued traveling exhibition of brand-new works by sixteen artists they considered trailblazers in the field. McMorris brought substantial credits to the enterprise; she had organized shows including nontraditional quilts as early

as 1976 and also served as host and producer of two PBS series on quilting that were televised nationally in 1981 and introduced viewers to the work of many new and innovative artists. Kile and McMorris were the first to use the term *art quilt* to describe the work of these modern quiltmakers. *The Art Quilt*, which opened at the Los Angeles Municipal Art Gallery in September 1986 and traveled to seven other sites over its three-year run, was even more influential than the *Quilt Digest* in bringing attention to the works of nontraditional quilters. The catalog, the first extensive scholarly exposé on the new art form, declared, 'The art quilt has emerged, and it heralds a dramatic and fundamental change in the history of quilts. It is art for walls, not beds, created by artists abandoning media like painting, printmaking, and ceramics to express themselves in original designs of cloth and thread'" (excerpted from Shaw's *The Art Quilt*, 1997).

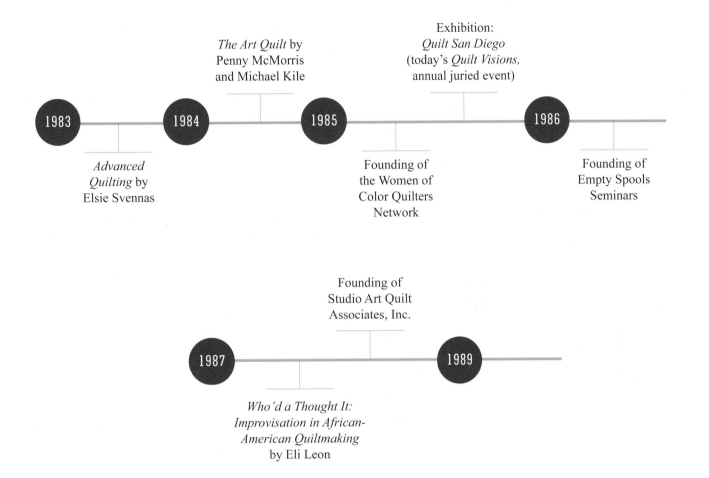

1983

1984 — *The Art Quilt* by Penny McMorris and Michael Kile

Advanced Quilting by Elsie Svennas

1985 — Founding of the Women of Color Quilters Network

Exhibition: *Quilt San Diego* (today's *Quilt Visions*, annual juried event)

1986 — Founding of Empty Spools Seminars

Founding of Studio Art Quilt Associates, Inc.

1987

1989

Who'd a Thought It: Improvisation in African-American Quiltmaking by Eli Leon

Although *Quilt National* did not tour during the 1980s, its exhibition catalogs made a national impact, especially *The New American Quilt*, published by Lark Books in 1981, illustrating quilts from the first and second *Quilt National* exhibitions. Three years prior to the McMorris and Kile touring exhibition, Charlotte Robinson curated *The Artist and the Quilt*, which opened in San Antonio and toured to other cities. The catalogue published by Knopf featured several essays, including art critic Lucy Lippard's "Up, Down, and Across: A New Frame for New Quilts." Somewhat ironically, this exhibition and its catalog publicized quilt artists in an unexpected fashion. Robinson had "quilters" such as Judy Mathieson and Wenda von

Weise collaborate with "artists" such as Lynda Benglis, Alice Neel, and Faith Ringgold (who collaborated with her mother as the quilter) to reproduce their works of art in fabric and expose these quilters to the art world. As one might imagine, some of the reviews were rather hostile. Al Paca wrote in *Fiberarts*: "Have these women ever looked out there into the real world to see what's really happening with the art of the quilt? There are already a helluva lot of mighty fine artists creating gorgeous quilts without their benevolence. This whole project patronizes and denigrates the real artists who create quilted art works." The art quilt had arrived.

Teresa Barkley | MAPLEWOOD, NEW JERSEY, USA

My parents have undoubtedly been my greatest influence. My mother taught me to sew when I was five years old, and the first thing I wanted to make was patchwork. My father encouraged me to collect postage stamps, which led to a passion for collecting all sorts of things. As a child, I admired my great-grandmother's Victorian scrapbooks, which led to a lifelong obsession with collecting pictorial textile materials. I think that I was attracted to patternmaking as a career because of my desire to master the art of fitting pieces together to make quilts as well as garments.

I am known for combining vintage found-object materials with contemporary fabric. These compositions are frequently designed to look

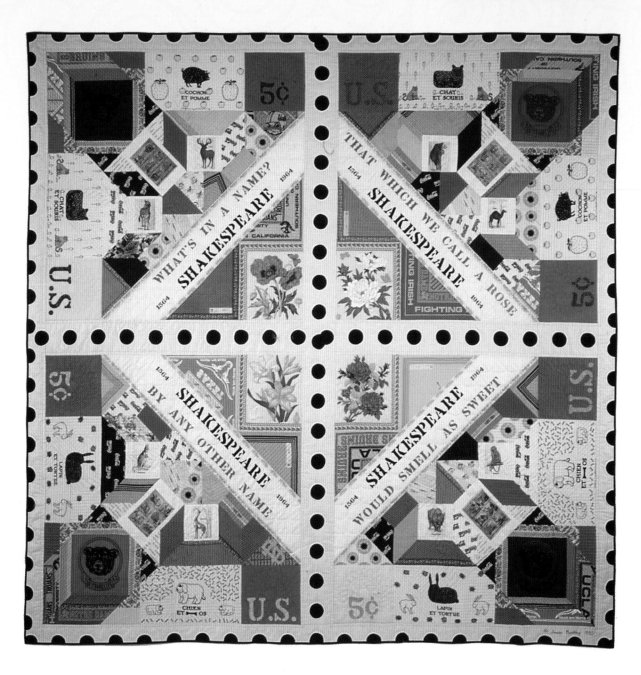

like a postage stamp. As such, they have lettering that is either painted or appliquéd. Also, they have a reverse-appliquéd scalloped border to resemble the perforated edges of a stamp. This series draws on the commemorative aspect that is shared by many postage stamps and many of the vintage textiles that I use.

My artist husband, Donald McLaughlin, was the inspiration for my becoming an artist. Time that we spent together in college changed my definition of art. I would like for my viewers to see the beauty of imperfection in worn materials, and to see familiar things in a new way. That would include appreciating fiber as art.

The Shakespeare Stamp. 1985. 103" x 103".
Cotton, cotton/poly blends (bandanas), antique linen book pages, linen tea towels, clothing labels, acrylic paint. Machine pieced, hand appliquéd, hand painted, hand quilted.
Photo: Karen Bell

Midtown Direct. 2005. 101" x 80".
Cotton, woven picture of the World Trade Center, Pullman Company towels, a headrest from the Pennsylvania Railroad, upholstery webbing, heat transfers of New Jersey Transit monthly train passes (1996–2005), acrylic paint. Machine pieced, hand appliquéd, stenciled, machine quilted.
Collection: Estate of Eileen Keely Hunnikin
Photo: Karen Bell

Joyce Marquess Carey | MADISON, WISCONSIN, USA

I started sewing art quilts after many years of art weaving. It was an easy transition, as I have sewn for most of my life. I thought that sewing my ideas would be faster than weaving them, but I was wrong about that. However, freed from the loom, I was able to increase the scale of my work, eventually making pieces as large as 13 by 25 feet for public spaces.

I've always found visual illusions fascinating, and I love working with gradations of color. I enjoy suggesting depth simply by playing with value. I was delighted when a friend of mine, upon seeing a photo of my two-dimensional *Glad Rags*, said, "I'd love to see the actual pieces to see how deep they are."

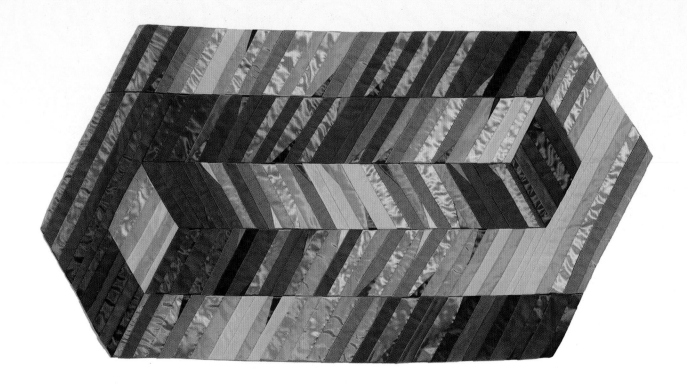

Flying Colors. 1986. 30" x 57".
Silk, polyester, metallic fabric. Machine pieced, hand stitched.
Collection: San Jose Museum of Quilts & Textiles, The
Marbaum Collection
Gift of Marvin and Hilary Fletcher
Photo: James Dewrance

I explored illusion early on in my work, gradually transitioning to narrative pieces. Some of these later works are about our fragile ecosystem. Others are commemorative, verbal and visual puns, or functional. My latest work is a liturgical stole for a friend's ordination.

The best piece of advice I received about creating artwork, or in fact about living, came from one of my students. She said, "When you make a mistake and have to fix it, just shut up and do it."

Passing Through. 1993. 40" x 52".
Satin, silk, polyester, rayon, metallic fabric. Machine pieced, hand stitched.
Collection: San Jose Museum of Quilts & Textiles, The Marbaum Collection
Gift of Marvin and Hilary Fletcher
Photo: James Dewrance

Gayle Fraas and Duncan Slade | BOOTHBAY, MAINE, USA

For a long time we've been painting places. Symbolic and ornamental elements respond to information gleaned from the history, geology, and culture specific to each place functioning as visual prompts that give meaning to the whole.

Textile surface and structure are a constant in our visual language, explored as material, subject, and metaphor. Medieval manuscript illumination, pop art, the Hudson River School, and the graphic language of flags also inform our work. The writing of Wallace Stegner and the music of Miles Davis inspire us as much as the work of any visual artist.

Flag—Departing Emily's. 2009. 18" x 24".
Dye, cotton fabric. Painted, sewn.
Collection: Eleanor Owen Kerr

OPPOSITE
Beach End. 1984. 40" x 40".
Dye, cotton fabric. Painted, sewn.
Collection: Merna and Joseph Guttentag
Photo: Dennis Griggs

The collaborative dialogue we share has been continuous since the mid-1970s. In the early 1980s our interest in creating quilts with a narrative of landscape and ornamental design coalesced when we combined painting, screen printing, block printing, and resist techniques using fiber-reactive dyes on cotton fabric.

Pieces are conceived and executed by either one of us or by both as a team. It is the content, intent, and meaning of the work that we share. Each work continues our visual conversation.

www.fraasslade.com

Judith Larzelere | WESTERLY, RHODE ISLAND, USA

I began quilting as a means of making art for sale. I hoped to do something unique and knew that specializing and years of involvement with a technique might lead to something. Combining Log Cabin construction and Seminole strip piecing was the basis for developing my signature style.

My processes and techniques have remained pretty much the same for nearly thirty years. I have worked with various fabrics: commercially dyed cotton broadcloth, hand-dyed muslin, cotton sateen, and silks, and, recently, "white goods"—undyed cottons, silks, and linens, off the bolt.

I like gathering fabrics for a palette, spreading them out on my work table and ordering them in ways that please me. It is exciting to work out

color combinations and set up a pattern for the strip piecing. My latest quilts consist of white fabrics exclusively, making a much more subtle surface with an emphasis on texture.

I used to be responsive to the natural world to generate color ideas and moods. My recent work is more of an intellectual exercise as I express intangible ideas such as "photons" or create minimalist quilts like those in the Translucency series. I don't keep a sketchbook of possible designs; instead I use a bound sketchbook to lay out a plan on paper to scale for the construction of each quilt.

I am committed to the process I have developed over the years, but I find that distractions of other media intrude and interrupt my production of new works.

www.judithlarzelere.com

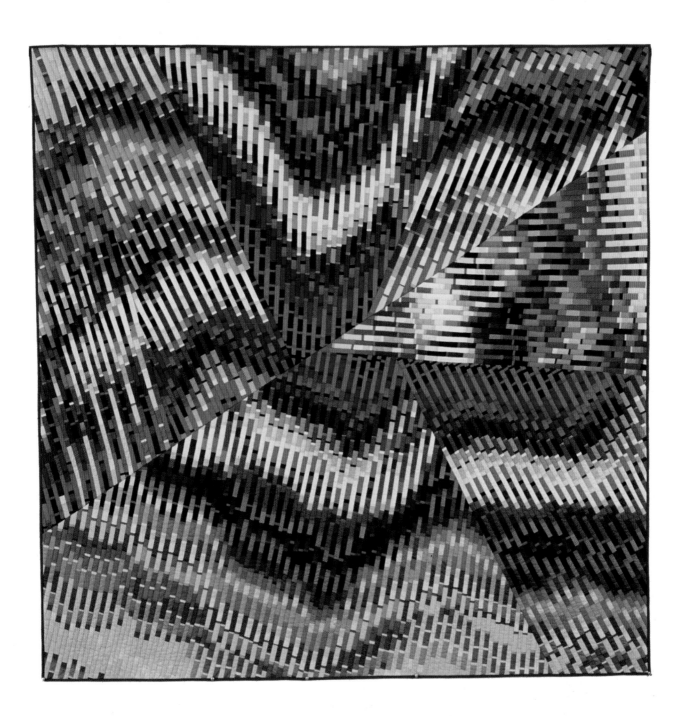

OPPOSITE
Full Spectrum. 1993. 58" x 58".
Cotton. Machine strip pieced and quilted.
Collection: San Jose Museum of Quilts & Textiles
Gift of P & B Fabrics
Photo: James Dewrance

Essex County April. 1986. 74" x 74".
Cotton. Machine strip pieced and quilted.
Collection: Museum of Arts and Design, New York
Photo: Jan Bindas

Terrie Hancock Mangat | EL PRADO, NEW MEXICO, USA

I enjoy hand stitching and find that I can take small parts of a big project along when I travel. I started working in this way when my children had soccer games, ballet lessons, other sports, etc. I could take a little stitching and be happy at the activities, and still be a good mom, get my work done. I still like to do hand embroidery, hand reverse appliqué, and hand piecing.

Embellishment is my passion, and for which I am best known. The other parts of my work that I enjoy are painting, embroidery, and the use of what I call conversational prints. These are more challenging to integrate into a composition but can also carry information about the idea being expressed. I was inspired to make quilts by looking at "scrap bag" traditional quilts and deciding which combinations of fabric I liked the best. The conversational prints are still what floats my boat.

*Dashboard Saints: In Memory of St. Christopher
(Who Lost His Magnetism)*. 1985. 99" x 124".
Commercial cottons, sequins, cotton embroidery thread, photo transfers,
scapulars, seed beads, malachite beads, milagros, coin beads, cotton
appliqués. Machine pieced, hand beaded, painted, embroidered, and quilted.
Collection: International Quilt Study Center & Museum

It takes a ton of time and work to finish a large art quilt. I have to be inspired by the idea and also the fabric and other materials. I enjoy supporting my current idea with the right materials. My monumental "mountain" quilt, for example, has shisha mirrors, pearls, and mica. These are symbols of water, so I put them in the mountain stream.

When I traveled to Bhutan, one of my favorite things I saw there was huge displays of very tall flags, maybe 20 feet high, dedicated to the dead. They were in the traditional number of 108, installed like a monumental art installation at the top of a pass, and in many mountain locations. On that trip I brought home a $15 bag of scraps from the men's traditional clothing. When I bought the scraps, everyone thought I was crazy. At first I thought I would just make a scrap bag from these symbolic Bhutan textile bits. Then last night it came to me to make a really tall flag quilt, using the precious handwoven traditional men's cloth for the poles of the flags. That one idea about the use of the fabric will inspire me to do the work of making the piece. So for me, the integration of the idea and the materials is important in committing to the work.

www.taosfolk.com/terrie-mangat/

Freedom Fireworks. 1998. 88" x 94".
Mud cloth, African tie-dyed fabric, cottons, acrylic paint, Oaxacan embroidered flowers, cowrie shells, fluff chicks, vintage stars, African lipstick beads, vintage glass beads, bugle beads, papier mâché, roundels, seed bead flowers, shisha mirror cloth, turquoise nuggets. Machine pieced, hand beaded, painted, embroidered, and quilted.

Medicine Bough Mountain Retreat.
2016. 23' x 12'.
Bugle and seed beads, commercial
and hand-dyed cottons, hand-screened
cotton, embroidery thread, acrylic
paint, sheer silk, mica, mountain
climbing cams, bugle beads, shisha
mirrors, canvas marigolds, pearls,
buttons, crystals, rhinestone necklace,
Oaxacan embroidered flowers, vintage
beaded dress, stones, rhinestones.
Machine piecing, hand piecing (small
squares), beading, hand embroidery,
silkscreen printing, machine quilting
by Nicole Dunn.

Taos Mountain Fireworks. 2012. 90" x 88.5".
Commercial silk and cotton, hand-dyed fabrics, acrylic paint, sequins,
vintage embellishments from India, shisha mirrors, rose buttons, ostrich
eggshell beads, rhinestones, pearls, rickrack, glass beads. Machine pieced
and quilted, hand beaded and embroidered.

Jan Myers-Newbury | PITTSBURGH, PENNSYLVANIA, USA

I like to be in control. Each aspect of the work that I do—from the dyeing to the piecing to the quilting—fits in with that basic need. Although the end result of my labors nearly always encompasses moments of inspiration and/or serendipity, I am always starting with elements of calculated process.

In the earliest days (late 1970s), this approach meant working with tightly spaced gradations within a gridded design format. As I began to explore patternmaking through the immersion dye process, however, I found that the fabrics and dyes interacted in sometimes unpredictable ways.

Carnival. 2011. 70" x 80".
Cotton. Hand dyed using *arashi shibori* techniques, underpainted and immersion dyed, machine pieced and quilted.
Collection: Mary Rubin and Sam Lieber
Photo: Sam Newbury

OPPOSITE
Cassiopeia. 1985. 74" x 60".
Hand dyed unbleached cotton muslin. Hand dyed in gradated sequences, machine pieced and quilted.
Collection: Honeywell Corporation, Minneapolis, Minnesota

It is a thrill for me when I unbind, wash, dry, and iron newly dyed fabrics and begin to put them together on my design wall. However, I most love the actual piecing once all the heavy lifting of composition has been completed. Give me a sewing machine and cotton fabric, and I am a happy gal.

I don't really feel that I have changed the *way* I work. What has changed is the *rate* at which I produce new work. And I have to admit that I am now less confident, since there are longer periods of time between initiating each new piece. Getting started is the hard part.

I have tried to make beautiful things that, I hope, bring joy to others, as well as to myself. It is an uncomplicated quest, really. I have never made topical or narrative work. I see my work as a potential oasis from all of the tragedy that seems to bear down on all of us with increasing frequency.

www.janmyersnewbury.com

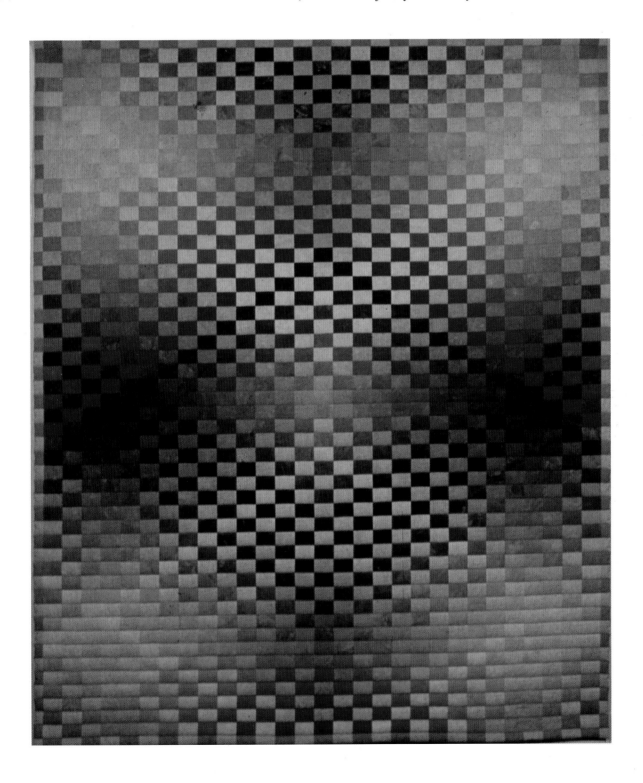

Mary Anhaltzer and Thirteen Moons Gallery

Born in Oshkosh, Wisconsin, in 1938 to Alberta and Miles Kimball, Mary Anhaltzer grew up under the influence of her philanthropic mother, who was directly responsible for the revitalization of downtown Oshkosh during the 1960s. When Miles Kimball died in 1949, Alberta assumed directorship of the Miles Kimball Co., a mail-order business still operating today. At the impressionable age of eleven, Anhaltzer observed her mother not only running a thriving business, but also anonymously donating millions of dollars to build a public library, opera house, and other civic improvements, as well as helping to support shelters for abused women.

In 1958 Mary married Herb Anhaltzer while attending Cornell University. They later moved to California, where she opened a gift shop in Portola Valley, expanding to locations in nearby Palo Alto.

Mary Anhaltzer certainly would have been aware of the quilt contests and patchwork fashion shows organized by Joyce Gross in the Bay area, which were well publicized.

Anhaltzer began her life in quilts by making traditionally patterned works, eventually experimenting with original designs, inspired by trips to Guatemala. The folk art and textiles of Guatemala are reflected in many of her quilts. In her philanthropic work, Anhaltzer often visited villages in Central America and elsewhere to encourage women as they attempted to build small businesses.

When Anhaltzer founded Thirteen Moons Gallery in Santa Fe in 1999, she intended for the gallery's profits to be donated to the Katalysis Fund, supporting women establishing textile businesses in Central America. Thirteen Moons, named after the thirteenth month in the Mayan calendar, was the first gallery dedicated exclusively to featuring contemporary quilt art. Its opening was hailed across the country by quilt artists, and the shows were extraordinary in the range of quilts presented. But in July 2001, Anhaltzer died in her sleep, and the gallery eventually changed hands, with a different focus for the exhibitions.

Mary Anhaltzer (d.)

USA
La Ofrenda para Maria Louisa. 1996. 71" x 42".
Cotton. Sewn.
Collection: Herb Anhaltzer
Photo: Deidre Adams

Founded by Lynn Lewis Young, *Art/Quilt Magazine*, with its high-quality illustrations on glossy paper, caused quite a sensation among quilt artists when the first issue appeared in 1994. Subtitled "a new magazine devoted to the art quilt," *Art/Quilt Magazine* was published intermittently in twelve issues until 2001.

As Young made clear in her first editor's statement, she was pretty much on her own in this ambitious undertaking, "Once I realized no one else was going to do what I had in mind, the idea for starting a periodical for art quilts became an obsession." Each issue contains forty-eight pages of articles, exhibition and book reviews, information on new products and services, upcoming events, and—most important for the Art Quilt Movement—a lengthy feature showcasing "New/ Works" that has become the most comprehensive documentation we have concerning art quilts from the 1990s.

In these pages we see masterful works by the first generation of quilt artists, alongside innovative quilts by new makers. Produced by Young herself on a Macintosh Quadra 800 computer, *Art/Quilt Magazine* was the timely result of advances in digital technology and one visionary woman.

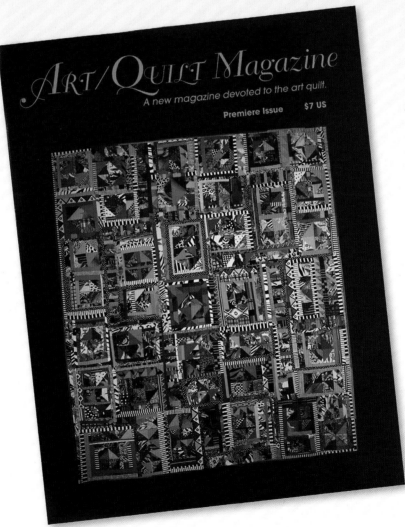

Art/Quilt Magazine
Cover of premiere issue
showing "Rules Broken:
Running Rampant"
by Ruth Smalley

Gallery 1980s

Françoise Barnes

Los Ranchos, New Mexico, USA
Zaire Songe Mask IV. 1989.
71" x 68.5".
Cotton, cotton batik, lamé.
Machine pieced, hand quilted.
Photo: Steven DeRoma

BELOW

Françoise Barnes

Zaire Songe Mask II. 1988.
72" x 72".
Cottons, handwoven fabrics from
Guatemala, Manuel Canovas
interior design fabric.
Machine pieced, hand quilted.
Photo: Steven DeRoma

Elizabeth Barton

Athens, Georgia, USA
Warm Light. ca. 1980. 57" x 43".
Cotton. Pieced and quilted.

BELOW

Sonya Lee Barrington

San Francisco, California, USA
Stairway to the Stars. 1988. 48" x 84".
Cotton. Machine pieced, hand
appliquéd, hand quilted.
Collection: San Jose Museum of
Quilts & Textiles
Gift of Sonya Lee Barrington
Photo: James Dewrance

Ross Palmer Beecher

Seattle, Washington, USA
7-Up Quilt. 1988. 72" x 54".
Metal, rubber, leather, and plastic. Cut and wired metal,
sewn inner tubes, cut and wired auto reflectors.
Collection: Hallie Ford Museum of Art, Willamette University,
Salem, Oregon, Maribeth Collins Art Acquisition Fund, 2012.019
Photo: Dale Peterson

Helen Bitar

Sheridan, Oregon, USA
Powerful Flowers. 1987.
50" x 56".
Satin, cotton. Appliquéd.

OPPOSITE

Dee Danley-Brown (d.)

USA
Metropolitan Postcard. 1989. 51.5" x 62".
Commercial and hand painted fabrics.
Machine and hand pieced, hand quilted.
Photo: Karen Bell

BELOW

Deborah Felix

Hadley, Massachusetts, USA
Discussing Plants for the Future. 1985. 69" x 90".
Canvas, cotton blends, painted and rubber
stamped with textile paints. Hand appliquéd,
machine quilted.

Nancy Halpern

Natick, Massachusetts, USA
Archipelago. 1983. 74.5" x 96".
Cotton, cotton blends, both
commercial and hand-dyed.
Hand and machine pieced,
hand quilted.
Collection: New England
Quilt Museum
Photo: David Caras

OPPOSITE

Jean Hewes (d.)

USA
Dancers. 1984. 94" x 86".
Silk, rayon, commercial cotton batik,
hand-painted cotton, Indian and
Afghan embroideries. Machine
appliquéd, pieced, and quilted.
Collection: International Quilt Study
Center & Museum, University of
Nebraska–Lincoln

BELOW

David Hornung

Woodside, New York, USA
Orange Construction. 1982. 66.5" x 56".
Cotton. Machine pieced and quilted
with hand appliqué.
Collection: International Quilt Study
Center & Museum, University of
Nebraska–Lincoln
Photo: International Quilt Study
Center & Museum

Katherine Knauer

New York, New York, USA
Flying Cadet, 1943. 1989. 67" x 67".
Cotton, silk, synthetic blends, textile paint. Painted, stencil
printed, sewn (machine pieced, hand embroidered, machine
embroidered), hand quilted (cross-stitch quilting).
Photo: D. James Dee

Shizuko Kuroha

Tokyo, Japan
The Sea of Japan in Winter. 1983. 78" x 79".
Collection: International Quilt Study Center &
Museum, University of Nebraska–Lincoln
Photo: International Quilt Study Center & Museum

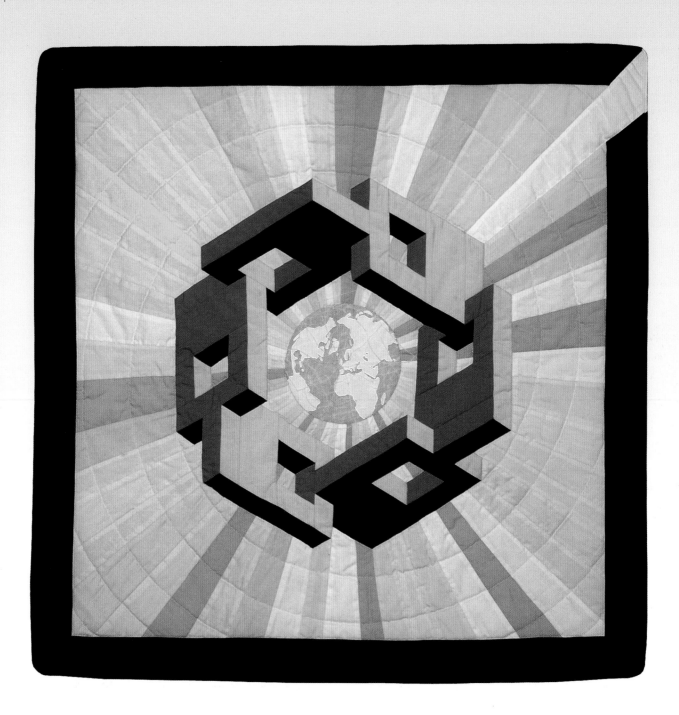

OPPOSITE

Irene MacWilliam

Belfast, Northern Ireland
Vision of the World. 1988. 39" x 39".
Cottons and polycottons. Machine
pieced, free-machine embroidered,
appliquéd, hand quilted.

Judy Martin

Sheguiandah, Ontario, Canada
self portrait. 1985. 44" x 42".
Maternity clothes, cotton, fabric
paint. Hand painted, machine
pieced, hand quilted.

Risë Nagin

Pittsburgh, Pennsylvania, USA
Dwelling. 1989. 76" x 96".
Silk, polyester, cotton, acetate, rayon, cellophane,
thread, acrylic paint, gouache. Stained, painted, pieced,
layered, appliquéd, embroidered, quilted, hand sewn.
Collection: Hermitage State Museum,
St. Petersburg, Russia
Photo: Sam Newbury

OPPOSITE

Jean Neblett

Santa Fe, New Mexico, USA
Primal II. 1989. 51" x 68".
Commercial printed and solid
cottons. Curved pieced, cut through,
then pieced. Machine quilted.
Photo: David Belda

Esther Parkhurst (d.)

USA
Reconstructed Rhythm.
ca. 1988. 47" x 66".
Collection: Denis Parkhurst
Photo: Denis Parkhurst

Deidre Scherer

Williamsville, Vermont, USA
Angel. 1985. 12" x 10".
Thread on layered cotton, silk.
Cut, layered, machine stitched.
Collection: Lillian Farber
Photo: Jeff Baird

David Walker

Cincinnati, Ohio, USA
The Other Side of Silence. 1989. 91" x 78".
Cottons, blends, metallic fabrics, control-bleached and hand-dyed
fabrics, yarn, beads, sequins, paint. Machine pieced and appliquéd.
Collection: National Quilt Museum
Photo: Victoria Caldwell, Horizon Media Group

Yvonne Wells

Tuscaloosa, Alabama, USA
Pieced Diamonds. ca. 1980–1990. 85.5" x 66.5".
Cotton and cotton blends. Pieced and appliquéd.
Collection: International Quilt Study Center & Museum,
University of Nebraska–Lincoln
Photo: International Quilt Study Center & Museum

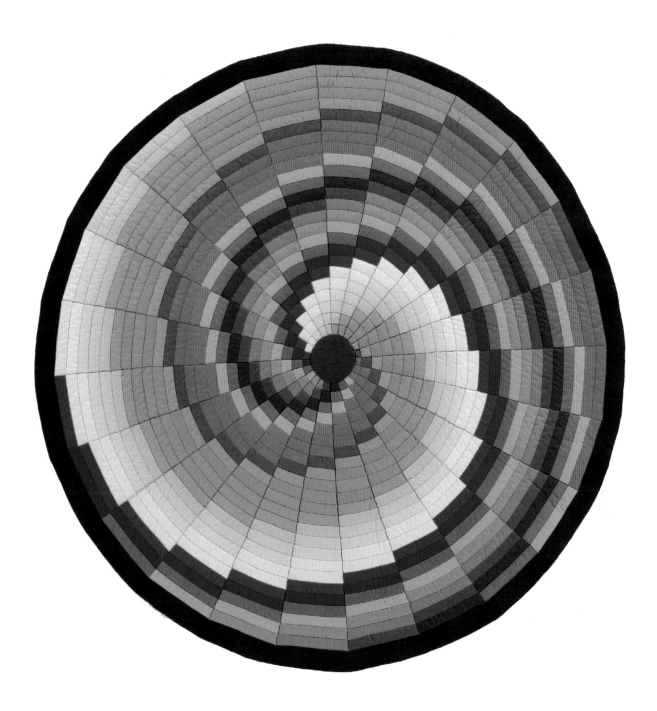

Virginia Randles

Athens, Ohio, USA
Helix II. 1984. 52" x 52".
Collection: International Quilt Study Center & Museum,
University of Nebraska–Lincoln
Photo: International Quilt Study Center & Museum

Charlotte Patera (d.)

USA
Tuxedo Junction. 1986. 72" x 72".
Cotton. Machine pieced, hand reverse appliquéd, hand quilted.
Collection: San Jose Museum of Quilts & Textiles
Gift of Charlotte Patera
Photo: James Dewrance

Rosie Lee Tompkins (d.)

USA.
Framed Improvisational Block. 1986. 82" x 74"
Velvet, velveteen, velour, panne velvet, chenille.
Hand pieced by artist, hand quilted by Willia Ette Graham.
Collection: Eli Leon
Photo: Sharon Reisdorph

Miriam Nathan-Roberts | BERKELEY, CALIFORNIA, USA

I have been interested over the years in creating illusions of three dimensions on flat or semiflat surfaces.* Perhaps this is partly because I had no depth perception until I was thirty years old; without prisms in my glasses, my eyes don't achieve normal fusion.

Since the early 1970s I have worked in multiple styles. The Interweave series from the 1980s is very controlled and intellectual, with a tight structure. I grew up in Pittsburgh, Pennsylvania, a city with three rivers. My father studied engineering and showed me the undersides of bridges; my Interweave quilts were inspired by these bridges. I found that as I worked in this series, I needed to rebel and let loose. Thus was born another group of quilts I call the Architectural series from the 1990s. These pieces use wild fabrics, which I love, and involved relatively little planning.

A third direction has been a departure from the first two series. I emphasized unusual fabric combinations and the play among colors throughout the quilt surface. I either do my designs on paper or compose on the working wall.

In the past few years, I completed several quilts based on photographic and scanned images, which I digitally manipulated on the computer. The final image was digitally printed on fabric and then machine quilted. I continue to explore the crossover between digital design and digital printing on textiles.

Although I also paint and create archival fine-art prints, when working in the quilt medium I feel like I am making a historical connection. I feel a sisterhood.

I'd like to be remembered for creating innovative work, and I'd like to feel that I have inspired other quilt artists.

www.miriamnathanroberts.com

*Based on the artist's website and on a December 2, 2009, interview with Nancy Bavor.

OPPOSITE
Lattice Interweave. 1983. 84" x 84".
Cotton, cotton blends. Machine pieced, quilting designed by artist and hand quilted by Sarah Herschberger.
Photo: James Dewrance

Salt and Pepper. 2012. 40" x 56".
Cotton, fiber reactive dye. Printed, machine appliquéd and quilted.
Photo: James Dewrance

Spin Cycle. 1998. 66" x 71".
Commercial cottons, hand-dyed and airbrushed
cottons. Machine pieced and appliquéd,
machine quilted.
Photo: James Dewrance

Ellen Oppenheimer | SAN FRANCISCO, CALIFORNIA, USA

I really enjoy manipulating fabric. I have a very tactile and simple reaction to sewing together different shapes and colors. I also love working with patterns.

There are a few different phases in developing my work. Initially, I sketch my ideas in a notebook. When I have an idea or image that I want to work on, I might need to create some silkscreens and also try a small sample to see if the colors, patterns, and textures are what I want. This can take quite a few attempts and sometimes is frustrating. When the fabric is all printed and washed, I can begin to sew everything together. Although I find the entire process compelling, my favorite part is seeing months of work come together the way I hoped it all would.

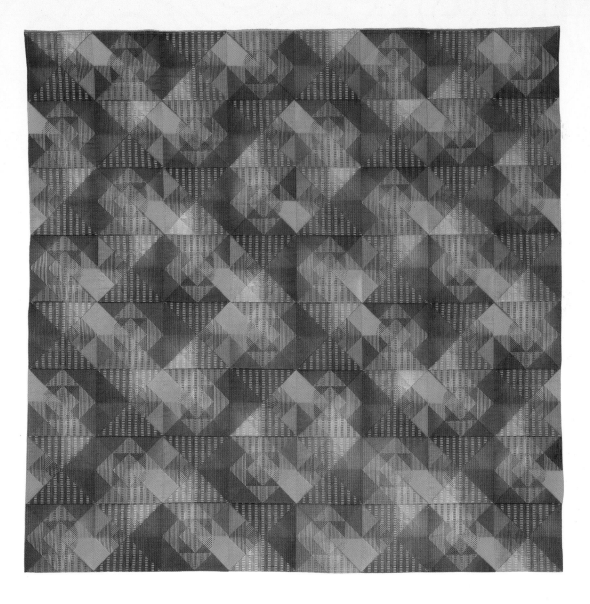

BR #1. 2010. 62" x 62".
Cotton fabric silk-screened with dyes and textile ink.
Silk-screened, machine sewn and quilted.
Photo: Deidre Adams

There were many people who influenced me as an artist. My mother was a professional harpist. Through my entire life her dedication and practice were ingrained in me. I am constantly aspiring to her professional grace and generosity. My wife is also an artist, and she has been a great inspiration as well as a mentor for me.

I took a class from the glass artist Marvin Lipofsky when he was teaching at the California College of Art. He emphasized the importance of learning the chemistry of glassmaking and creating a unique palette, something not accessible to anyone else. If I applied that same principle to quilting, I had to learn to dye and print my own fabric. So I began to do that, which allowed me to develop a unique visual vocabulary.

https://ellen-oppenheimer.squarespace.com

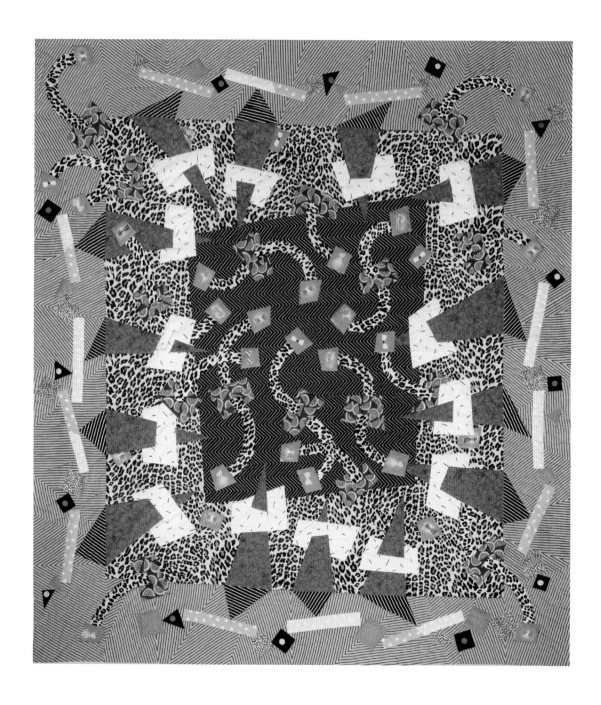

New Years Eve Party. 1987. 84" x 76".
Commercial fabric. Machine pieced, hand quilted.
Photo: James Dewrance

Yvonne Porcella | (d.)

Although I had been weaving and making clothes with fabric I wove myself, by 1980 I abandoned weaving and focused on wearable art and quilt making.* I took the plunge and bought 150 yards of 150 different colors from a mail-order fabric store owned by Elly Sienkiewicz. I had my palette. All I knew was how to do Log Cabin blocks, strips, squares, and eventually a half-square triangle. Because I just put strips together, my design had to rely on color. I made *Takoage* with the only shapes I knew how to do—strips and triangles. I also made my first kimono-shaped quilt after seeing an exhibition at the Asian Art Museum in San Francisco.

Come Again Kabuki. 2005. 85" x 77".
Raw edged, fused, appliquéd. Machine pieced and quilted.
Collection: San Jose Museum of Quilts & Textiles, gift of the Artist
Gift of Yvonne Porcella
Photo: James Dewrance

By the 1990s, I started focusing more on themes and creating my own imagery, as in *Chili, Purple Dog, Chili, Chili* and *Termites Ate the Purple Dog*. Over the years, I have used a wide variety of techniques from piecing, appliqué, and fusibles. I also did machine piecing and quilting as well as hand quilting.

My strong Catholic faith helps my work. When I get stuck, I pray. I think I live my faith, as you can see from what's on the walls of my studio. I get emotional when I talk about this, but I have been blessed. My work is very positive, happy, and sometimes imbued with fantasy. I will continue doing what I do because it makes me happy.

I always told my students four things that would help them find their voice and be a successful artist. One, you have to have the drive. Two, you have to be prolific. You could have the drive and not create, but you have to create. Three, you have to be free of creative constraints, and four, you have to have your own space.

My son Don, who is also an artist, gave me some good advice: "You've got to keep yourself current and active." I hope I have done that in my career.

www.yvonneporcella.com

*Based on an October 24, 2009, interview with Nancy Bavor. Yvonne Porcella, who died in 2016, founded Studio Art Quilt Associates in 1989.

Robe of the Dragon Rider. 1982.
60" x 48".
Cotton and metallic fabrics.
Machine pieced, hand-painted lining.
Collection: Robert Porcella
Photo: James Dewrance

OPPOSITE
Taking the Train to Bakersfield. 1986.
74.5" x 70".
Cotton. Machine pieced and quilted.
Collection: Robert Porcella
Photo: James Dewrance

Razzle Dazzle. 1981. 39" x 34".
Cotton. Machine pieced and quilted.
Collection of: Sandra Sider
Photo: Deidre Adams

Faith Ringgold | ENGLEWOOD, NEW JERSEY, USA

I became an artist in the tumultuous 1960s. By the early 1970s I had developed both vision and voice as a black woman artist in America.

I went to West Africa in the 1970s and returned home inspired to write my memoir. *We Flew over the Bridge: The Memoirs of Faith Ringgold* was published in 1995—it took me fifteen years to get it published. During that time I wrote and painted Story Quilts and began to create masked performances to tell my story. I had been working in collaboration with my mother, Mme. Willi Posey, a dressmaker and fashion designer. We made our first quilt in 1980.

News of the great jazz saxophonist Sonny Rollins, a childhood friend, blowing his horn on the Manhattan Bridge so that he would not disturb his

neighbors inspired my painted Story Quilt, *Tar Beach*. That story of Cassie Louise Lightfoot flying over the George Washington Bridge became my first children's book. I have published fourteen children's books to date. The year 1990 found me in France painting the French Collection and writing the story of Willia Marie Simone, an African American woman who went to Paris to be an artist in 1920 during the Harlem Renaissance. The American Collection came next and the Story Quilts and children's books continued to document my artistic production.

In 1992 my husband, Birdie, and I moved from Harlem to Jones Road in Englewood, New Jersey, to build a studio. However, our white neighbors (unsuccessfully) sought to deny us the freedom to live there. Freedom, you know, is not free. It took me six years to realize my dream of a beautiful studio surrounded by a beautiful garden. Inspiring images of my ancestors on the Underground Railroad now appeared in my new landscape paintings of *Coming to Jones Road under a Blood Red Sky*. Icons of black men and women making the music the whole world loves, the music we brought to America along with the pain of slavery, were now a new inspiration. *Mama Can Sing* and *Papa Can Blow* are the ever-reassuring realities of black life I depend on during difficult times.

Recent work includes *Our Ancestors* (a quilt project): stories about the world's children who, faced with life in a world at war, have forgotten how to play. We call upon our ancestors, who would surely bring love and happiness into their lives. Where would we have been without them?
www.faithringgold.com

Dancing at the Louvre from the series
The French Collection #1. 1991. 73.5" x 80.5".
© 1991 Faith Ringgold
Acrylic on canvas. Stitched.
Private collection

Joy Saville | PRINCETON, NEW JERSEY, USA

I was inspired as a child to work with fabric by my mother, who encouraged me to make art. Since the age of seven, I have worked with fabric and the sewing machine. As an artist, I developed my strip-piecing technique to assemble abstract images and use vibrant color as my focus.

It took me ten years to figure out what I wanted to do with fabric. After making a commission of four communion tablecloths and pulpit hangings for my church, I realized that color was my focus. That passion has continued to evolve ever since. Creating my fabric constructions involves me completely: spiritually, intellectually, and emotionally. When people see my pieces, I hope that they find something relevant in my work and that they are inspired to be creative, too.

The best advice I ever had was from my husband, who said, "Do what excites you!"

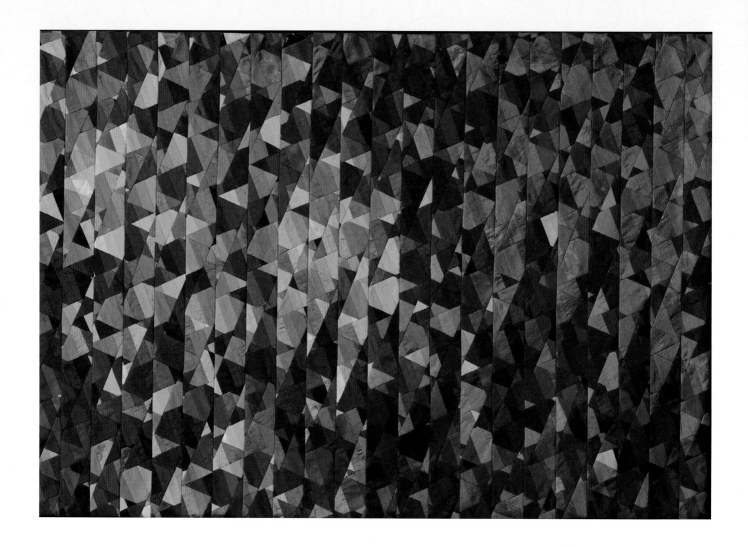

Spring Moss. 2011. 38" x 50".
Silk. Machine pieced.
Collection: Dr. and Mrs. Jim Hastings

Seminole Study III: Gravity & Grace. 1982. 92" x 68".
Silk. Machine pieced.
Collection: Museum of Arts and Design, New York
Photo: William Taylor

Studio Art Quilt Associates, Inc. (SAQA)

Studio Art Quilt Associates (SAQA)
Conference attendees.

Founded in 1989 by California artist Yvonne Porcella, SAQA expanded nationally during the 1990s to include some 500 members. In 1993, SAQA co-sponsored a symposium with the Los Angeles County Museum of Art that featured artist Miriam Schapiro as a speaker along with museum curators, collectors, and other artists. Other events during the next 14 years prompted conferences and symposia by SAQA, and the organization has held an annual conference since 2007.

The membership has now reached more than 3400 individuals in 40 countries, with twenty percent of the membership residing outside the United States. SAQA achieved recognition from the National Endowment for the Arts in 2010 with an award in the Visual Arts category to support a touring exhibition, and today SAQA's numerous juried exhibitions of art quilts travel to more than a dozen countries, accompanied by full-color printed catalogues containing essays on quilt culture and aesthetics.

SAQA's mission is to promote the art quilt through education, exhibitions, professional development, documentation, and publications. To achieve these goals, SAQA focuses on projects that support its members and provide educational outreach, such as *SAQA Journal* and *Art Quilt Quarterly* magazine. Online resources include webinars, an annual six-week Seminar, and back issues of the *SAQA Journal*. Regional groups form the backbone of SAQA, providing local networking opportunities, workshops, and mini-conferences. SAQA had 23 regional exhibitions touring in 2017 alone.

SAQA's archives are housed at the International Quilt Study Center & Museum at the University of Nebraska, Lincoln.

www.saqa.com

SAQA™
Studio **Art** Quilt Associates

Eight years after the first *Quilt National*, a new juried art quilt competition was founded on the West Coast in 1987 with the title *Quilts in the Grand Tradition*, featuring eight-two pieces by sixty-eight artists and exhibited at Grand Tradition Estate near San Diego. By 1990 the main title of the show had become *Visions* with various thematic subtitles, a biennial competition.

From 1990 until 1998, *Visions* premiered at the Museum of San Diego History, then at the Oceanside Museum of Art from 2002 until 2010. Since then, the exhibition has been hosted by Visions Art Museum: Contemporary Quilts + Textiles, in San Diego. Like *Quilt National*, *Visions* publishes each exhibition in a full-color catalog including statements from the jurors, who have included (in chronological order) such luminaries as Jonathan Holstein, Nancy Crow, Paul J. Smith, Robert Shaw, Rebecca Stevens, Jane Sauer, Patricia Malarcher, Marci Rae McDade, and Katie Pasquini Masopust.

Unlike *Quilt National*, with its expansive space at the Dairy Barn, which can accommodate numerous quilts, *Visions* selects no more than approximately forty quilts for each exhibition, lending an air of exclusivity to the competition. The *Visions* exhibitions do not tour, prompting collectors, curators, and quilt artists to include Visions Art Museum in their travel plans when the show is on display.

www.visionsartmuseum.org

CHAPTER THREE

1990s: Discovery and Experimentation

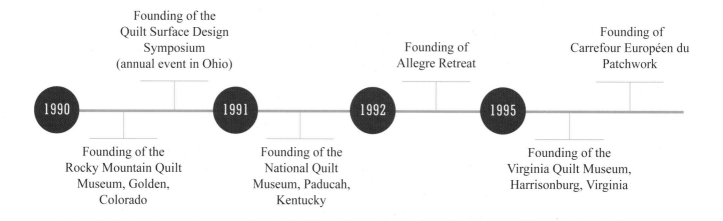

Founding of the
Quilt Surface Design
Symposium
(annual event in Ohio)

Founding of
Allegre Retreat

Founding of
Carrefour Européen du
Patchwork

1990   1991   1992   1995

Founding of the
Rocky Mountain Quilt
Museum, Golden,
Colorado

Founding of the
National Quilt
Museum, Paducah,
Kentucky

Founding of the
Virginia Quilt Museum,
Harrisonburg, Virginia

Quilt artists Nancy Crow and Linda Fowler founded the Quilt Surface Design Symposium (QSDS) in Ohio in 1990, offering a wide variety of educational opportunities. During the first decade of QSDS, hundreds of students experimented with new techniques and processes in studio workshops. By the 1990s, Quilting by the Lake (founded in 1981) in upstate New York had also become a popular destination for quilters in general, with many classes focusing on art quilts by the end of the decade. Other inspirational studio classes expanding the creativity of quilt artists were being taught at Empty Spools Seminars in Asilomar, California (founded in 1986), and at Art Quilt Tahoe (1998). Many of the artists in this book were teaching those classes during the 1990s.

This decade saw five quilt institutions founded across the country, beginning with the Rocky Mountain Quilt Museum in Golden, Colorado, in 1990. The following year, the National Quilt Museum was founded in Paducah Kentucky, then in 1995 the Virginia Quilt Museum in Harrisonburg. The La Conner Quilt Museum in La Conner, Washington (now the Pacific Northwest Quilt & Fiber Arts Museum), opened its doors in 1997, the same year in which philanthropists and quilt collectors Robert and Ardis James were instrumental in founding the International Quilt Study Center & Museum (IQSCM) at the University of Nebraska, Lincoln. These venues, which exhibit quilts of all types, have long provided quilt artists with refreshing new avenues to explore.

Quilt makers embraced innovation and experimentation. They strove to create original designs and develop new or adapt familiar techniques to serve their creative purposes. In doing so, these artists transformed quilts from a functional bedcover, produced at home for domestic use, to an aesthetic art object. As such, the art quilt represents a

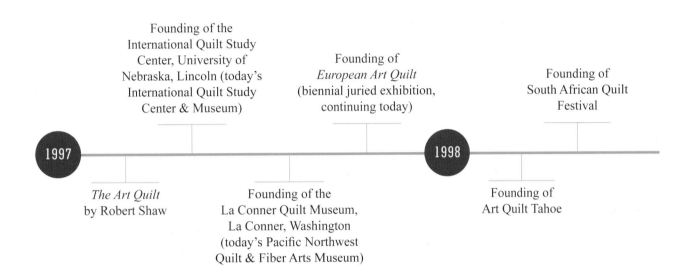

Founding of the International Quilt Study Center, University of Nebraska, Lincoln (today's International Quilt Study Center & Museum)

Founding of *European Art Quilt* (biennial juried exhibition, continuing today)

Founding of South African Quilt Festival

1997

1998

The Art Quilt by Robert Shaw

Founding of the La Conner Quilt Museum, La Conner, Washington (today's Pacific Northwest Quilt & Fiber Arts Museum)

Founding of Art Quilt Tahoe

continuum both of quilt history and art history. By the 1990s, the art quilt had received broader acceptance in the art, craft, and quilt worlds, and for the most part quilt artists in the 1990s were not working in isolation as their predecessors often did. The trailblazers frequently inspired the later artists, often through the earlier artists' teaching, publications, or quilt exhibits. While some in this next generation of artists may have started by learning traditional quilt-making techniques, they quickly developed their own distinctive style, embracing the new art form.

Experimentation with materials, techniques, and processes resulted in dynamic surfaces and vivid imagery. Tafi Brown applied cyanotype chemicals to fabric in her interpretations of architectural structures, extending the concept of "blueprint." Jane Burch Cochran attached gloves, ribbons, gold leaf, doilies, pockets cut from clothes, plastic watches, playing cards, and many other embellishments to her expressive quilts. Arturo Alonzo Sandoval wove fabric by hand for his 1992 flag quilt, and Jane Dunnewold printed transparencies for her quilt celebrating the medieval mystic Hildegard von Bingen. During the 1990s, Wendy Huhn was becoming known for her political quilts based on xerographic imagery, and John Lefelhocz incorporated paper packets of sugar, nylon window screening, and dental floss to represent US currency in one of his astonishing mixed-media quilts.

Quilt artists often endorsed the postmodern tendency to embrace unorthodox materials and pop culture, working in a collage or pastiche mentality. The assemblage nature of quilts encourages this approach to art making, which was flourishing in the last decade of the 20th century.

Elizabeth Busch | GLENBURN, MAINE, USA

Instead of having a regular schedule for doing my work, I trust that inner voice to tell me when it's time. That signal gets me into the studio, to put paint on a blank piece of fabric, and so the process begins. The steps are always the same and always new, and each is pleasurably a part of my subconscious.

The Maine environment is extremely important to me and influences my work; helps it to evolve. I draw, paint, sew, and sculpt space. I do not know how that happens, but I recognize that it has happened when I look at new pieces and see they are quite different from earlier work. I know that I will make a lot of work, and some of it will be good and some of it won't. It doesn't matter. I simply need to make piece one before I can make pieces two, three, etc. It may not be until four or five that a piece really works. I simply had to make one through three to get there.

If I am fully present with my work, I believe it will connect with others. If I'm not 100 percent with the piece while I'm painting and composing, that energy will not be there . . . and neither will the viewer's interest.

www.elizabethbusch.com

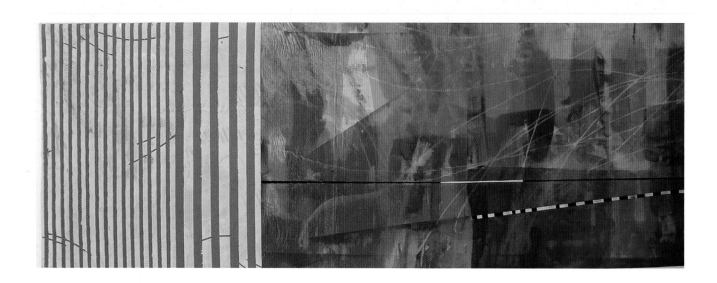

Heat Wave. 2014. 26" x 70".
Cotton canvas, textile paint, gray and black Trigger cloth.
Hand painted, machine pieced, hand quilted.

When We Were Young. 1988. 80" x 68".
Cotton canvas, acrylic paint, hand-dyed cotton. Hand painted, airbrushed, machine pieced, hand quilted.
Collection: Museum of Arts and Design, New York
Photo: Dennis Griggs

Spring. 1998. 69.5" x 67".
Cotton canvas, acrylic paint, cotton
fabric, metal leaf. Hand painted,
airbrushed, hand quilted.
Photo: Dennis Griggs

OPPOSITE
Summer. 1998. 70" x 68".
Cotton canvas, acrylic paint, cotton
fabric, metal leaf. Hand painted,
airbrushed, hand quilted.
Photo: Dennis Griggs

BELOW
Winter. 1998. 69" x 67".
Cotton canvas, acrylic paint, cotton,
metal leaf. Hand painted, airbrushed,
hand quilted.
Photo: Dennis Griggs

Dorothy Caldwell | HASTINGS, ONTARIO, CANADA

The land is the subject of my work. Art is a process of searching and exploration that allows me to learn and to experience place in many different ways. There's a physical aspect to it, being in a landscape and touching the plants, rocks, and soil. Identifying my own personal landmarks through gathering, touching, and recording is how I create a unique sense of place.

The vocabulary for my art is drawn from textile traditions and practices. I have a deep respect for cloth. It's very powerful when cloth retains traces of its previous life, gathers history, and becomes something new. I am drawn to cloth that has been repaired and reconstructed. In that ongoing process, the cloth encodes time and the richness of lives lived.

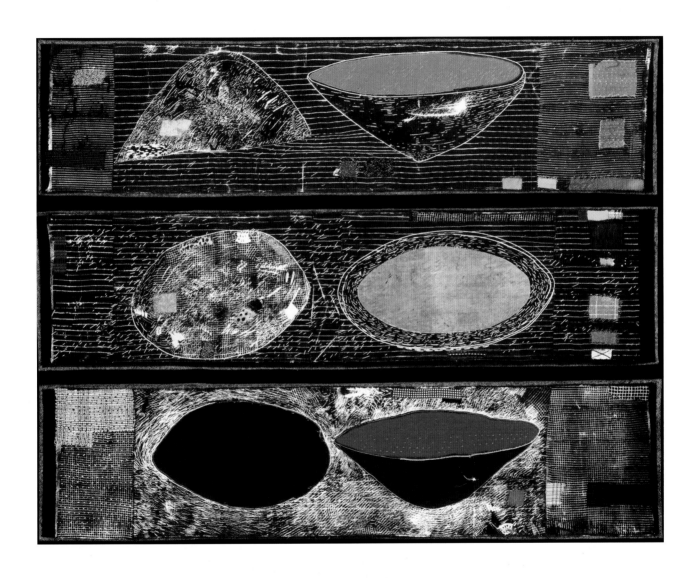

I love the graphic quality that is possible with silkscreen and discharge batik. Tools such as tjantings for drawing, found and made printing blocks, and paint brushes are used to apply hot and cold wax to make my fabric. These tools support the feeling that a mark is very personal and an extension of one's body energy. I juxtapose the direct quality of the drawn mark with the slower, more contained mark of the stitch. Slow growth is inherent in my process.

Through working in remote environments where human traces are few and silence is palpable, my work has become more quiet and subtle. The drama and graphic quality of my black-and-white discharge batik has softened over time into less confrontational gray washes and small-scale patterns.

In some ways, the land is like a mended piece of cloth. Mending is supposed to be invisible, but there's always a trace of human intervention.

www.dorothycaldwell.com

133

OPPOSITE
Four Patch: Hay/Wheat/Rye/Barley.
1994–1995. 96" x 98".
Wax resist and discharged cotton with stitching
and appliqué. Hand quilted by Evelyn Martin,
Ruth Lamont, Grace Foxton, Lydia Kelder.
Collection: Eleanor McCain
Photo: Gulf Reflections Studio, Inc.

*Triptych: A Hill / A Lake; A Lake / A Bowl;
An Island / A Pond.* 2002. Each 24" x 60".
Wax resist and discharged cotton with stitching and appliqué.
Collection: *A Hill / A Lake* and *A Lake / A Bowl* are in collection
of Ron Fitzgerald; *An Island / A Pond* is in the collection of
Museum of Civilization, Hull, Quebec
Photo: Thomas Moore

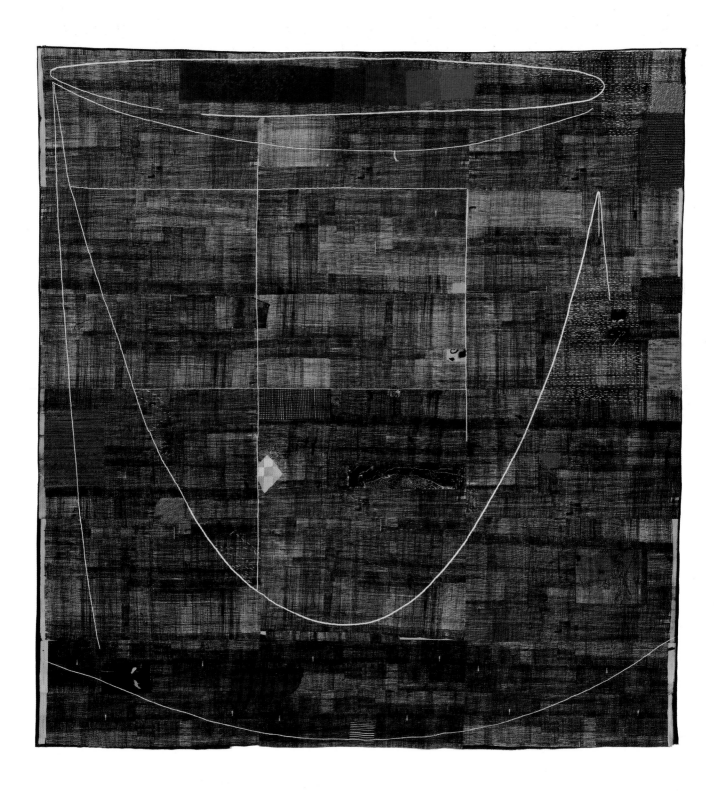

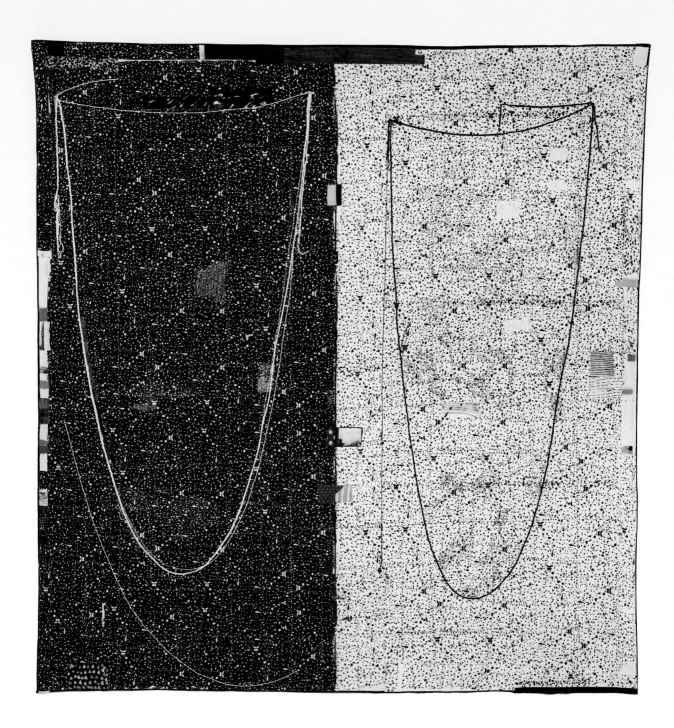

OPPOSITE
Fjord. 2008–2009. 8.5' x 8.6'.
Wax and silkscreen resists on cotton.
Discharged, stitched, appliquéd.
Photo: Leslie Michaelis Onukso

Fjord (detail)

How Do We Know When It's Night? 2010. 10' x 9.5'.
Wax and silkscreen resists on cotton. Stitched, appliquéd.
Photo: Leslie Michaelis Onukso

Jane Burch Cochran | RABBIT HASH, KENTUCKY, USA

My grandmother was a painter and encouraged me to paint watercolors when I visited her in the summers. I was a painter until 1978 and then wanted to try making a quilt containing my father's ties. I was friends with Terrie Hancock Mangat (we both lived in Cincinnati) and had never seen an art quilt until I saw hers. I started making small pieces that were called fiber collages, but then began assembling quilts.

I like using recognizable objects and clothing, such as gloves and dresses, along with the abstraction of random patchwork, and, in most quilts, I have

a strong central image as a focal point. Although most of my work is narrative, I am not telling a specific story. My quilts are highly embellished with beads, buttons, recycled fabric items, and paint to enhance the narrative with a unique and personal texture. Because my surfaces are so densely embellished, they prompt viewers to look closely at the details. I like for viewers to experience an element of surprise, of discovery, as they approach my quilts.

My advice to artists: Don't worry about what other people think and don't ask for critiques!

www.janeburchcochran.com

OPPOSITE
Moonlight. 2007. 77" x 61".
Fabrics, recycled fabric items, beads, buttons, paint.
Machine pieced, machine appliquéd, hand appliquéd using beads, hand embellished with beads and buttons, hand quilted and tied with embroidery thread.

Life Line. 1994. 62" x 82".
Various fabrics and old clothing that had been treated with paint and colored pencil, beads and buttons.
Machine pieced, hand appliquéd, embellished by hand.
Collection: Dorothy Gleser, Seattle

Jane Dunnewold | SAN ANTONIO, TEXAS, USA

Early on, I recognized that sewing was a challenge for me. Slight dyslexia and my impatience kept me from perfecting technique where the sewing machine was concerned. When I learned to paint fabric, and then later to work with dyes and other wet media processes, I found my sweet spot. I also recognized that if I wanted to make a living, I needed to focus on one area and not spread myself too thin.

I latched onto painting with textile paints and then learned to dye, and gradually worked my way through techniques—never really "getting it" that the main driving force eventually has to be content. Maybe it's color or form, or maybe it's hoping your work will change how viewers think

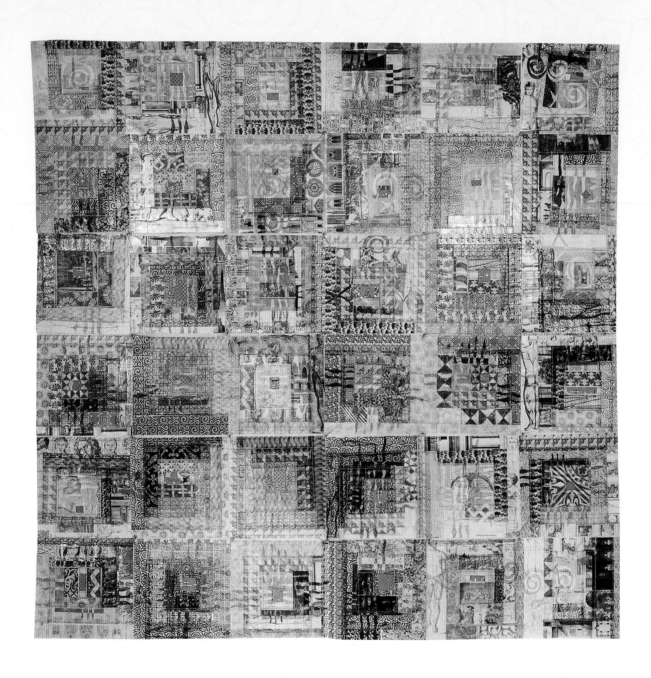

about the world, but without the passion to drive the process and materials, it's a hollow experience. When I discovered, around 1999, that I could build a visual series around my visceral response to the *Tao Te Ching* (an ancient spiritual guide from China), my world, along with my understanding of the power of visual media, rocked. I love knowing how to make materials respond to what I want, which takes time to understand. But then, once

I understand, I love what materials can do serendipitously. It's an ongoing dance back and forth.

Barbara Lee Smith was the first serious artist I ever met who encouraged me to follow my interests, and to her I am eternally grateful. I create art because of what I think and how I feel inside. If what I make moves someone, or makes anyone laugh, I'm happy.

www.complexcloth.com

OPPOSITE
Ode to Hildegard. 1996. 48" x 48".
Lutradur, acetate transparencies, thread, beads. Photocopies on Lutradur and acetate, stitched, beaded.

Refraction #1. 2017.
48" x 78".
Vintage quilt blocks, vintage Bible pages, felt, spackling, gold, leaf, textile pigment.

BELOW
Receptacles of Memory. 2015. 18" x 72".
Vintage quilt, spackling, gold leaf, paper. Fused, spackled, gold leaf applied, hand painted.
Photo: Zenna Duke

Caryl Bryer Fallert-Gentry | PORT TOWNSEND, WASHINGTON, USA

I'm probably best known for dyeing my own fabric and for my colorful, curved-seam designs using many gradations. In 1989 I developed a technique for sewing fast, easy, and accurate curves that I call "applipiecing." I have taught this technique to thousands of students since then. I also invented a technique I call High Tech Tucks. I made several hundred quilts in this style, and the technique is still being taught today in a number of quilt shops. My quilting has become an important element in my finished artwork.

Early on, most of my quilting was done with invisible thread and was just enough to hold the layers together so the quilts hung straight. Today I am using dozens of different colors of thread, and the stitching adds the final touches of pattern, texture, and color to the finished quilt.

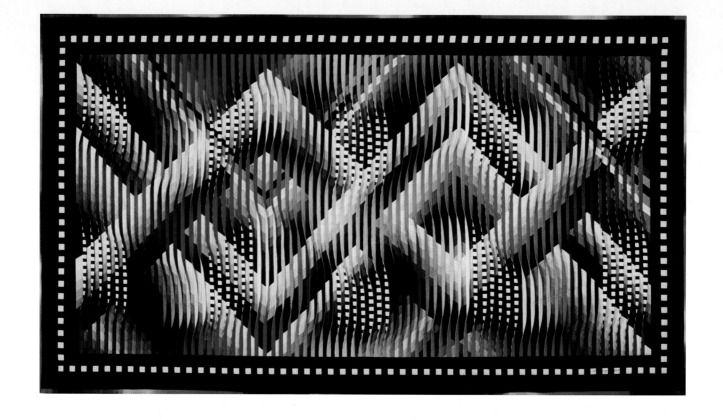

High Tech Tucks 35. 1994. 44" x 79".
Cotton. Hand dyed and painted,
machine pieced and quilted.
Collection: R. R. Street & Co.,
Naperville, Illinois

OPPOSITE
Corona #2: Solar Eclipse. 1989. 94" x 76".
Cotton, dye. Hand dyed and painted, machine
pieced and quilted.
Collection: National Quilt Museum, Kentucky

I have always made art of one kind or another. Even when I was a very young child, my favorite activity was drawing. I never wanted to make anything exactly like someone else, even if I had a pattern, so making quilts as art just seemed much more interesting than making traditional patterns. As a child growing up in Chicago, I was exposed to Georgia O'Keeffe and the French impressionists at the Chicago Art Institute. In my early twenties, I saw the original *Op Art* exhibition at the National Gallery in Washington and never recovered. My first exposure to the whole art/quilting subculture was in a lecture by Jean Ray Laury in Buffalo, New York, in 1982.

That opened my eyes to the whole world, not only of making quilts as art, but also the possibility of actually making a career of it.

From the beginning of my quilting journey forty years ago, I made things that I thought would be fun and interesting. What almost all of my work has in common is color and luminosity, the illusion that the light comes from inside the quilt rather than from an outside source. Whether my quilts are abstract or pictorial, I portray positive, uplifting images. I am constantly searching for the most beautiful image I can create in my mind.

www.bryerpatch.com

OPPOSITE
Celebration #2. 2015. 84" x 64".
Cotton. Hand dyed and painted, machine
pieced and quilted.

New Dawn. 2000. 78" x 63".
Cotton, synthetics. Hand-dyed and painted,
machine pieced and quilted.

Wendy Huhn | DEXTER, OREGON, USA

I use such a mixed bag of techniques! I decide which ones would probably work best, make test samples, and go from there. Often I will begin to work and be well into a project, only to determine that the techniques are not working, and start all over again. Problem solving is my favorite aspect of the creative process, using my signature techniques of image transfer and screen printing. I am excited by the prospect of transferring a story or thought into concrete form. Recently I have enjoyed working in different media, from painting the City of Eugene (Oregon) traffic boxes to making 14-foot-high papier-mâché giraffes.

Most of my work can be seen as double-entendre narratives. Some people find my pieces offensive, while others do not. My sense of humor often doesn't run with the mainstream. The self-taught artist Henry Darger has been my strongest influence—his sense of poignancy and depictions of innocence in a harsh world, with a penchant for graphic figurative imagery.

Of all the advice I have been given as an artist, what stays with me is something that Barbara Lee Smith said: "You never know who is in the room."

www.wendyhuhn.com

OPPOSITE
Housework. 1994. 28" x 28".
Paint, glitter, phosphorescent paint, fabric, monofilament.
Photo-copied fabric, stenciled, sewn.
Collection: Museum of Arts and Design, New York
Photo: Lovell Photography, Eugene, Oregon

Mary, Mary, Quite Contrary. 2014. 20" x 20".
Canvas, acrylic paint, beads, horsehair netting, monofilament thread. Stenciled, screen printed, bound with beads, sewn.
Photo: Dennis Galloway Photography, Prescott, Arizona

Art quilts are my most visible collection—I now own thirty. I also like clay pottery with matte glazes, hammered metal items, and hooked rugs made with wool on linen. Paintings and drawings by local artists are another favorite collection. My showroom gallery in Omaha, 21st Century Quilts, was open from 2010 through 2012. It was my greatest joy to imagine the space and then create it in 2009, sharing the quilts with new audiences. Many visitors were surprised at the depth of meaning in the works, their visual impact, and the artists' locations from around the world.

I began collecting art quilts in 2004, my first acquisition being *Seascape* by Australian artist Dianne Firth. It was part of an exhibit at the Houston International Quilt Festival, displayed on hard white walls, resulting in a fabulous gallery. I kept going back to look at this quilt throughout the weekend. Finally, I purchased it, with a little trepidation. Would I actually see it again, after the quilt traveled for three years? I acquired *Seascape* for its simplicity, elegance, and brilliant color. It hung in our home for several years, and then in the 21st Century Quilts showroom. When we downsized to move to a condo, I sold some art quilts, and this was one of them. Firth's beautiful quilt now hangs in a new home in Clearwater, Florida.

Noriko Endo

Tokyo, Japan
Radiant Reflections. 2008. 66" x 80".
Cotton, polyester, tulle, luminescent fibers. Small pieces covered with tulle, machine embroidered and quilted, painted.
Collection: Shirley Neary
Photo: Masaru Nomura

Pokey Bolton

Patricia (Pokey) Bolton founded *Quilting Arts Magazine®* in 2001 as a way to share her love for embellished quilting and crazy quilting. The first issue focused heavily on crazy quilting (all but one article) but included a piece by Lisa Siders Kenney, *Creation Dream*, which was definitely an art quilt. As Bolton traveled to local regional quilt shows to promote the new magazine, she realized the need to broaden the magazine's focus to include more art quilts.

For the second issue, she expanded the focus to include art quilting. Bolton interviewed Barbara Barrick McKie at her studio in Lyme, Connecticut, and profiled Yvonne Porcella's most recent book published by C&T. The third issue was published shortly after 9/11, and the following issue showcased some of the art quilts that were made as a tribute to the victims.

Those issues set the tone for the magazine, which now focuses exclusively on art quilts and how readers can use various techniques to create their own art. There are no patterns and no exhibition reviews. Articles on design, composition, art theory, or professional advice are provided in every issue.

Both the magazine and the later *Quilting Arts* TV series, premiering in 2007 and originally hosted by Bolton, offered something for everyone, covering a wide variety of fiber art and mixed-media techniques—from sewing, surface design, and embellishing to hand and machine stitching.

The *Quilting Arts* media provide an important showcase for established artists, support for emerging artists, and a market for artist/writers and teachers.

Quilting Arts Magazine
Cover of Issue 1.

Gallery 1990s

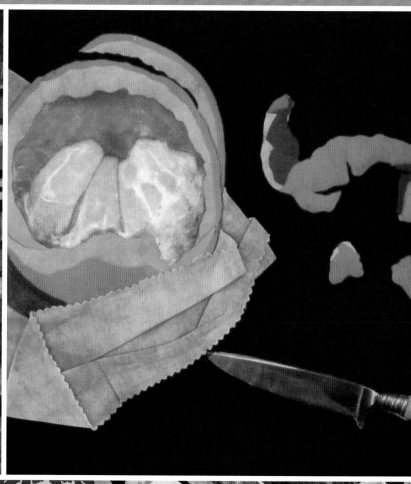

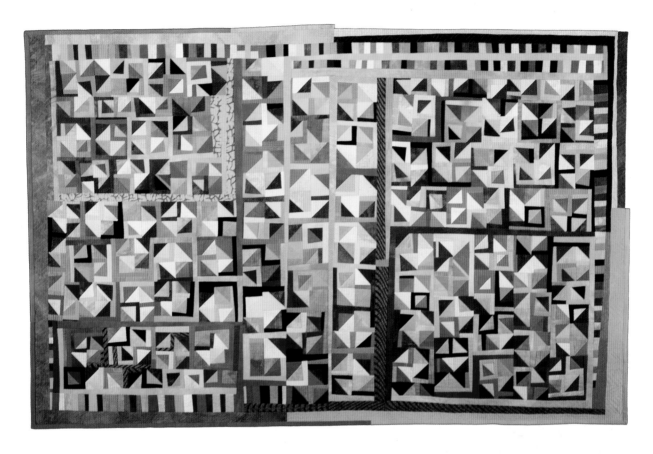

Liz Axford

Clinton, Washington, USA
Mumbo Jumbo 3: Renaissance Thinking.
1995. 49" x 77".
Hand-dyed cotton. Improvisationally
machine pieced, machine quilted.
Photo: Hester + Hardaway

BELOW

Karen Berkenfeld (d.)

USA
The Black and Blinded Birds of Night.
1991. 62" x 55".
Cotton. Block printed, pieced, quilted.
Collection: Museum of Arts and Design,
New York, Gift of Barbara and
Ray Ranta in 2001

Tafi Brown

Alstead, New Hampshire, USA
Beam Team. 1992. 54" x 53".
Cotton. Cyanotype photographs and
photograms on cotton.
Photo: Jeff Baird

OPPOSITE

Kyoung Ae Cho

Milwaukee, Wisconsin, USA
Aged: Covered by Wisdom. 1996. 108" x 108".
Wood, fabric, linen cord. Worked wood, hand and machine sewn.
Collection: John M. Walsh III

BELOW *Aged: Covered by Wisdom* (detail).

DETAIL

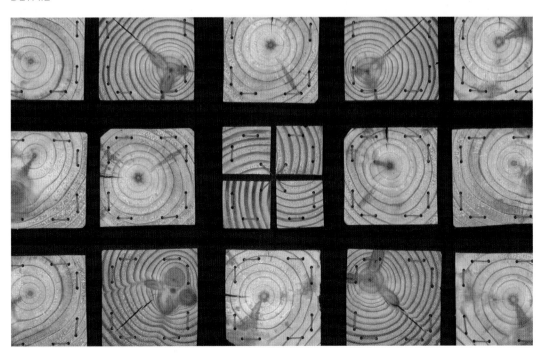

Rhoda Cohen

Weston, Massachusetts, USA
Groundwork. 1993. 108" x 83".
Cotton blends, commercial and hand-dyed.
Pieced, appliquéd, quilted by hand.
Photo: David Caras

OPPOSITE

Maryline Collioud-Robert

Boudry, Neuchâtel, Switzerland
Quelques Herbes. 1998. 46.5" x 64".
Cottons, cotton blends. Reverse
seams sewing technique.

BELOW

Judy B. Dales

Greensboro, Vermont, USA
Fantasy Form 1634. 1995. 40" x 57".
Cotton, chiffon, tulle. Machine
pieced and appliquéd, hand quilted.
Photo: Karen Bell

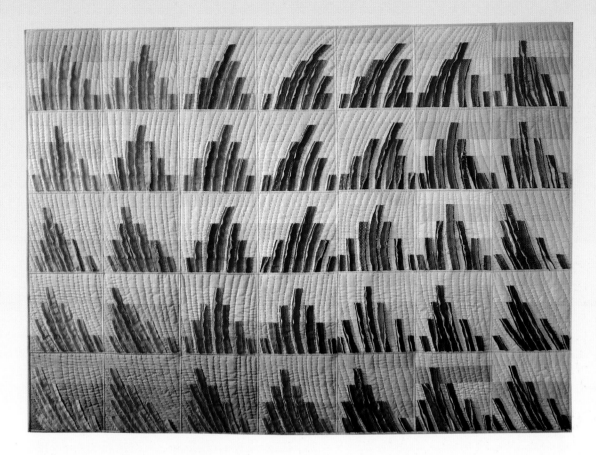

Katriina Flensburg

Storvreta (Uppsala), Sweden
Frozen Heart. 1994. 59" x 47".
Commercial cottons. Machine pieced
and appliquéd, hand and machine quilted.

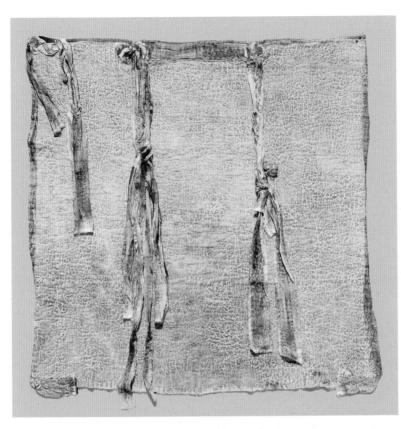

Suzan Friedland

San Francisco, California, USA
Tibet. 1996. 48" x 48".
Linen. Hand painted, machine quilted.
Collection: San Jose Museum of
Quilts & Textiles
Gift of Penny Nii and
Edward Feigenbaum
Photo: James Dewrance

BELOW

Linda Gass

Los Altos, California, USA
After the Gold Rush. 1998. 21" x 26".
Silk crepe de chine, acid dyes. Silk
painted using resist and dyes, salt and
alcohol techniques, machine quilted.
Photo: Don Tuttle

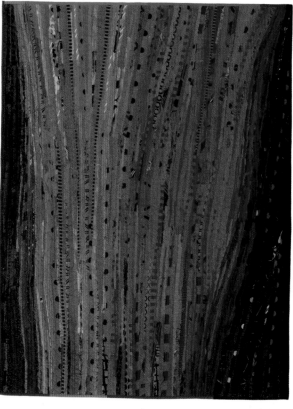

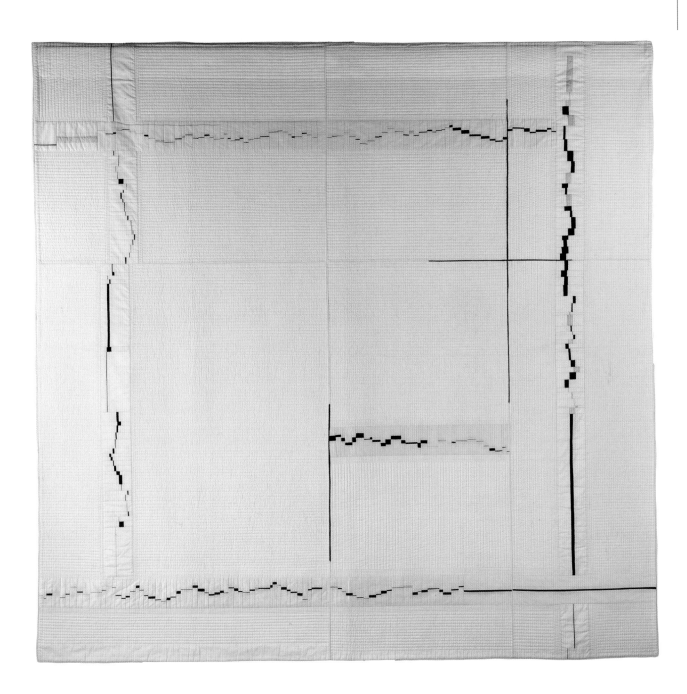

OPPOSITE

Marilyn Henrion

New York, New York, USA
Innuendo. 1998. 35" x 50".
Silks. Hand pieced and quilted.
Collection: Museum of Arts and
Design, New York, gift of D. C.
Earle and J. L. Henrion, 2000
Photo: Karen Bell

BELOW

Judy Hooworth

Morisset, New South Wales, Australia
*Mother and Daughters: Kate and Sarah
(diptych)*. 1998. 54.5" x 41" each.
Commercial cotton. Torn, layered,
stitched, machine quilted.
Collection: San Jose Museum of Quilts
& Textiles, The Marbaum Collection
Gift of Marvin and Hilary Fletcher

Yoshiko Jinzenji

Kyoto, Japan
Sound. 1999. 77" x 79.5".
Silk, cotton, gold foil, bamboo dye.
Hand dyed, machine pieced and quilted.
Collection: Museum of Arts and Design,
New York, Gift of the artist, 2003
Photo: Ed Watkins

Natasha Kempers-Cullen

Topsham, Maine, USA
Revelations, one of twelve panels in the Saints
and Sinners series. 1996. 48" x 48".
Fiber-reactive dyes and textile paints on cotton,
tulle, glass beads. Printed using block printing,
monoprinting, monotypes, silk-screened,
cyanotypes, machine and hand quilted and beaded.
Collection: San Jose Museum of Quilts & Textiles
Gift of Penny Nii and Edward Feigenbaum
Photo: James Dewrance

Patricia Kennedy-Zafred

Murrysville, Pennsylvania, USA
Innocenza Presa. 1994.
21.5" x 16.5".
Acetate, plastic vinyl, hand-dyed
fabric. Hand dyed, layered,
machine pieced and quilted.
Photo: Peter Shefler

BELOW

Judy Langille

Kendall Park, New Jersey, USA
Indigo Leaves. 1999. 50" x 40".
Cotton. Rice paste resisted, indigo
dyed, machine and hand quilted.
Photo: Peter Jacobs

Hsin-Chen Lin

Tainan City, Taiwan
Dream Catcher. 1994.
53" x 50".
Commercial fabrics.
Hand appliquéd, pieced,
and quilted.

OPPOSITE

Emiko Toda Loeb

New York, New York, USA
Transparent Sunbeams. 1998. 82.5" x 62".
Old Japanese cotton; new Japanese,
American, French, and Indonesian cotton;
cotton satin; old Japanese silk; synthetic
blends. Special reversible technique:
simultaneously pieced and quilted.
Photo: Karen Bell

RIGHT *Transparent Sunbeams* (reverse).

BELOW

Judy Mathieson

Bristol Stars. 1999. 81" x 81".
Commercial cottons.
Machine pieced and quilted.
Photo: Jack Mathieson

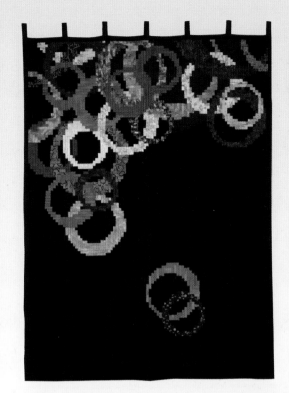

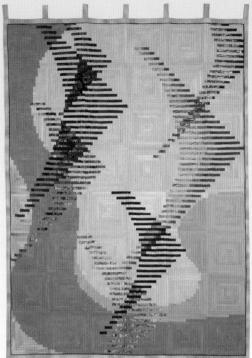

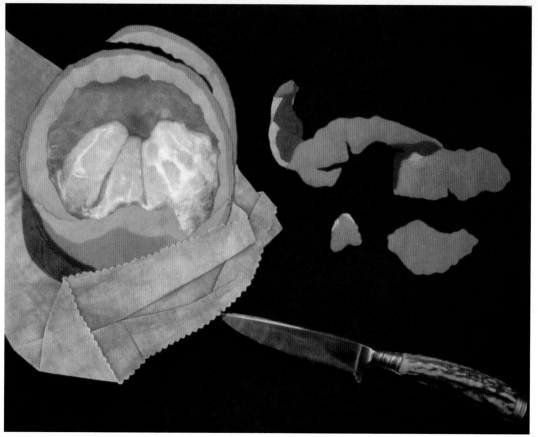

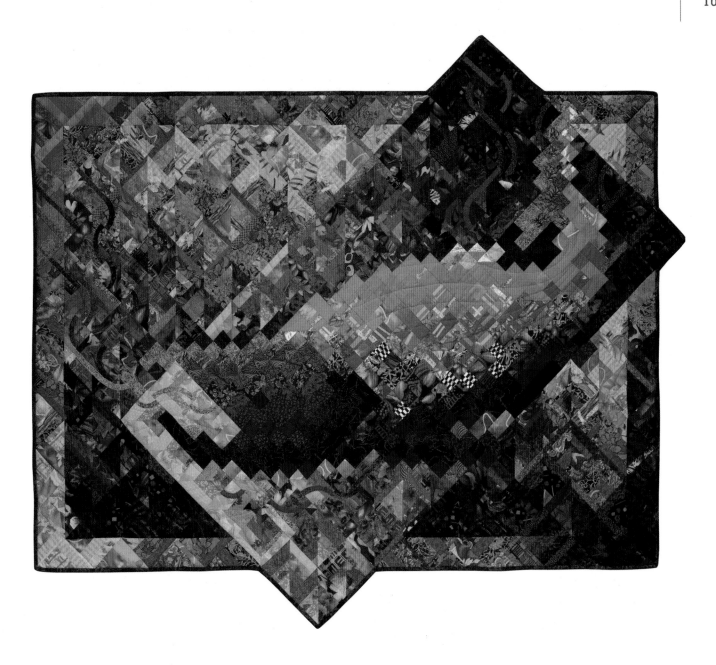

OPPOSITE

Carolyn L. Mazloomi

West Chester, Ohio, USA
Blues at Annie's Place. 1997. 52" x 66".
Commercial cotton, beads, buttons,
acrylic paint, metallic fabric. Machine
pieced, machine and hand appliquéd,
hand painted, machine quilted.
Collection: Michigan State
University Museum of Art
Photo: Courtesy of MSU Museum of Art

BELOW

Barbara Barrick McKie

Lyme, Connecticut, USA
An Orange for Lunch. 1997. 12" x 18".
Disperse-dyed polyester, hand-dyed
cotton. Trapunto, printed, machine
appliquéd and quilted, fused.

Ree Nancarrow

Fairbanks, Alaska, USA
Creation. 1993. 64.5" x 74".
Commercial cotton. Machine pieced,
fusible appliquéd, machine quilted.
Photo: Eric Nancarrow

OPPOSITE

Dominie Nash

Bethesda, Maryland, USA
Peculiar Poetry 4. 1993. 43" x 43".
Cotton, silk organza. Surface design
processes, machine appliquéd and quilted.
Collection: Smithsonian American Art
Museum, Renwick Gallery
Photo: Mark Gulezian/Quicksilver
Photographers

BELOW

Karen Perrine

Puyallup, Washington, USA
Forest Flowing. 1992. 75" x 138".
Cotton fabric, dye, pigment, metallic
knit mesh. Dye and pigment painted,
stamped, stenciled, resisted, hand
appliquéd, machine pieced and quilted.
Collection: Waltron, Ltd.
Photo: Mark Frey

Olga Prins Lukowski

Molenschot, Netherlands
The Holy Grail. 1997. 22" x 27".
Hand-dyed cotton
Photo: Peter Braatz

Jonathan Shannon (d.)

USA
Amigos Muertos. 1994. 89" x 89".
Cotton. Hand appliquéd, machine pieced, hand quilted.
Private collection
Photo: Sharon Riesdorph

Ricky Tims

La Veta, Colorado, USA
Songe d'Automne. 1999. 86" x 86".
Hand-dyed 100% cotton fabric. Machine pieced, machine
appliquéd, free-motion machine quilted.
Collection: Quilts, Inc., Texas

DETAIL

Meiny Vermaas-van der Heide

Tempe, Arizona, USA
Fields of Color III: a GREEN QUILT. 1991.
72" x 72".
Cotton. Machine pieced and quilted.

BELOW *Fields of Color III: a GREEN QUILT.*
(detail)

Nelda Warkentin

Phillips, Maine, USA
Chinese Tiles. 1996. 54" x 44".
Raffia, plastic bags. Raffia inserted into
plastic bags, machine stitched and hand tied.
Collection: Janet Werner
Photo: John Tuckey

Carol Watkins

Lafayette, Colorado, USA
Passages II. 1999. 68" x 39".
Hand-dyed and commercial fabric.
Machine pieced and quilted.
Photo: Ken Sanville

Kathy Weaver

Highland Park, Illinois, USA
Guns Are Us, Funerary Piece One. 1994.
83" x 85" x 3".
Cotton, fibers, found plastic skeletons, found
plastic rings, found paper tags, string, ribbon,
thread. Silk-screened, Xeroxed, appliquéd.
Collection: Museum of Arts and Design,
New York, Gift of an anonymous donor, 2001
Photo: Ed Watkins, 2007

Anne Woringer

Paris, France
Le Labyrinthe de Merlin. 1998.
61" x 60".
Hemp and linen from the 19th
century (hand woven), hand dyed
by artist. Appliquéd and stitched.
Private collection
Photo: Bruneau Jarret

BELOW

Ardyth Davis

Horizon X Amber. 1992.
32" x 48".
Silk. Hand pleated and hand tied.
Collection: John M. Walsh III
Photo: Joseph Coscia

Libby Lehman | HOUSTON TEXAS, USA

For me, quilting has been all about play . . . about freedom and spontaneity.

I started quilting more than forty years ago when my mother signed us up for a class. She and I began quilting together, and she eventually opened a shop. It was nice to have something in common with her that we learned as adults, as peers rather than as mother and child.

Like most quilters, my shift from hand quilting to machine quilting was an evolution. I have always loved to experiment, and as sewing machines became more sophisticated and computerized, they offered an ever-increasing range of possibilities. I loved the freedom (and speed!) that machine quilting provided.

Joy Ride. 1986. 80" x 80".
Cotton, metallic threads. Machine
embroidered, machine quilted.
Photo: Bill Arnold

When I worked on a quilt, I often carried on a conversation with it. It might not have been a deep conversation about the meaning of life, but it was more "Do you need more red? Yes or no?"

I love threads. Thread companies loved me because my techniques ate thread. When I saw metallic threads for the first time, I became very excited. I wanted to learn how to use them, and it really became a matter more of problem solving because they are brittle threads. It took me about six months to figure out how to work with them.

I would like to say how much the quilting community means to me. Quilting has been my art for more than forty years, but it has also been my salvation over the past few extremely difficult years. Thank you all from the bottom of my heart.

Watch Your Step—Mushrooms. 2012. 42" x 42".
Cotton, metallic and other threads. Machine stitched and quilted.
Collection: Carolyn Wallwyn
Photo: Bill Arnold

M. Joan Lintault | NEW PALTZ, NEW YORK, USA

I begin my work with white fabric because I see its possibilities. Fabric can be used in many different ways. It is an obedient, forgiving material. I want every process and technique that I use to contribute to the content of my work, so I dye, print, and paint my own images.

Fabric is sensual and can be manipulated. It can be made to have weight, mass, and texture. It creates atmosphere by reflecting and changing its appearance in light. For me, the result is a material with the potential for an infinite expansion of expression and form.

Alphabet Soup. 1998. 98" x 74".
Hand-dyed, screen-printed, hand-painted cotton.
Airbrushed, appliquéd, sewing-machine lace.
Photo: Dan Overturf

I place myself solidly in a textile tradition, and because of that I feel free to use any textile technique that would contribute to my work. I look back in history to see where I came from, but the new comes through my experience of working.

As it was with my predecessors, the embroiderers, quilters, and lace makers who worked with fabric and thread, time is not a factor when I work. I do not choose to reject a technique simply because it is laborious. Using the technique of free-motion embroidery on the sewing machine has allowed me to introduce texture and lace in my work and to build the quilts in a unique way. The lace work that joins the pieces takes advantage of the resulting negative space. This enables me to eliminate the background that is usually used to hold the image together.

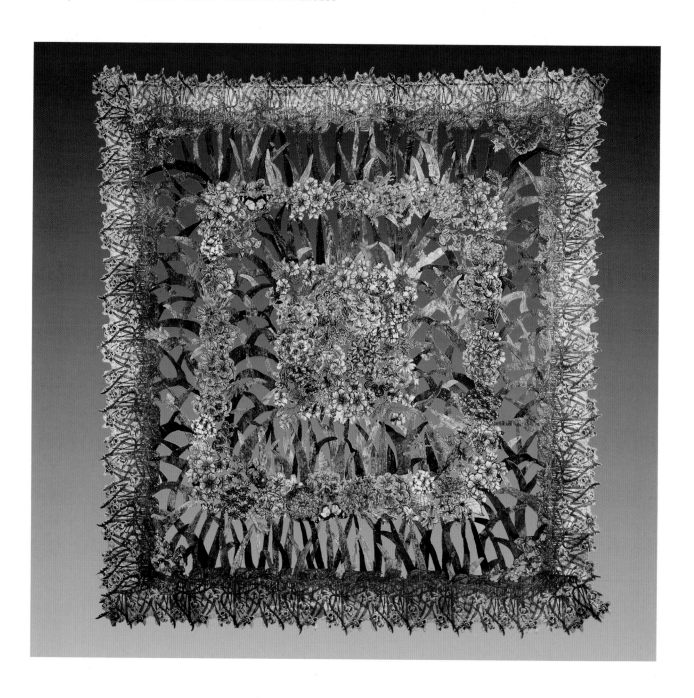

OPPOSITE
In the Grass. 1992. 93.5" x 99.5".
Hand-dyed, screen-printed, hand-painted cotton.
Appliquéd, quilted, sewing-machine lace.
Collection: Jack M. Walsh III
Photo: Chris Maitzen

When the Bee Stings. 1996. 87" x 95".
Hand-dyed, screen-printed, hand-painted cotton. Pieced, quilted.
Collection: Jack M. Walsh III
Photo: Dan Overturf

Ruth McDowell | COLRAIN, MASSACHUSETTS, USA

I love the way in which the construction of a pieced quilt fractures the total image, background and foreground. The lines of the construction seams, which derive from the lines of the image I'm working with, give a unity and integrity to the surface of the whole piece. The extension of these lines across the surface of the quilt can be very gestural, enhancing movement and flow.

I use a wide range of commercially and hand-done printed and patterned fabrics. They give detail, texture, complexity of color, and an extraordinary richness to the quilt. Quilting, by hand or machine, is a chance to add a linear pattern to the surface and develop a low relief if that is desired. It adds texture and detail and unifies the surface.

Poppies. 1988. 67" x 69.5".
Cotton, silk. Machine pieced, hand appliquéd and quilted.
Photo: David Caras

My quilts have developed along several paths of overlapping and interweaving interests: geometry, botany, the natural world, color and pattern, abstraction, and composition. Geometry was an early interest, beginning with the idea of repeated blocks, although the blocks quickly became shapes other than squares.

Much of my work is inspired by what I see around me in my rural New England town. I've walked past the small barn depicted in *Passages* for sixty-five years. It has a slate roof, which is why it still is standing. But the physical barn is just the impetus for a meditation on passages—time and space, wind and rain and weather, lives past and lives coming.

www.ruthbmcdowell.com

Passages. 2016. 37.5" x 32".
Cotton. Machine pieced and quilted.
Photo: John Polak

Velda Newman | NEVADA CITY, CALIFORNIA, USA

For me, creating art quilts continues to be challenging, rewarding, and exciting. I love the versatility of fiber, exploring color in the dyeing process and developing ideas for new pieces, as well as the craft of stitching.

Appliqué is the basis for most of my work. I approach each piece as a "painting," using fabric, thread, paint, and ink to create a realistic close-up of the subject matter. I begin conventionally by breaking down a design into its most basic elements. However, somewhere in the process my vision skews and the scale becomes much larger and more amplified, and color is exaggerated for greater impact.

Sunflower State. 1996. 54" x 114".
Hand-dyed cotton sateen, paint, ink.
Hand and machine stitched.
Photo: James Dewrance

My favorite part of the creative process is working on the composition. My focus has always been on nature, things that live and grow. We all relate easily to natural subjects, whether portrayed in a painting, decorative arts, or a quilt. I go beyond realism, to elaborate on nature and capture the essence of a subject without attempting to replicate it. Deciding on color choices and where to place them to achieve balance in the work is always exciting, and dyeing the perfect fabric color—it's the best! These two skills are key to making a successful piece; the rest of the work requires good stitching techniques, and persistence!

www.veldanewman.com

DETAIL

Zinnia. 2010. 88" x 211".
Hand-dyed cotton sateen, paint, ink.
Hand and machine stitched.
Photo: C&T Publishing.

Zinnia. (Detail)

Jane Sassaman | HARVARD, ILLINOIS, USA

From an early age I knew I wanted to be an artist and a master of some arcane craft. In college I concentrated on textiles and jewelry. By the time I left school, neither medium had stepped forward. Then in 1980, Nancy Crow's quilt was on the cover of *American Craft* magazine. One look and I knew I'd found my medium. This approach is exactly what I had been doing in paper, but it had never occurred to me to do it with pieced fabric.

I quilted "in the closet" when my children were small, so I didn't go to classes and learned the hard way, by trial and error. Sometimes I think that this isolation kept my voice clearer. But all artists and designers learn a lot by looking at other people's work.

Garden Spiral. 1988. 50" x 50".
Cotton, lamé. Machine pieced, appliquéd, and quilted.
Photo: Gregory Gantner

I was a designer of decorative accessories for many years—plates, vases, picture frames. I looked at lots of work and incorporated decorative motifs in my own work, especially from the Arts and Crafts Movement. The decorative arts have been a major influence on my work. That sense of formality is a definite characteristic of what I do.

I work in a collage technique inspired by shapes. Shapes are my stimulus. Once they start talking to each other, the composition begins to evolve. Creative decisions must be made from beginning to end. This isn't the fastest way to work because you are always reacting and heading off in other directions. But I find it a very entertaining and satisfying way to work. The results are always a surprise.

One of my favorite books is *Dawns and Dusks*, 1980 interviews with Louise Nevelson. She says that it is impossible to do everything, so we must make our choices and be at peace with them. I read this book in college and it prepared me for life as an artist.

www.janesassaman.com

Willow. 1996. 75" x 75".
Cotton. Machine appliquéd and quilted.
Collection: Fairfield Processing, Connecticut
Photo: Gregory Gantner

Pamela Studstill Quest | PIPE CREEK, TEXAS, USA

My maternal grandmother, June Magnolia Vawter, taught me how to piece quilts. She would also recline on her couch and paint miniature landscapes from memory on index cards. By example she taught me that all colors "go" with all other colors.

Using hand-painted fabrics with traditional piecing techniques was a bridge between the quilt making I learned as a child and the painting I pursued as a young college student. Discovering the color theory work of scholars such as Johannes Itten and Josef Albers was a turning point. Discovering that color harmonies could be composed, not just intuitively but according to the laws of color theory, gave me a great deal to explore.

I found what I was interested in early on, and I worked on various ideas about changing color and patternmaking forms for about twenty years. I liked all that pattern: dots, curved and wavy lines. I liked the way the pattern moved. Each of my quilts was a study in light inspired by the local landscape around me.

I enjoy how the creative process can combine elements and activities that are very systematic and precise with those that are very personal and that occasionally can seem chaotic. As I grew older, my work grew looser, changing from grid-based designs to some freeform appliqué work. Now I find I'm more interested in working in different mediums. Ceramics in particular is fascinating.

My motto is this: Work hard. Work for fun. Work every day. I hope that when viewers see my art they feel a sense of the variety, the intricacy, and the wonder that make up our world.

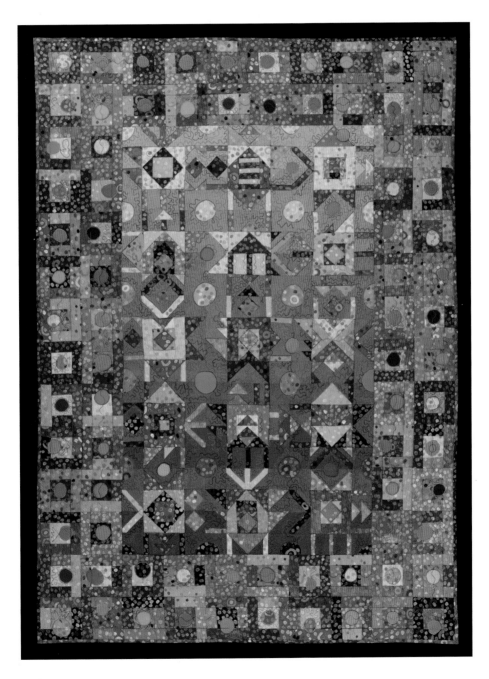

OPPOSITE
Quilt No. 26. 1983. 40" x 40".
Cotton. Hand painted, machine pieced,
hand quilted.
Photo: Deidre Adams

Quilt No. 145. 2002. 56" x 40".
Cotton. Hand painted, machine pieced,
hand quilted.
Photo: Deidre Adams

It all started with a postcard. Rick Gottas, who owned American Art Company in Tacoma, Washington, sent us a postcard announcing a contemporary art quilt show at his gallery. The postcard was a wonderful photograph, filled to the edges of the card, of a quilt by Erika Carter titled *Intertidal Wilderness*. We had never seen anything like the photograph on the card and were intrigued.

Nancy flew up to Tacoma to see what this contemporary art quilt genre was all about. Rick represented a number of artists, and most were at the opening. It was a great opportunity to talk with the artists and learn more about what they were doing. All the artists were from the Pacific Northwest. Nancy came home with three art quilts.

Buying three art quilts did not make us collectors. That evolved over time. In the first fifteen years we purchased about 140 pieces. We have always enjoyed meeting and getting to know the artists. Their written and verbal input is an important part of the artwork they have created, and enhances our appreciation of the medium.

Over the last ten years we have purchased just a few pieces. At some point one has no more room and, frankly, keeping quilts rolled in the closet is not very satisfying. Even switching pieces out becomes a bit of a chore. We now have about forty pieces on display, and that's our collection. We have donated the balance to Visions Art Museum in San Diego to be part of its permanent collection. The highlight of our collecting history was purchasing the fifty-four works in *Playing with a Full Deck* and ensuring that this unique collection would remain intact. It is now at Visions Art Museum.

Our advice for anyone purchasing any art is "buy what you like." And, no, we did not always both like what we purchased. One or the other of us would like it and that was enough.

Caryl Bryer Fallert-Gentry

Port Townsend, Washington, USA
Three of Diamonds, Playing with a Full Deck collection. 1993. 28" x 18".
Cotton. Hand dyed and painted, machine pieced and quilted.
Collection: Visions Art Museum, Brakensiek Collection
Photo: Visions Art Museum

Surface Design: Dyeing Fabrics by Hand

Hand-dyed fabrics have been a significant aspect of the repertoire of quilt artists since the early 1960s, when practitioners such as Joan Lintault and Katherine Westphal became known for their expertise in the various processes. Indigo dyeing appealed to some, such as Ed Johnetta Miller, who traveled to Nigeria in the 1960s to study with native experts.

Caryl Bryer Fallert-Gentry's quilts are distinguished today by her hand dyeing, a process that she has perfected during four decades of creating quilt art. In Sue Benner's junior year of college, she learned how to work with Procion dyes (which do not require steaming), and hand dyeing is among her favorite methods of introducing color into her quilts. Debra Lunn's quilt *Counterpoint*, containing her own dyed fabrics, was accepted for the first *Quilt National* in 1979. She began hand-dyeing fabrics for her quilts because at that time she was not pleased with the availability of solid-color cottons in fabric stores. Along with her partner Michael Mrowka, she founded Lunn Fabrics, which has been supplying hand-dyed fabrics to quilt makers for more than twenty-five years.

Gayle Fraas and Duncan Slade pioneered the use of paintbrushes with dyes, producing studio quilts with realistic imagery and some astonishing *trompe-l'oeil* effects, beginning in the late 1970s. As a college student, Judith Content studied surface design with Constance Crockett and Ana Lisa Hedstrom. She became enamored with arashi shibori dyed pole-wrapped silk, experimenting with broom handles and wine bottles. Procion dyes have also been important for Jan Myers-Newbury, especially in her first eight years of quilt making. The tonal effects she created with her geometric compositions could be precisely controlled during the dyeing process. Joan Schulze hand-dyed some of her fabrics during the 1970s and created batik landscapes.

While several vendors, such as Uta Lenk in Germany, have offered hand-dyed fabrics for quilt makers in the twenty-first century, Mickey Lawler of Skydyes has been in business since 1984. Her sky, cloud, and landscape motifs painted in dye have long appealed to quilt artists.

The *Quilt Digest*

Launched in 1983 by Roderick Kiracofe and Michael Kile in San Francisco, the *Quilt Digest* presented antique, contemporary traditional, and contemporary art quilts in a single publication. This bold step heightened awareness and increased appreciation of the quilt in American art and culture. While this annual publication continued only until 1987, it provided a crucial springboard for the Art Quilt Movement.

Most of the articles discussed antique and traditional quilts, but the compelling "Showcase" of images compiled for each volume by Kiracofe broke new ground among quilt publications. Readers could see the suggestion of an Amish palette in a 1982 piece by Sonya Lee Barrington, with her quilt facing an antique *Bars* composition; treatments of three-dimensional space by Linda MacDonald and Judy Mathieson; the energetic rhythm of a Therese May creation facing a turn-of-the-twentieth-century crazy quilt; and, recent quilts by other leaders of the Movement, including Françoise Barnes, Pauline Burbidge, Ed Larson, Terrie Hancock Mangat, Jan Myers-Newbury, Miriam Nathan-Roberts, Joan Schulze, and Pamela Studstill Quest.

Kiracofe remembers, "We wanted the articles to be well written, thought provoking, and useful and practical, and to explore new territory. Equally important to us was our desire . . . for this new publication to be beautifully photographed, designed, printed, and produced. I feel extremely satisfied that we accomplished those goals, creating a platform for excellent articles and presenting examples of the finest quilt making at the time."

CHAPTER FOUR
2000s: Art Quilts and Galleries

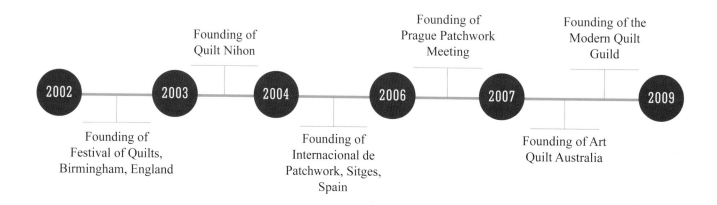

Founding of
Quilt Nihon

Founding of
Prague Patchwork
Meeting

Founding of the
Modern Quilt
Guild

2002　2003　2004　2006　2007　2009

Founding of
Festival of Quilts,
Birmingham, England

Founding of
Internacional de
Patchwork, Sitges,
Spain

Founding of Art
Quilt Australia

Only approximately 30 percent of the US galleries selling quilt art are on or near the East or West Coast, something of a puzzle when we consider the many art galleries in cities such as New York, Miami, Los Angeles, and San Francisco. Interestingly, 65 percent of quilt artists reporting sales are local artists, similar to the successes of local makers with art consultants and public art projects (probably because site visits are easier, usually leading to stronger proposals). Two-thirds of the sales are for representational quilts containing recognizable imagery, often depicting nature. Collectors acquiring quilts for their residences seem to prefer this style, rather than abstract designs, and occasionally commission artists to create one or more additional quilts in the same mode.

Partly because very few galleries exclusively show quilt art, artists typically exhibit in gallery spaces showing other mediums, often paintings, photographs, and prints. Several artists have had great success selling their work in frame shops, even when the quilts are not framed or on stretchers. This success makes sense because many people coming into a frame shop already have acquired art and should be receptive to pieces conveniently displayed in such an environment. Location of galleries plays a crucial role in impromptu purchases, and a storefront at street level obviously brings in the most traffic. If the gallery is situated in an arts neighborhood or near popular restaurants or other attractions, so much the better.

More quilts seem to be purchased out of solo shows than group shows, perhaps because a body of work can be both impressive and informative. In 2012, Kate Stiassni sold her first quilt for $2,800 from a solo show in a Connecticut gallery that had never before exhibited fiber art. Nearly all of her pieces were purchased during the exhibition, causing the gallery to change its attitude toward representing contemporary art quilts.

Quite a few quilts on the smaller side are purchased by tourists, who prefer to bring home something special by a local or regional artist. To this end, quilt artists sometimes incorporate local imagery or themes into their quilts, such as architecture, landscapes, seascapes, and even cuisine. Quilt artists working in abstract modes who sell to the tourist market tend to keep their works relatively small, allowing the buyer to transport the work home in a suitcase.

Galleries appreciate and support artists who are willing to cooperate with them in developing markets for their work. Some galleries employ a corporate sales director, as mentioned by quilt artist Nelda Warkentin, whose quilts have been placed in the offices of a hospital, credit union, bank, and other businesses by her gallery.

While quilt artists consistently report higher prices from their work purchased from the nationally juried art quilt exhibitions, especially *Quilt National*, in general they express satisfaction with their gallery sales. Gallerists usually earn their commissions, and since the later 1990s they gradually have been expanding the market for contemporary quilt art. Many artists have sold their first gallery quilt in the twenty-first century, including several who had been trying to enter the gallery market earlier. Not only are more galleries offering quilt art, but also more professional artists have found their voice in this medium.

The ArtQuilt Gallery • NYC. was run by Cathy Izzo and Dale Riehl from 2011 through 2014.
Photo: Dale Riehl

B. J. Adams | WASHINGTON, DC, USA

I'm known for my free-motion machine embroidery. I prefer the process even if it is very slow. I enjoy drawing and painting and have always loved hand embroidery. When I discovered that you could "paint" and "draw" with the sewing machine, I switched to machine embroidery. I'm excited by fabrics and other flexible materials because they can be manipulated into something else. They can be hard or soft, flat or highly textured, or three-dimensional and have simple or complicated designs. When people view my artwork, I want them to be surprised by the transformation, to have a sense of wonder.

I keep looking for a simpler way to work, maybe a technique that takes less time. Perhaps the simplicity I am looking for comes down to how I design, along with my techniques, and both might need to be simplified. My fiber sensibility was influenced by Joan Michaels Paque. She explained how one shape or form can be seen in many of the textile techniques—for example, the chain is a looping technique used in embroidery, crochet, knotting, tatting, basketry, netting, and probably more. These associations appeal to me.

www.bjadamsart.com

Kage Hinata. 1986. 29" x 60".
Various kinds of fabrics and a variety of threads.
Manipulated fabrics including twisting, pleating and tucking, appliquéd, pieced, embroidered.
Collection: Steven and Edna Baruch
Photo: Joel Breger

OPPOSITE
Traveling from Dawn to Dusk. 2009.
38.5" x 24.5".
Thread and various fabrics, painted canvas, zipper. Free-motion machine embroidered, appliquéd, quilted.

Pauline Burbidge | DUNS, BERWICKSHIRE, UNITED KINGDOM

A secondary-school teacher inspired me to become an artist. His name was Albert Clamp and he was a fabulous teacher, full of enthusiasm and excitement for the arts. It was he who opened up the world of art for me and encouraged me with my art practice.

I began my quiltmaking through books and started making traditional blocks. Soon I began designing my own blocks, but I was wedded to the straight-edged geometric form and pieced all of my blocks. However, there came a time when I needed to free up my imagery, so I began collaging, rather than piecing. Today I work in a very spontaneous way, allowing the images to develop directly with the cloth, without too much planning.

Because I surround myself with my work, I have a continual dialogue with it. Once I am linked into a subject, I become attracted to it and search for more—water reflections, plant forms, grasses, or hedgerows, for example. I like to explore one theme for quite a while, and then there comes a point when I need to explore new things, although they could be related to the current theme.

I love working with fabric and combining drawing and stitch. I have always loved immersing myself in the making of things; I like being able to use my craft skills as well as my art skills. I am happy working and developing my visual language—using color, shape, texture, and line and linking this to my inspiration of rural landscape and plant forms. It is satisfying to feel that my work can be made only by using textiles as my medium.

www.paulineburbidge-quilts.com

OPPOSITE
Dancing Lines. 1998. 80" x 80".
Cotton. Collaged, stitched, quilted.
Collection: National Museums of Scotland,
Edinburgh, United Kingdom
Photo: Keith Tidball

Mirrored Steps. 1983. 83" x 79".
Cotton. Machine quilted, hand finished.
Collection: Shipley Art Gallery, Tyne & Wear
Museums, United Kingdom
Photo: John Coles

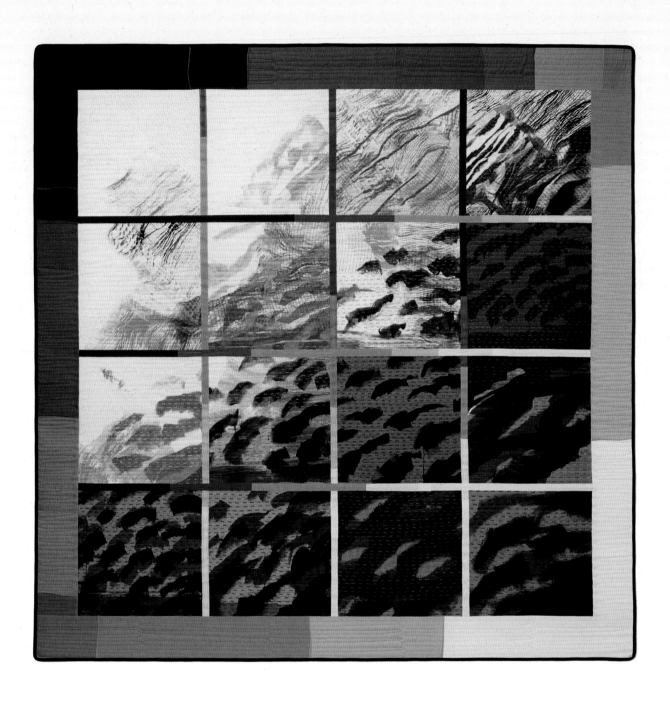

Wind-over-Water. 2003. 77" x 77".
Cotton, silk. Collaged, pleated, painted, machine and hand quilted.
Collection: International Quilt Study Center & Museum,
University of Nebraska–Lincoln
Photo: Keith Tidball

Starscape. 2015. 76" x 76".
Cotton, silk. Monoprinted, cyanotype printed,
painted, collaged, stitched by hand and machine.
Photo: Philip Stanley Dickson

Hollis Chatelain | HILLSBOROUGH, NORTH CAROLINA, USA

I moved back to the US in 1996, after living and working with humanitarian organizations in Africa for twelve years. Once I was back in the States, I really missed the African people and wanted to portray them in my art. Since I had a drawing background, I decided to try to teach myself to paint images with dyes. My first three years were spent just learning to manipulate the dyes, so my work was purely representational.

Then my "statement" dreams started appearing in monochromatic color schemes. These dreams led me to paint my quilts in one-color schemes and quilt them with hundreds of different colors of thread.

When designing my quilts, I search for strong graphics that can be seen from a distance. The details in the quilting will then appear as the viewer approaches. Dye painting allows me to paint people with boldness and depth to the image, while the quilting supports the subtleties and color variations I am searching for in my art.

I believe that we can educate and bring awareness through art. Much of my work is based on my dreams that tell a story or make a statement. To support these statements, I always research the subjects first. Having greater knowledge about the issues is so interesting and gives me more understanding as I start my drawings. I adore the individual aspects of research, drawing, designing, painting, and quilting that is my evolution for each piece.

Parched. 2013. 27" x 72".
Hand dye-painted fabric, denim.
Machine appliquéd, hand dye-painted
accent fabric, machine quilted.
Photo: Jack Alterman

OPPOSITE
Sahel. 1997. 80" x 60".
Cotton. Hand dye-painted with thickened
fiber-reactive dyes, machine quilted.
Photo: Lynn Ruck

Art quilting is a medium that exists between two and three dimensions. It isn't flat like painting, and most quilt art isn't three-dimensional like sculpture. It is also one of the few mediums that allow us to have thousands of nuances of color added with quilting, and I strive to push these characteristics as far as possible. Over the years, I have experimented with different techniques outside of dye painting, including creating the images with just quilting and fabricating large faces by using blue jeans.

My greatest desire is that each person will react emotionally to my art. I hope that the viewer will relate personally to the images and be affected by the quilt.

www.hollisart.com

Blue Men. 2001. 58" x 78".
Cotton. Hand dye-painted with thickened
fiber-reactive dyes, machine quilted.
Collection: Sally Davey
Photo: Lynn Ruck

Precious Water. 2004. 77" x 85".
Cotton. Hand dye-painted with thickened
fiber-reactive dyes, machine quilted.
Collection: Private collection
Photo: Lynn Ruck

Noriko Endo | TOKYO, JAPAN

I began making my art quilts when I had the chance to visit Hyogo in central Japan, which is famous for traditional Banshu-Ori weaving. I purchased lots of fabric and went home with a bagful. I wanted to make my naturescape quilts look like oil paintings, so I cut the fabrics into small toothpick sizes. I found that a layer of black tulle held the small pieces in place when I used it to cover the surface of the quilts and stitched through it.

Since I had plenty of Banshu-Ori fabric, the next year I entered their contest. I won the Silver Award, which gave me lots of energy to work on more quilts. I have won many other awards since then, and it has been my privilege to teach thousands of students around the world.

Recently, I have been experimenting with a variety of new techniques. My work now has even more quilting, and I use paint to add texture and depth.

I am worried about the environment; so many of my recent works highlight the issue of disappearing woodlands and the threats to the animals and birds who live there.

When I see natural landscapes, especially woodlands and reflections in water, I am eager to express that beauty in my quilts. Trees are a recurring image. I believe that a mature tree is one of the boldest graphic sights that any human will witness.

www.norikoendo.com

OPPOSITE
Forest in New England. 1996. 55" x 84".
Cotton, tulle. Small pieces covered with tulle and machine quilted.
Photo: Nagamitsu Endo

Sylvian Ambience #2. 2006. 49" x 60".
Cotton, tulle. Small pieces covered with tulle and machine quilted.
Collection: Kathlyn Dowson
Photo: Nagamitsu Endo

Cherry Blossoms and Moon. 2015.
41" x 59".
Cotton, polyester, silk, tulle, paints.
Small pieces covered with tulle and
machine quilted, painted, appliquéd.
Photo: Yuji Nomura

OPPOSITE
Birds of a Feather Flock Together. 2015. 53" x 78".
Silk, paint, silk flakes, wool yarn, cotton. Whole cloth quilt,
stitched and painted, couched, birds are made separately
and appliquéd.
Photo: Yuji Nomura

Tim Harding | STILLWATER, MINNESOTA, USA

Stretching my own canvases in art school started my interest in fibers. I was intrigued with the tactile quality, the inherent grid of the woven structure, and the pliable plane. I soon realized I was more interested in the canvas than the paint. I became fascinated with the apparent juxtaposition of textile's preciousness and vulnerability. My next experimental projects were intended to violate basic cultural taboos about how one handles fabric. These included scorching silks with an iron, then with a blowtorch, staining, and blasting layered fabrics with a shotgun.

I eventually developed my technique of building up fabrics and cutting through them to reveal layers of color. I had no training in sewing techniques. I figured out how to manipulate fabrics with coaching from my wife,

Kathleen. Tearing and ripping and cutting and slashing broke the continuity of warp and weft, freeing the individual yarns from the woven grid structure. They could morph into new chaotic textures.

This technique evolved to be very textural and very painterly. It unifies structure with surface. It incorporates my interest in color theory and is perfectly suited for developing the potential of simultaneous contrast color work.

When the various elements work together in a balance, it's a compelling visual experience. With my technique, there is an element of surprise that's always in the background. You control the fabrics as much as you can, and then you kind of let things happen. That's the fun part—that unexpected twist within all the intent.

www.timharding.com

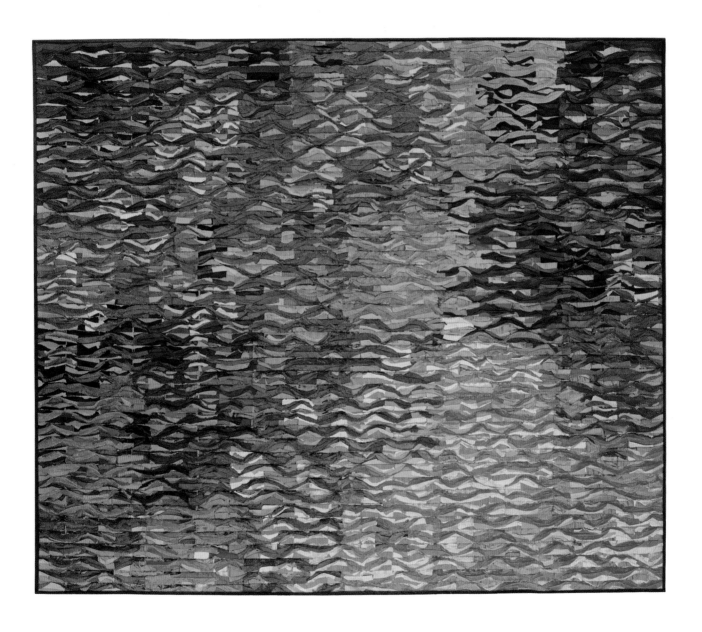

OPPOSITE
Swimmers. 1986. 60" x 80" x 1.5".
Silks. Collaged, reverse appliquéd.
Private collection
Photo: Petronella Ytsma

Garden Shimmer. 1997. 42" x 49".
Silks. collage, reverse appliqué.
Private collection
Photo: Cecile M. Hooker

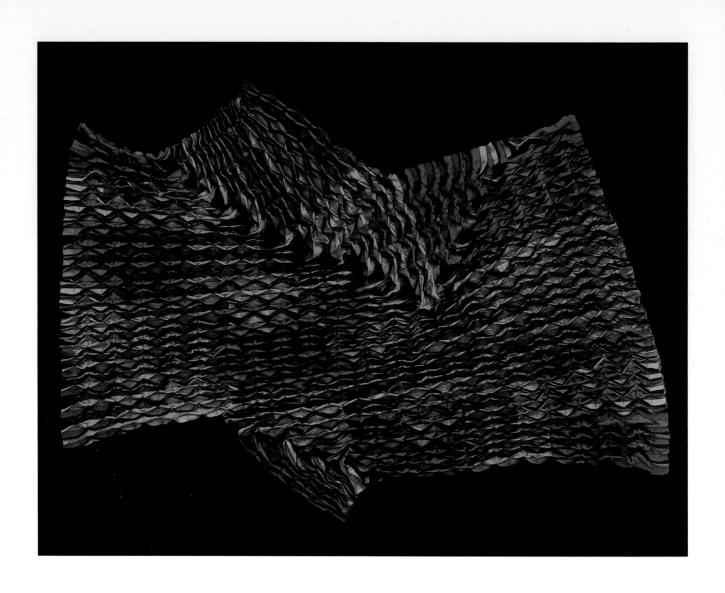

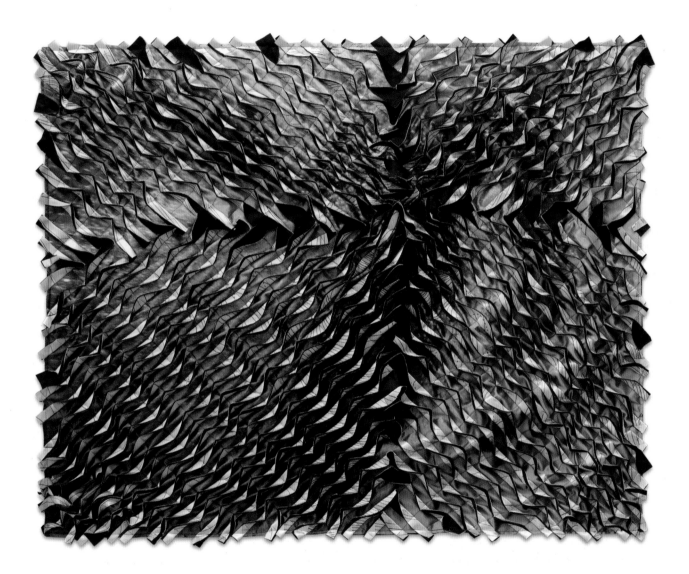

Artifact # 22. 2004. 34" x 48" x 1".
Silks and cotton. Collage, reverse
appliqué, collapse quilting.
Photo: Cecile M. Hooker

Submerged. 2014. 43" x 54" x 2".
Polyester and cotton. Dye sublimation print,
collage, reverse appliqué.
Photo: Cecile M. Hooker

Collector Maureen Hendricks

I am very optimistic about the Art Quilt Movement. I think it is just a matter of getting the word out to people who collect fine art. Anyone who has visited our residence or our Gateway Canyons Resort in Colorado and sees art quilts on the walls instead of paintings is surprised and impressed. The response is usually something like, "I had no idea that this form of art was even out there!" Over time this form of visual art—characterized by its dimensionality, vibrant color, warmth, and creative expression—is sure to become a favorite among fine-art collectors.

I have collected 200 quilts from artists around the world. Ninety quilts from various SAQA artists are framed in shadow boxes and exhibited at the resort. I have another 175 SAQA 12-inch-square quilts displayed in different homes. In addition to collecting quilts, I collect elephant memorabilia. After the Discovery Channel in 1988 produced *Ivory Wars*, a study on elephant poaching, I fell in love with elephants and started collecting stone and wooden sculptures depicting elephants. My husband and I travel extensively, and I try to buy artwork from each country. I have always loved handmade art and crafts.

Katie Pasquini Masopust

Fortuna, California, USA
Grapes. 1996. 60" x 96".
Cotton, blends. Machine appliquéd and quilted.
Hendricks Collection
Photo: Hawthorn Studio

Collection of International Quilt Festival (IQF): Quilts, Inc.

For nearly four decades, Karey Bresenhan and her cousin Nancy O'Bryant Puentes have been acquiring quilts for their corporate collection. They discovered many of these works in exhibitions at the Houston International Quilt Festival, of which Bresenhan is founder and president and O'Bryant Puentes is executive vice president.

These two quilt enthusiasts are also cofounders of the Texas Quilt Museum in La Grange, a noncollecting museum featuring exhibitions from worldwide sources. Of more than 600 quilts in the IQF collection, approximately 200 are art quilts. Bresenhan says that her collector's eye is inspired by color. She and O'Bryant Puentes don't recall making a conscious effort to include art quilts in their rapidly expanding collection of traditional quilts during the early 1980s. O'Bryant Puentes explains, "I don't think it was a conscious decision, but more a natural progression as we saw more and more wonderful art quilts that appealed to us being made. That stirred the acquisitive instincts of natural-born collectors!"

Artists in the collection include SAQA past presidents, Houston prizewinners, and emerging quilt artists. Bresenhan and O'Bryant Puentes have a knack for supporting talented young artists, both foreign and domestic, who later make a name for themselves.

Virginia Greaves

Roswell, Georgia, USA
White Raven. 2013. 32" x 40".
Cotton. Fused, machine appliquéd and quilted.
Collection: Quilts, Inc.

Gallery 2000s

Pamela Allen

Kingston, Ontario, Canada
The Snake Charmer. 2006.
46" x 42" x 2".
Recycled and commercial
fabrics. Raw edge appliquéd,
machine free-motion quilted.

BELOW

Geneviève Attinger

Pontivy, France
Ado-l'Essence. 2001.
51" x 51".
Chintz, cotton, denim, cotton
braid. Free-motion machine
embroidered, curved strip
woven, layered, buttonhole
stitched, machine quilted.

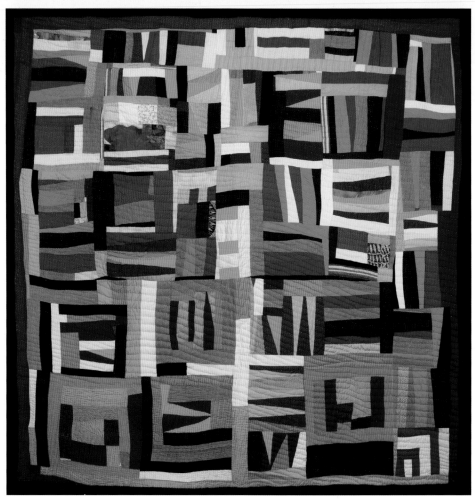

OPPOSITE

Izabella Baykova

St. Petersburg, Russia
Theatre. 2004. 78" x 98".
Silk, rayon. Appliquéd, machine
sewn, hand embroidered.

BELOW

Mary Lee Bendolph

Huntsville, Alabama, USA
Grandma Strips. 2009. 75" x 77".
Fabric. Quilted.
Courtesy of Greg Kucera Gallery
Photo: S&S Photography,
Alabama

Jenny Bowker

Garran, Australian Capital Territory, Australia
Mohamed Sa'ad: Caretaker of the Mosque.
2009. 59" x 66".
Cotton, synthetics, hand-dyed and painted
fabrics. Burned, machine appliquéd, pieced,
and quilted.
Photo: Daniel Heather

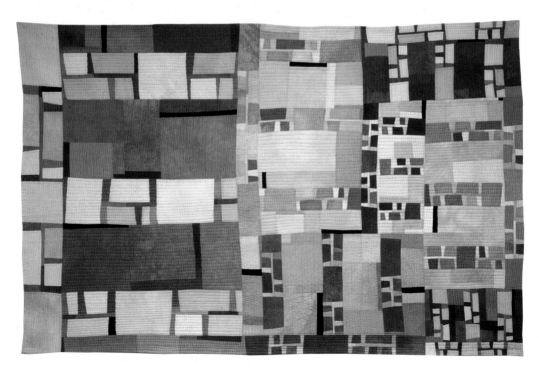

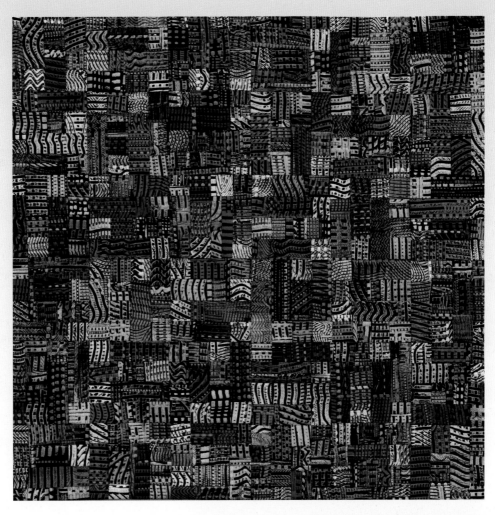

Rachel Brumer

Seattle, Washington, USA
Coral Pollen Pearls. 2002. 60" x 60".
Hand-dyed cotton, textile paint. Silk-screened,
rubbing, drawn, French knots, machine pieced,
hand quilted.
Photo: Deidre Adams

Lisa Call

Kapiti Coast, New Zealand
Structures #11. 2002. 47" x 72".
Dye, fabric. Freehand cut, pieced and quilted
on a home sewing machine.
Collection: Theodore McMinn

Benedicte Caneill

Larchmont, New York, USA
Units 9: Cityscape. 2009. 34" x 34".
Cotton, fabric paints and inks. Monoprinted,
machine pieced and quilted.
Photo: D. James Dee

BELOW *Units 9: Cityscape*. (Detail)

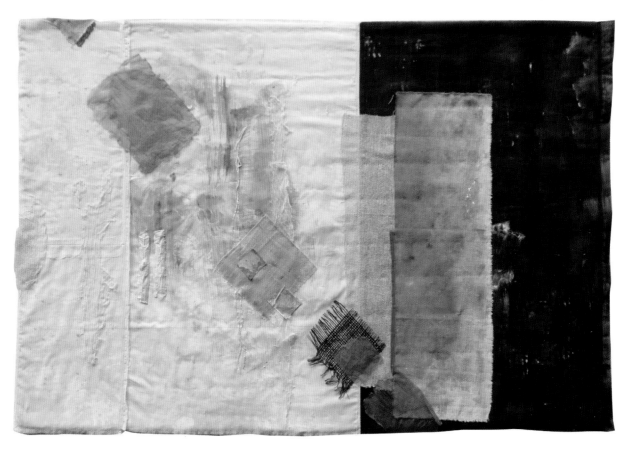

OPPOSITE

Linda Colsh

Middletown, Maryland, USA
Journey. 2006. 44" x 64".
Cotton printed with altered computer
images and screens from the artist's
photographs. Dyed, painted, and printed
by the artist, machine pieced and quilted.
Photo: Pol Leemans

BELOW

Fenella Davies

Bath, United Kingdom
Venice Light. 2009. 35" x 54".
Cotton, silk pods, Japanese
matting, cotton, paper.
Collaged, hand stitched,
painted, and dyed.

Ruth de Vos

Perth, Western Australia, Australia
Not Even Solomon. 2007. 59" x 72".
Fiber-reactive dyes, cotton
homespun. Hand dyed, machine
pieced and quilted.
Thomas Contemporary Quilt
Collection
Photo: Victor France

Sue Dennis

Brisbane, Queensland, Australia
Anthills—Study in Gold. 2008. 31" x 30".
Hand-dyed cotton, hand-rusted fabric,
fabric paint. Monoprinted, hand stitched,
machine quilted, hand painted.
Photo: Bob Dennis

Radka Donnell

Rites of Spring. 2005. 74.5" x 64".
Cotton, satin. Hand pieced, hand
appliquéd, machine quilted.
Collection: San Jose Museum of Quilts
& Textiles
Gift of Radka Donnell
Photo: James Dewrance

OPPOSITE

Chiaki Dosho

Kawasaki-shi, Kanagawa-ken, Japan.
Light & Dark II 1-6. 2009.
47" x 12" x 1.5" each.
Old Japanese kimono. Direct appliquéd.
Photo: Akinori Miyashita

BELOW

Karin Franzen

Fairbanks, Alaska, USA
A Time to Dance—September 9th.
2008. 48" x 55" x 4".
Silk organza, synthetic sheers, recycled
clothing, cotton, dyes, paints. Silk-
screened with thickened dyes, machine
appliquéd, printed, hand embroidered,
machine quilted.
Collection: Signe Franzen
Photo: Eric Nancarrow

OPPOSITE

Valerie S. Goodwin

Tallahassee, Florida, USA
African Burial Ground II. 2009.
44" x 32".
Sheer and opaque fabrics, paint.
Digitally printed, painted, hand
and machine sewn and quilted.
Photo: Richard Brunck

BELOW

Gloria Hansen

East Windsor, New Jersey, USA
Squared Illusions 6. 2007.
44" x 34".
Silk, cotton, pigmented inkjet ink,
paint, fabric pastels. Machine
pieced and quilted.

Jim Hay

Takasaki, Gunma, Japan
Mystery. 2009. 90.5" x 90.5".
Kimono and Obi cloth, Mexican
tablecloth, iridescent cloth, thread,
lace. Thread line drawn, collaged,
appliquéd.

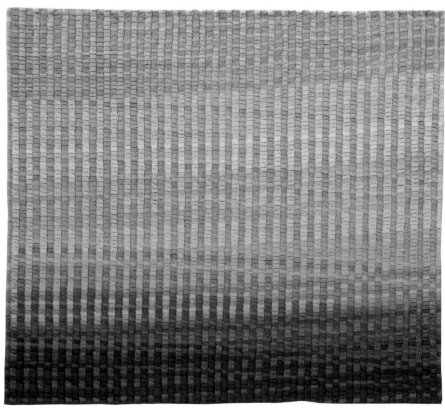

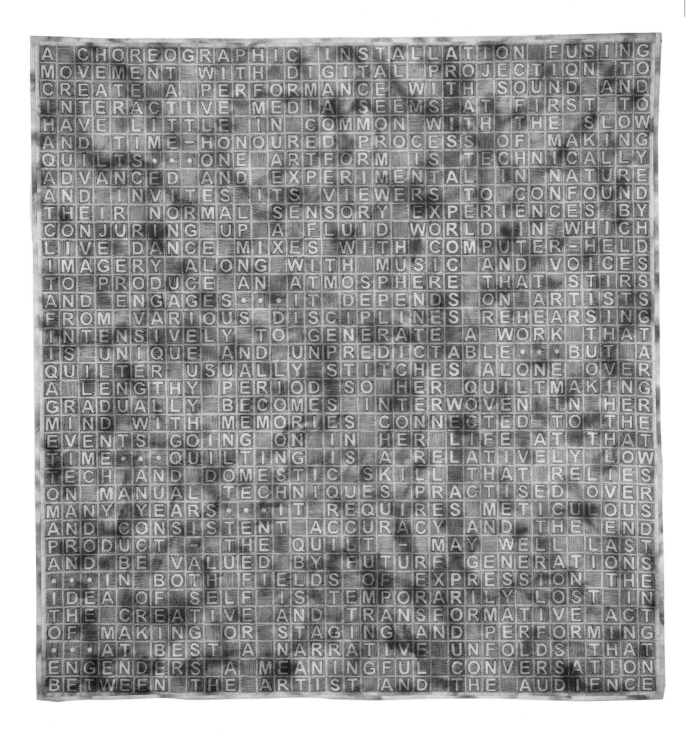

A CHOREOGRAPHIC INSTALLATION FUSING MOVEMENT WITH DIGITAL PROJECTION TO CREATE A PERFORMANCE WITH SOUND AND INTERACTIVE MEDIA SEEMS AT FIRST TO HAVE LITTLE IN COMMON WITH THE SLOW AND TIME-HONOURED PROCESS OF MAKING QUILTS...ONE ARTFORM IS TECHNICALLY ADVANCED AND EXPERIMENTAL IN NATURE AND INVITES ITS VIEWERS TO CONFOUND THEIR NORMAL SENSORY EXPERIENCES BY CONJURING UP A FLUID WORLD IN WHICH LIVE DANCE MIXES WITH COMPUTER-HELD IMAGERY ALONG WITH MUSIC AND VOICES TO PRODUCE AN ATMOSPHERE THAT STIRS AND ENGAGES...IT DEPENDS ON ARTISTS FROM VARIOUS DISCIPLINES REHEARSING INTENSIVELY TO GENERATE A WORK THAT IS UNIQUE AND UNPREDICTABLE...BUT A QUILTER USUALLY STITCHES ALONE OVER A LENGTHY PERIOD SO HER QUILTMAKING GRADUALLY BECOMES INTERWOVEN IN HER MIND WITH MEMORIES CONNECTED TO THE EVENTS GOING ON IN HER LIFE AT THAT TIME...QUILTING IS A RELATIVELY LOW TECH AND DOMESTIC SKILL THAT RELIES ON MANUAL TECHNIQUES PRACTISED OVER MANY YEARS...IT REQUIRES METICULOUS AND CONSISTENT ACCURACY AND THE END PRODUCT — THE QUILT — MAY WELL LAST AND BE VALUED BY FUTURE GENERATIONS ...IN BOTH FIELDS OF EXPRESSION THE IDEA OF SELF IS TEMPORARILY LOST IN THE CREATIVE AND TRANSFORMATIVE ACT OF MAKING OR STAGING AND PERFORMING ...AT BEST A NARRATIVE UNFOLDS THAT ENGENDERS A MEANINGFUL CONVERSATION BETWEEN THE ARTIST AND THE AUDIENCE

Marina Kamenskaya

Wauconda, Illinois, USA
Edge # 7. 2009. 72" x 72".
Cotton. Pieced, machine
quilted.

Misik Kim

Seoul, Korea
The Story of My Life. 2007. 54" x 54".
Hand-dyed cotton. Machine stitched,
appliquéd, pieced, and quilted.

Ellie Kreneck

Lubbock, Texas, USA
*Exiting Eden with Eve Firing Up
the Pick-Up*. 2008. 54" x 42".
Hand-dyed and commercial cotton,
fiber-reactive dyes, water-soluble
resists. Drawn, painted, appliquéd,
hand quilted.

OPPOSITE

Viola Burley Leak

Washington, DC, USA
Addressing Hair. 2008. 62" x 46".
Cotton. Machine appliquéd,
machine quilted by
Juanita Canfield.
Photo: Mary and Chas. E. Martin

BELOW

Linda Levin

Wayland, Massachusetts, USA
Walking the Dogs / Summer. 2000. 49" x 64".
Cotton. Procion-dyed, raw-edge appliquéd.
Collection: San Jose Museum of Quilts &
Textiles, The Marbaum Collection, Gift of
Marvin and Hilary Fletcher
Photo: Joe Ofria

Inge Mardal and Steen Hougs

Struer, Denmark
Facing North. 2008. 49" x 65".
Cotton, paint. Whole cloth painted,
machine quilted.

Kathleen McCabe

Coronado, California, USA
In His Shadow. 2008. 29" x 33".
Commercial cottons, nylon tulle.
Raw-edge machine appliquéd,
machine quilted.

OPPOSITE

Eleanor McCain

Shalimar, Florida, USA
6 Color Grid Study 1. 2006. 22" x 44".
Hand-dyed cotton. Improvisationally
cut, machine pieced and quilted.
Collection: Dorothy Caldwell
Photo: Luke Jordan

BELOW

Reiko Naganuma

Utsunomiya, Tochigi, Japan
A Scorching Sun. 2007. 85" x 65".
Cotton, linen, nylon, organza, real
branches. Machine pieced, quilted,
appliquéd, and embroidered; hand
woven.

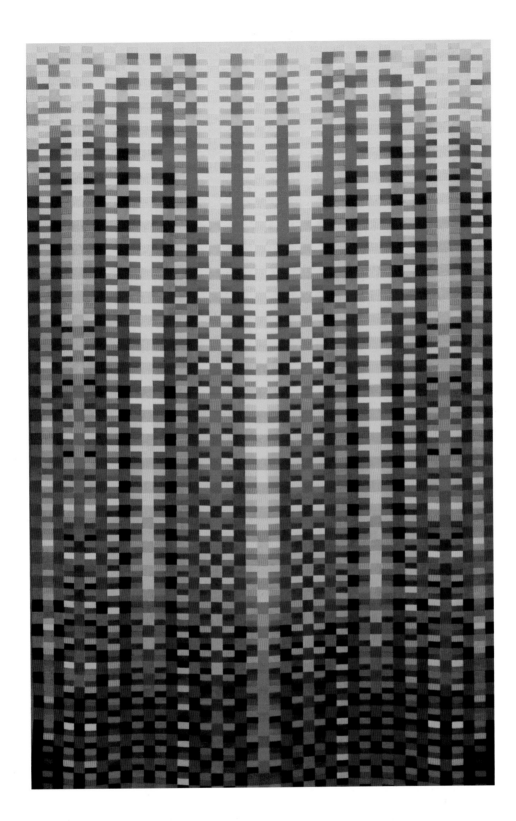

OPPOSITE

Anne McKenzie Nickolson

Indianapolis, Indiana, USA
Woman Still Seated. 2002. 57" x 57".
Cotton. Machine pieced, hand
appliquéd through all layers.
Collection: San Jose Museum of Quilts
& Textiles, The Marbaum Collection,
Gift of Marvin and Hilary Fletcher

BELOW

Kathy Nida

El Cajon, California, USA
Here. 2009. 55" x 47".
Commercial and hand-dyed cottons, ink,
cotton embroidery thread. Fused appliqué,
machine stitched, machine quilted, inked,
hand embroidered.
Photo: Gary Conaughton

Dan Olfe

Julian, California, USA
Cascade. 2002. 64" x 41".
Whole-cloth cotton. Hand
painted with transparent textile
paints, machine quilted.

Amy Orr

Philadelphia, Pennsylvania, USA
Twist Tie Quilt #6: Double Vision. 2005. 54" x 36.5".
Paper and metal twist-ties that are used to close bags.
Hand stitched into Log Cabin blocks, then assembled and
stitched onto whole cloth. Quilted through four layers.
Photo: J. Woodin

Lori Lupe Pelish

Niskayuna, New York, USA
Bad News. 2003. 54" x 44".
Cotton commercial fabrics. Machine appliquéd,
embroidered, and quilted.
Photo: David Pelish

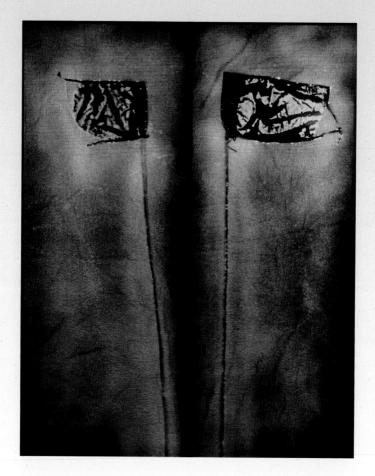

Clare Plug

Napier, New Zealand
Ice Crack 2. 2008. 71" x 55.5".
Cotton. Machine appliquéd, discharge
dyed, machine quilted.
Collection: Antarctica New Zealand
Photo: David Evans

Shawn Quinlan

Pittsburgh, Pennsylvania, USA
Jesus Get Your Gun. 2004.
49" x 36".
Altered fabric wall hangings,
commercial fabrics. Pieced,
appliquéd, machine quilted.

Sara Rockinger

Lafayette, Colorado, USA
Two-Sided War. 2008. 90" x 34" x 26".
Nylon organza, silk gauze. Hand-dyed
fabric, free-motion machine stitched,
layered, appliquéd.
Photo: Joe Mendoza

RIGHT *Two-Sided War* (reverse)

Pam RuBert

Springfield, Missouri, USA
Paris—Wish You Were Hair.
2008. 38" x 49".
Cotton, vintage button. Layered
fabric, cut, fused, free-motion quilted.
Photo: Russ RuBert

BELOW

Lynn Setterington

Manchester, United Kingdom
Mums Are Heroes. 2005. 67" x 53".
Cotton. Hand stitched.
Collection: International Quilt
Study Center & Museum
Photo: Stephen Yates

Joan Sowada

Gillette, Wyoming, USA
Cosmic Bicycle (left side).
2005. 35" x 22".
Commercial fabrics. Fused,
machine raw-edge appliquéd
and quilted.
Collection: Shirley Neary
Photo: Ken Sanville

BELOW *Cosmic Bicycle* (right side).
22" x 35".

Robin Schwalb

Brooklyn, New York, USA
Chinese Characters. 2006. 67" x 93".
Fabric, fabric paint. Stenciled, photo silk-
screened, hand and machine
appliquéd, machine pieced, hand quilted.
Collection: John M. Walsh III
Photo: Karen Bell

Virginia A. Spiegel

Byron, Illinois, USA
Boundary Waters 48. 2009. 37" x 54".
Cotton, acrylic paint, felt, cheesecloth, cotton
yarn, upholstery fabric, duck cloth, polyester,
silk, recycled pieces of artist's art quilts.
Painted, screen printed, burned, dyed,
crocheted, hand and machine stitched.
Photo: Deidre Adams

Laurie Swim

Lunenburg, Nova Scotia, Canada
*Breaking Ground, the Hogg's Hollow Disaster,
1960*. 2000. 84" x 240".
Cotton, silk, man-made fabrics. Photo transfers,
free-motion stitched, machine and hand
embroidered, machine quilted.
Collection: City of Toronto Art Collection
Photo: Signature Studios

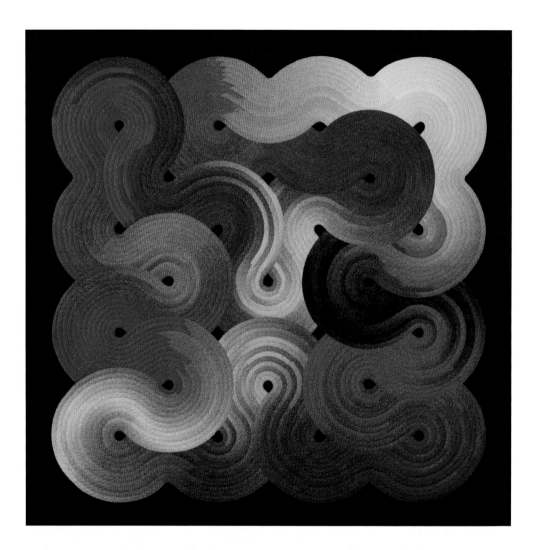

Etsuko Takahashi

Yokohama, Kanagawa, Japan
Waves #4. 1998. 78" x 78".
Cotton. Direct appliquéd, machine stitched, pieced and appliquéd on whole cloth.
Collection: San Jose Museum of Quilts & Textiles, The Marbaum Collection, Gift of Marvin and Hilary Fletcher
Photo: Dairy Barn Center for the Arts

Carol Taylor

Pittsford, New York, USA
Windfall. 2008. 43" x 86".
Hand-dyed fabrics. Pieced, fused, appliquéd.
Private collection

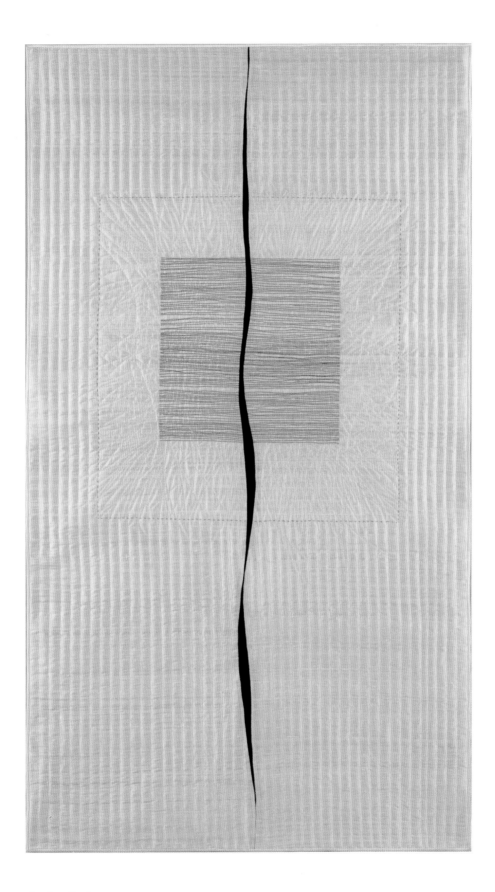

Daphne Taylor

Montville, Maine, USA
Quilt Drawing #9. 2009. 50.5" x 25.5".
Silk, cotton. Pieced, hand embroidered, hand quilted.
Photo: Karen Bell

DETAIL

Ulva Ugerup

Malmö, Sweden
Angels of Wrath. 2008. 29" x 43".
Mixed fabrics, vintage lace and
necklaces, sequins, buttons, beads,
shells, caps, found items. Machine
pieced and quilted, hand embroidered.
Photo: Deidre Adams

BELOW *Angels of Wrath* (detail)

Anna Von Mertens

Peterborough, New Hampshire, USA
Madame X's Aura, after John Singer Sargent. 2009. 83" x 43".
Hand-dyed, hand-stitched cotton.
Hand dyed, hand quilted.
Collection: Museum of Fine Arts, Boston
Photo: Don Tuttle

OPPOSITE

Kent Williams

Madison, Wisconsin, USA
Sine Me Up. 2008. 82" x 55".
Cotton. Machine pieced and quilted.
Collection: San Jose Museum of Quilts & Textiles, The
Marbaum Collection, Gift of Marvin and Hilary Fletcher
Photo: Eric Tadsen

Ita Ziv (d.)

Israel
Fire Fingers. 2009. 39" x 39".
Organza hand-dyed by the artist, commercial cotton
fabric. Fused curved strips, appliquéd, screen
printed, machine free-motion quilted.
Collection: Ela Ziv

Ann Johnston | LAKE OSWEGO, OREGON, USA

I have gradually expanded the kinds of quilts that I make. In the 1970s my focus was traditional quilts, and I dyed fabric in traditional ways. In the 1980s I made mostly whole-cloth quilts, hand painted and printed with thickened dyes, still exclusively hand quilted. In the 1990s I continued to learn freehand construction and machine quilting while developing a simple method of low-water immersion dyeing with fiber-reactive dyes.

I began experimenting with raw-edge appliqué in the early twenty-first century because this technique offers a variety of lines and shapes. I began to realize that I could make any quilt I can imagine, adapting my sewing and dyeing to the idea and not the other way around.

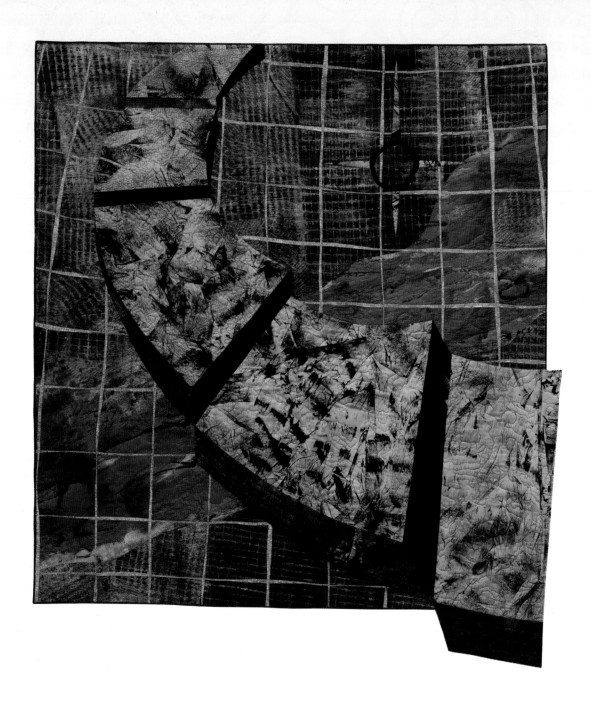

In 2010 the Martin Museum of Art at Baylor University invited me to do a solo exhibit three years into the future. This opportunity gave me a reason to start on a new body of work, concentrating on a subject I had studied my whole life but that was too ambitious for a single quilt. I spent a year collecting notes and photos, and sketching and dyeing new fabrics. This process has stretched me and continues to—there were fourteen quilts in the 2013 exhibition and thirty-two in my exhibit at the Bellevue Arts Museum in 2017.

Every piece has been a new chance to learn. Each step, from idea to final quilt, presents many choices, each leading to even more choices. This process is challenging and fun. I finish my quilts because I want to know what they will look like.

www.annjohnston.net

OPPOSITE
North Is Up. 1997. 65" x 75".
Cotton broadcloth. Hand painted and printed with dye, machine pieced and quilted.
Photo: Bill Bachhuber

The Contact: Cross Polarized Gabbro. 2014. 85" x 25".
Cotton sateen, silk organza. Hand painted and printed with thickened dyes, raw-edge machine assembly, hand and machine quilted.
Photo: Bill Bachhuber

Chunghie Lee | SEOUL, SOUTH KOREA

The antique patched *bojagi* or *pojagi* (Korean traditional wrapping cloth) made many generations ago in Korea are a source of great inspiration to me. They were made by our female ancestors, who are not remembered by history: no names or reputations. In their time they had little independence, but they were faithful to their situation and endured. Using carefully saved scraps of precious fabrics, they played with color and shape naively, naturally, creating pure and innocent artworks. My art pays tribute to these ancestors, and I often incorporate their photographic images to honor them in my work.

No-Name Women (30 panels). 2005. Each panel is 40" x 12'.
Hemp, silk. Photo images hand silk screen printed.
Photo: Jiyoung Chung

OPPOSITE
No-Name Women—Red. 2005. 44" x 44".
Silk. Hand silk-screen printed.
Collection: Ruth and Bill True
Photo: Garith Yang

In the early 1990s I was chosen to travel to the United States to lecture about Korean fiber art. *Pojagi* was suggested, but I knew little about it. I spoke to the director of the Museum of Korean Embroidery, Dr. Hur Dungwha, who had started to collect *pojagi* in the 1960s. It was through his invaluable efforts that these *pojagis* were preserved.

In order to make my own *pojagi*, I had to go to the market and buy traditional Korean fabric. I discovered how beautiful the fabrics were. I had not paid much attention to my own culture's fabrics and colors until that moment. It was like finding treasure in my backyard.

Traditionally *pojagi* is made of just two pieces of fabric. I have expanded and applied this technique to making clothes, wall hangings, and three-dimensional installations. I see this patchwork as a metaphor for human life. We may feel ourselves to be as random pieces of fabric, alone and without meaning, but God's hand places us together in a beautiful composition that has great harmony and meaning.

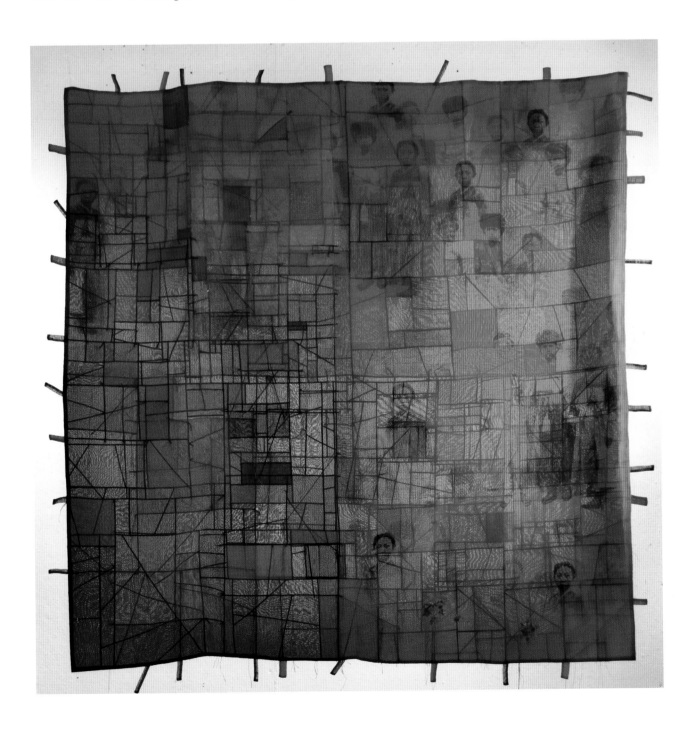

Linda MacDonald | WILLITS, CALIFORNIA, USA

My artwork has changed over the years. As a child, I was inspired by women in my family from Ohio and Indiana who made quilts of repeating patterns. I wanted to create large landscape images with planes of space and patterns combined. I wanted to create visual three-dimensionality in the quilt. I hadn't seen this done in quilts, so it was my challenge. After I achieved this goal in my early work, I then moved on to creating image and pattern through paint and hand quilting. I was trying to merge paint with the quilt.

Going to graduate school led me to question my voice and intent. The issues that were important to me were environmental and local. I live in rural Northern California, where there were marches protesting clear-cutting in the forests and a movement to designate the spotted owl as an endangered species. Realizing that I had to make artwork about these important issues, I made many quilts with trees and owls. The redwood tree is now my focus; it is a symbol of environmental change, greed, threatened species, and immense beauty. I do not know where portraying these trees will take me, but it will be an adventure.

There is so much advice about how to find your voice, how to find your personal style, and how to create your unique art. It is all true: work hard, go to school, take many art classes, take art history classes, take risks in your art making, try many art mediums, experience many

OPPOSITE
Clear Palisades. 1987. 92" x 92".
Cotton. Hand dyed, hand pieced and quilted.
Photo: Sharon Risedorph

Tree Park. 2002. 48" x 36".
Cotton, paint. Airbrushed, hand painted, hand stitched.
Photo: James Dewrance

teachers, and visit museums and galleries. But the most important advice of all is to create art about what truly interests you. What do you think about, worry about; what do you love? What is your passion? Then forget about all the art you have ever seen, forget about all the classes you have taken, forget about all the advice people have given you about your art, and get in the studio and work on your own. You want to stay fresh and make work that is uniquely yours and, above all, honest. That is a big challenge.

The greatest compliment a friend gave me was that no matter what medium I used—oils, watercolors, textiles, pencils—she always knew it was my work. It had the feel and presence of my art statements and was recognizable as my style. Art is a vehicle for self-discovery and much joy. The path is revealed as you walk it.

www.lindamacdonald.com

Migration of CA Red Legged Frog. 2002. 39" x 36".
Cotton, dye, paint. Airbrushed, hand painted, hand stitched.
Collection: Robert and Kathleen Kirkpatrick
Photo: Robert Comings

Paula Nadelstern | BRONX, NEW YORK, USA

When an artist works in a series, the questions become more complex but the answers become simpler. I have been absorbed in a series of kaleidoscopic quilts since 1987. The unplanned perks of this degree of focus include sudden, intuitive leaps of understanding—actual breakthroughs to new and deeper perspectives of problems that you did not even realize needed to be resolved.

State-of-the-art kaleidoscopes have been not only my inspiration but also my classroom. I've learned to manipulate physical properties such as rhythm and line to inject a feeling of motion into an otherwise static image. I'm always trying to learn more about the unique qualities of what might be called the kaleidoscopic personality: surprise, magic, change, and chance. To conjure an

Kaleidoscopic XVI: More Is More. 1996. 64" x 64".
Cotton, silk. Machine pieced and hand quilted.
Collection: American Folk Art Museum, New York
Photo: Karen Bell

instant of luminous and fleeting spontaneity, I have learned to trust in symmetry, rely on detail, commit random and staged acts of color, and understand that the whole will always be greater than the sum of its parts.

One of my design strategies is to camouflage seams and create seemingly seamless connections. This tactic encourages an uninterrupted flow of design or color from one section to another. The result is a smooth transition, with the illusion that there is no seam at all. A "seamless" surface draws the viewer physically closer to the quilt, inviting inspection and enjoyment of its organization. My quilts combine the symmetry and surprise of a kaleidoscope with the techniques and materials of quilt making. I try to free myself from a conventional sense of orderliness, seeking a random quality to imitate the succession of chance interlinks and endless possibilities synonymous with kaleidoscopes.

I travel extensively within the US and abroad teaching my idiosyncratic patchwork sensibility. Most classes explore the possibilities offered by complex textiles while demystifying the nature of symmetry. I've written five books about my signature style and have designed fabric collections for Benartex for more than twenty years.

http://paulanadelstern.com

Kaleidoscopic XL: Her Self / A Radiation Mask. 2016. 19" x 14" x 10".
Cotton kaleidoscopic fabrics designed by the artist, beads, sequins. The foundation is the intact, hard-plastic radiation mask (including the original attached clips) worn by the artist during treatments. Hand stitched, hand beaded, glued, fused.

Kaleidoscopic XL: Her Self / A Radiation Mask (reverse)

Developing a personal style began by weaning myself away from the strong influence of my abstract-painting professor and mentor, Hale Woodruff, during my undergraduate and graduate years at New York University. I was drawn to the surrealist works at New York's Museum of Modern Art as a teenager and eventually became a neosurrealist in my psychedelic work. Decades later, exploring imaging on the computer, I found that integrating disparate photographic images to create new gestalts brought me spiraling back to those early inspirations.

My distinctive techniques include photomontage that is heat-transferred onto sheer and opaque fabrics with tiled compositions. I also create deconstructed quilts with multiple layers of each block suspended individually, requiring the

Mount Koya San: Ancestors. 2001. 29.5" x 37".
Photo montage, heat transferred on cotton, glass beads,
sequins. Hand-sewn, quilted.

invention of unique support systems that are installation ready. In addition to the problem-solving aspects of composition and construction, l value the meditative quality of time spent in my studio.

The art quilt genre gives me a world of possibilities incorporating tactile sensibilities and layering. It can include my earlier painting and printmaking techniques and certainly challenges me to go through new doors. Surprisingly, I am going larger in my installations, even though that scale poses more challenges.

www.arlesklar.com

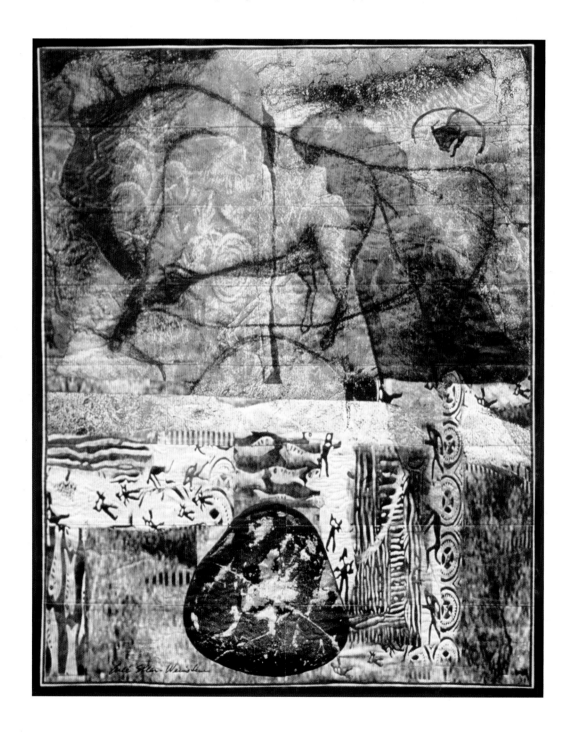

Cave Wall: Bison. 1999. 52" x 42.5".
Photo montage on canvas. Heat transferred, quilted.

Barbara W. Watler | PEMBROKE PINES, FLORIDA, USA

I was raised in the 1930s and '40s, when children were told to be seen and not heard. I learned not to speak up. Making pictures was a way for me to speak, and that is still true today. I make art in the hope that someone will "hear" what I have to say by stopping to look at the art that my experiences have taught me to express.

In my early years as a quilt artist, I wanted my quilts to look as if they were paintings. I concentrated on painting the fabrics and using a direct appliqué process in a collage technique, as in *Catch a Falling Star*. That quilt includes thread painting, with rayon and metallic threads on the background, shell, rocks, and figure. Later I mastered whole-cloth reverse appliqué, as in many of my Fingerprint series.

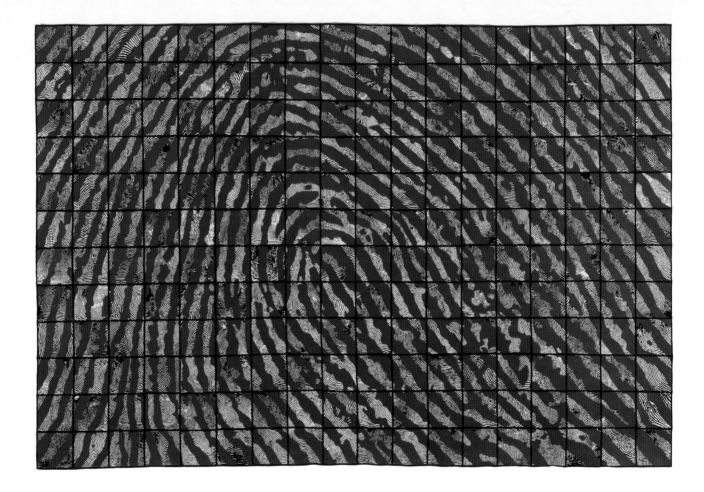

Fingerprint #50: UNITY. 2005. 60" x 90".
Cotton canvas. Straight-stitched to cover all fabric.
Collection: Coral Springs Museum of Art, Florida
Photo: Gerhardt Heidersberger

Barbara W. Watler | PEMBROKE PINES, FLORIDA, USA

That series also features thread painting, using machine running stitches that completely cover the foundation fabric. Recently I have focused on hand-stitched projects based on dense, random running stitches, as in *Convergence*. I am most excited by the finishing process. It amazes me each time I have persisted enough to finish a quilt, especially with hand-stitched surfaces requiring approximately six months.

As a child, I was encouraged to experiment with soft pastels by my family, and that hooked me on painterly compositions. Michael James and Dorothy Caldwell have been very influential. He suggested that I try working in a larger format, and she taught me the value of playing with design.

www.barbarawatler.com

Convergence. 2014. 45" x 33.5".
Linen/cotton canvas, #5 perle cotton. Hand-worked random running stitches covering entire surface.
Photo: Gerhardt Heidersberger

OPPOSITE
Catch a Falling Star. 1996. 72" x 50".
Lamé, cotton, blends, velvet, ribbon floss. Painted, colored with pencils, hand and machine stitched and embellished.
Photo: Gerhardt Heidersberger

California art quilt collector Del Thomas now owns 330 works, including the largest group of quilts by Ruth McDowell in a private collection. The Thomas Contemporary Quilt Collection covers more than three decades and has been shared across the country in numerous museums and quilt show exhibitions.

Thomas purchased her first quilt in 1985, enthusiastically acquiring quilts ever since then. She favors works in which the quilting complements the composition, and tends to purchase pieces with bright color and graphic forms. Artists in her collection include Elizabeth Barton, Sylvia Einstein, Noriko Endo, Caryl Bryer Fallert-Gentry, Ann Johnston, Jean Ray Laury, Libby Lehman, and Jane Sassaman.

Del Thomas is a popular leader of quilt workshops, especially in California, and has generously lectured on her collection for many years during exhibitions and other quilt-related events. Her support of Visions Art Museum: Contemporary Quilts + Textiles in San Diego has been noteworthy, most recently her matching grant to produce a catalog for the latest *Visions* exhibition. Beth Smith, curator of the museum, comments: "When Visions Art Museum opened as Visions Art Quilt Gallery in San Diego in April 2007, Del supported the organization's location from the beginning. She has been a sponsor of the *Quilt Visions* biennial exhibitions in recent years, as well as offering an award from the Thomas Contemporary Quilt Collection for the quilt she admires most in the *Quilt Visions* exhibitions. In 2011 Del made a substantial financial contribution with an ongoing pledge to name the largest gallery in the museum as the Del Thomas Gallery.

Ruth McDowell

Colrain, Massachusetts, USA
A Rash of Flamingos. 2000. 52" x 100".
Cotton. Machine pieced and quilted.
Thomas Contemporary Art Collection
Photo: Deidre Adams

OPPOSITE *A Rash of Flamingos* (detail)

John M. Walsh III has been collecting art quilts since the early 1990s, guided by the unerring eye of curator and author Penelope "Penny" McMorris. His collection now has more than 100 works, and Walsh has generously shared them with the public through museum exhibitions and publications.

He comments: "Quilt artists frequently bring to their works academic training and professional skills in the fine arts in addition to their quilting skills. John Lefelhocz, for example, was educated in the fields of painting, drawing, sculpture, photography, film, and art history. I own two of his quilts. In addition to the layers of fabric in art quilts, there are frequently also layers of meaning. Lefelhocz's quilt *Mona in the Age of Social Butterflies* in my collection illustrates that at several levels: Mona Lisa taking a selfie, the tiny letters comprising the pixels in Mona Lisa's self portrait spelling out a quotation from Leonardo da Vinci, and blue butterflies with humorous tweets and posts from five hundred years ago to the present, such as [this one] from Mona Lisa herself: 'Sitting here for this portrait . . . I'm in a slightly weird mood, grinding my teeth.'"

"I differentiate between collecting and accumulating. Collecting to me is a serious endeavor requiring focus and study. It is a discipline engaging the mind and the spirit. It is a true avocation. I collect art quilts. 'Accumulating' in this context for me connotes gathering together related items—not necessarily as a discipline and frequently whimsical. I accumulate elephants. My grandfather was a New York state senator, and friends often gave him elephants because he was a Republican and that party's symbol is the elephant. As a child I was enthralled with those elephants, which came to me when he died. My elephant parade now numbers approximately 250—my fun collection. Art quilts are my passion."

John Lefelhocz

Athens, Ohio, USA
Mona in the Age of Social Butterflies. 2012. 64" x 64".
Cotton sateen, with pixelated image of the *Mona Lisa* by Leonardo da Vinci under text by da Vinci on the nature of art. The butterfly wings are printed with made-up social media quotes from individuals "living" in the 1500s. Image designed by the artist and printed by Spoonflower, butterflies made from glass beads and printed card stock. Hand stitched and embellished.
Collection: John M. Walsh III

CHAPTER FIVE
2010s: Looking Forward

Founding of Quilt Expo
Beaujolais (today International
Biennial of Quilt and Textile
Art, Villefranche, France)

Founding of Quilt and Craft
Show, Curitiba, Brazil

2010

2011

2016

Founding of the
Texas Quilt Museum,
La Grange

Founding of the
Wisconsin Museum
of Quilts & Fiber
Arts, Cedarburg

Founding of the
Iowa Quilt Museum,
Winterset

Like contemporary artists working in other media, many quilt artists working in the twenty-first century use the quilt medium to address important social, political, economic, and environmental issues of the new millennium. Whether the artworks are created by artists who have spent decades exploring the quilt format, or are created by artists who embraced the art form more recently, global issues often are at the forefront of their subject matter.

The broad range of subject matter parallels the wide variety of materials and techniques used in these works. Materials include silk-screened, hand-dyed, painted, repurposed, found, commercial, and digitally printed fabrics. Artists continue to explore new technology, such as digital photography, and they use computer software to create or manipulate images, which then can be transferred or printed onto fabric. Art quilts can incorporate LED lights, sound, and movement for additional impact. Artists continue to challenge the definition of a "quilt," with some works intended to be hung away from the wall or viewed as three-dimensional objects.

New technologies more widely available after 2010, such as programmable longarm quilting machines, digital textile-printing services, and high-resolution digital cameras on mobile phones, also are having an effect on work produced. However, while some artists are intrigued by these new technologies, others embrace handwork, preferring evidence of the human touch to communicate their message.

In the second decade of the twenty-first century, the emergence of the Modern Quilt Guild (MQG), founded in 2009, had a far-reaching effect on all aspects of the quilt-making industry, energizing a new generation that seeks to take its place in the continuum of quilt history. Like many of the art quilt pioneers, MQG leaders began making functional quilts for their homes and then quickly developed their own personal styles. Drawing on historical, modern, and contemporary design, quilts by MQG members can be functional objects of beauty and individual expression as well as powerful displays of social and political comment. MQG makers often blur the lines between fine art and functional craft. MQG's phenomenal growth and influence, made possible by the internet and social-media platforms, is likely to continue for years to come, taking a significant place in quilt history.

Whatever materials, techniques, form, or subject matter today's quilt artists choose, the lines between art and craft are not just blurring but disappearing. Artists are choosing the appropriate materials and techniques for what they want to express. Today's artists who choose to work in the quilt medium pay tribute to their predecessors as they look to the future and the limitless possibilities of the art form.

Sue Benner | DALLAS, TEXAS, USA

During college while majoring in molecular biology, I learned to batik and dye fabric, first from a friend and then more formally in a University of Wisconsin fabric design class. I went on to pursue more art classes, often using science as subject matter and inspiration. These experiments with fabric led to my first art quilt: a batik plant cell complete with nucleus and organelles.

I developed my personal style over many years and by making lots of work. I often worked in series, exploring the same idea and changing just a few variables. Over the years I have created structures of biological and geometric abstraction, landscape, still life—a variety of styles and subject matter as well as work driven by pure process.

Watchful Eye VII: Ogalu Blue. 1996. 43" x 63".
Silk, cotton, found fabrics, dye, paint. Dyed, painted,
fused, machine quilted.
Collection: Lakeview Health, Jacksonville, Florida

Today, my work is created primarily with silk and cotton that I have dyed and painted, incorporating estate sale and thrift store fabrics. I compose the surface of the quilt with layers of textile collage and paint. I work on five to ten quilts at a time, often in two different series. Ideas naturally overlap and play off one another to push my creative process forward.

I am always trying to stretch myself, but at the same time I periodically recycle the themes in my work, not because I want to, but because I can't help myself. It seems like a natural process. I think that our lives circle back around based on our history (our experiences), what is important to us (our values), and how our brains are wired (our natures). But there is always something new to bring to the table—or at least that is what I hope for.

A recent body of work conveys my love of plaids and grids. Metal mesh and chain-link fences are things that I photograph all the time, including the world seen through them. The fences form a scrim for the scene behind—instant units, instant analysis . . . an instant quilt.

www.suebenner.com

View from Grand River Road. 2015. 35" x 103".
Silk, cotton, polyester, rayon, found fabrics, dye, paint. Dyed, painted, fused, machine quilted.
Collection: Mayo Clinic, Rochester, Minnesota
Photo: Eric Neilsen

ABOVE *View from Grand River Road.* (Detail)

Regina Benson | GOLDEN, COLORADO, USA

I don't create alone. I bring the enormous stream of past and ongoing art creation into my own artwork, sometimes consciously and sometimes subliminally.

Baltic Seaside is one of my first works that combined mark making on fabric laid directly on the land with dimensional presentation and quilting. I view this work as embryonic to my consequent practice of marrying my subject with the making process itself. I believe that this collaborative process further informs the vision and concept of the piece. The surface cloth was first dyed, then laid on the grass with river rocks, twigs, and reeds set down as resist; then the entire cloth was discharged, painted, layered, quilted, and stitched.

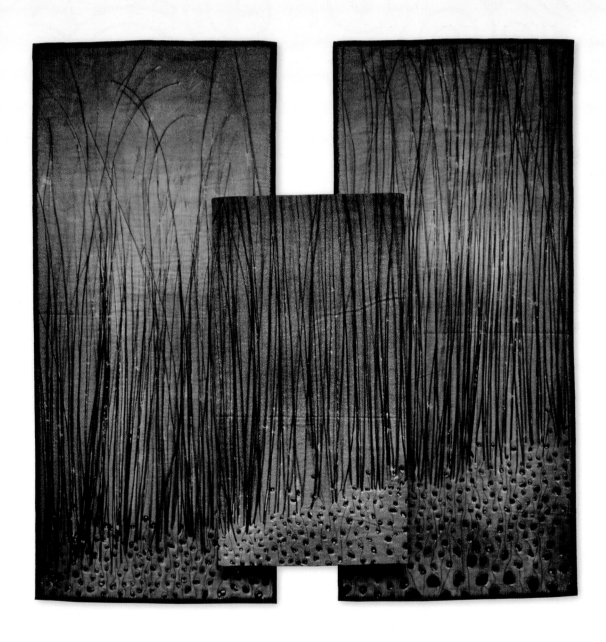

Baltic Seaside. 2006. 43" x 43" x 4".
Cotton sateen. Painted, bare-needle stitched.
Collection: Galante Family
Photo: John Bonath

My rusted series on ancient messages includes *Unearthed.* This series explores the remains of culture, art, and language we see and rediscover around the world. Being Lithuanian born, and having Sanskrit as the closest ancestral link to my native language, has brought a special appreciation of the artistry of surviving written markings on stone, scrolls, and ruins. I try to inform my own marks with this sense of ancestral history, survival, and connectedness.

My pieces are very graphic and intricately detailed at the same time. I want the viewer to feel the overall piece from 10 to 15 feet away and, as the distance gets closer, discover more and more details of color and texture to enhance those first impressions. I am coaxing the viewer into sharing a physical space with my visions. I want the viewer to be enveloped, surrounded, and drawn inside my work.

www.reginabenson.com

Unearthed. 2008. 44" x 44" x 8".
Cotton, silk, linen, polyester, paint. Soy wax resisted, rusted, appliquéd, pieced, stitched, burned.
Photo: John Bonath

Eszter Bornemisza | BUDAPEST, HUNGARY

I have been always fascinated by contemporary art. I originally pursued the field of mathematics, earned a PhD, and worked as a researcher for nearly twenty years. In the late 1990s my attention turned to textile arts, and I started to experiment with surface design on fabric and with making quilts.

My main sources of inspiration are the layers of history and age in the earth—signs and traces of the past, and their meanings for us. I like to use maps of ancient settlements and dwellings that preserve the spirit of the people who lived there. City plans, map fragments, and labyrinths all have a very graphic appearance while representing the very complex relationship of city and citizen.

Cosmic Embrace. 1999. 54" x 64".
Re-dyed commercial and painted cotton fabrics. Pieced, appliquéd, machine quilted.
Photo: Tihanyi & Bakos

Eszter Bornemisza

Unlike the archaeologist who uncovers deeper and deeper layers of time, I superimpose layers on my quilts. I focus on the process of understanding the course of time through the assumed meanings of its signs, considering these reminiscences part of our common, ancient knowledge.

In recent years I have begun to create large-scale, transparent, and translucent textiles as a way to explore our patterns of urban living. I am exposing the multilayered networks of cities in these three-dimensional objects and installations. These works include recycled paper, reprinted newspaper, discarded threads and yarns, and even gut. As urban structures develop, widen, thicken, clot, and create subsystems in history, the cities that live with us undergo an endless and continuous evolution.

www.bornemisza.com

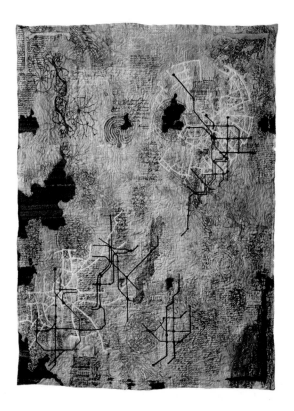

Palimpsest. 2009. 80" x 60".
Cotton damask tablecloth, cotton and synthetic fabrics. Dyed, distorted, screen printed, appliquéd, machine quilted.
Photo: Tihanyi & Bakos

BELOW
March. 2012. Each 72" x 40" x 4".
Sketch paper, newspaper, paint, dust, nets, cotton, copper pipes, pipe insulation, brick. Dyed, painted, glued.
Photo: Tihanyi & Bakos

I always use my personal, contemporary interpretation of the traditional *arashi shibori* Japanese dye technique for the surface of my work. I have been exploring this process since encountering it while studying textiles at San Francisco State University in the late 1970s. Recently I have begun experimenting with *itajime shibori*, whereby actual shapes are secured to the wrapped silk and dyed or discharged.

The processes involved in creating my work can be divided into several parts: pleating the silk in preparation for dyeing/discharging, dyeing/discharging the silk, piecing together the composition, quilting and occasional appliqué, and the final finish. I enjoy each part equally, but for different reasons. I can work on two wall pieces at a time, or multiple individual combinations, until the piece begins to resonate and should not have any other visual competition. Call it piecing, call it collage, this stage is all about composition.

Cenote Turquesa. 2011. 46" x 56".
Thai silk. *Arashi-shibori* dyed, discharged, overdyed,
pieced, machine quilted and appliquéd.
Hendricks Collection
Photo: James Dewrance

I use quilting to add texture to the surface of the piece and to define areas in the composition, bringing them to the foreground. Alternatively I use stitching to diffuse and blend patterns in the silk. Previously I used only black thread to quilt, but as my work has become more colorful, I now employ a vast combination of colors. I store all my threads in antique typeset drawers installed immediately to the left of where I sew. In this way I can find the precise color I need in an instant.

Another change to note in my recent work is the increased density of my quilting. I am fortunate to belong to several groups of artists who gather to critique each other's newest work. I have learned a lot from these gatherings, and I'm sure I have gained new insights into the beauty of the quilted surface. My older work had much less stitching and large expanses of subtle gradations of dyed silks. My new work expresses a different level of appreciation for the stitched line.

I find inspiration in the natural world around me. Canyon walls, rocky pinnacles, wintry hillsides, as seen from a distance or in close proximity, provide ideas. However, water in its many forms (ice, fog, rain, waves, snow) remains my primary source of inspiration.

www.judithcontent.com

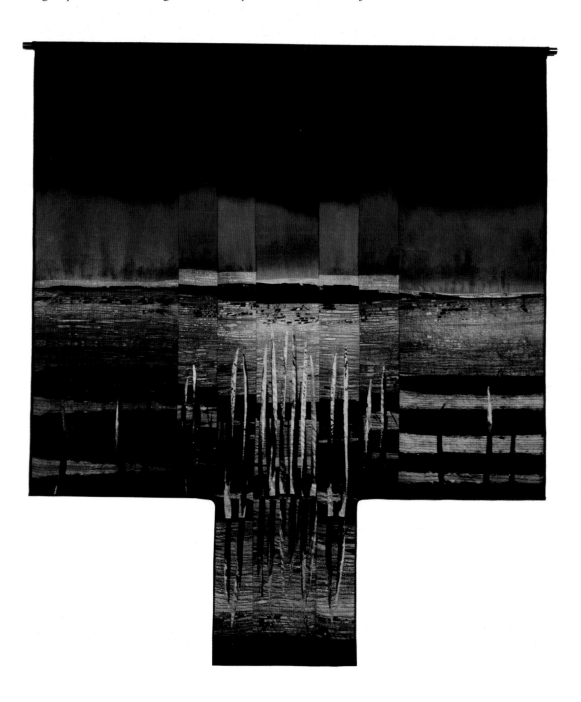

OPPOSITE
La Briere. 2004. 57" x 66".
Thai silk. *Arashi-shibori* dyed, discharged, overdyed,
pieced, machine quilted and appliquéd.
Photo: James Dewrance

Corn Dance. 1993. 66" x 54".
Thai silk. *Arashi-shibori* dyed, discharged,
overdyed, pieced, machine quilted and appliquéd.
Photo: James Dewrance

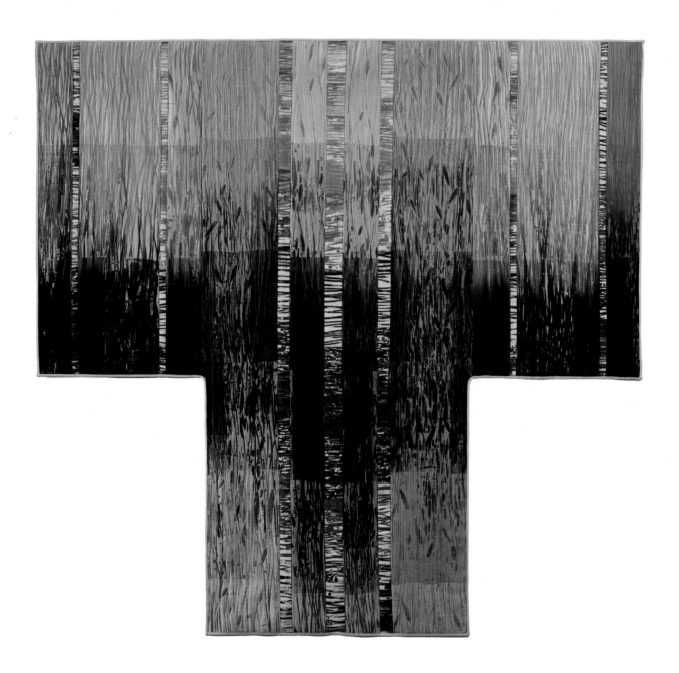

Indigo Ice. 2016. 70" x 74".
Silk charmeuse, Thai silk facing. *Arashi*
and *itajime shibori* dyed, discharged,
overdyed, pieced, quilted, stitched.
Photo: James Dewrance

Michael Cummings | NEW YORK, NEW YORK, USA

I construct my quilts using the appliqué technique, with embellishments, textile paints, and written texts. This approach allows me to transfer my compositions into quilts that capture my vision. Prior to creating quilts in the 1970s, I had been making collage works for several years, using pieces of paper, photos, and fabric to make collaged narratives. It was an easy transition from collage to appliqué construction in fabric. Appliqué enables me to build my composition on top of a foundation fabric, giving me more freedom than I would have with a traditional pieced technique. What I like best in quilt making is attaching three-dimensional objects to embellish my designs and enhance the narrative. To visualize an idea and see it develop as my hands physically construct it is both exciting and gratifying.

I'll Fly Away. 1991. 90" x 82".
Wool, painted canvas, African prints, cotton/blends, beads, buttons, hand-dyed silk and cotton, antique quilt blocks.
Collection: Museum of Arts and Design, New York
Photo: Karen Bell

I allow for spontaneity, for exciting surprises. To step back and see what your imagination has created is an exhilarating moment.

My style of quilting is influenced by a variety of art forms and artists. I listen to all types of music when I'm working, but jazz is my favorite, and I have made several quilts on the theme of jazz. The songs of folk music (e.g., Bob Dylan) caused me to appreciate narrative structure, and I gradually introduced that into my art. In the beginning I was constructing quilts by hand for about a year, and then I purchased a sewing machine from Macy's. After thirty years I am still using my domestic-model sewing machine. I call it my "dance partner" because of all the large swaths of fabric that I swirl around.

No one inspired me to become an artist. I always had an inner voice telling me to make art. By the age of ten, I had decided my career in life. Vincent van Gogh's painting of sunflowers made a profound impression on me as a child. His brilliant colors and brushstrokes dancing on canvas reinforced my desire to be an artist. The greatest influence on my quilt making has been Carolyn Mazloomi. She founded the Women of Color Quilters Network (WCQN), of which I am a member. She is considered the leading expert on African American quilts and has developed venues over many years that exhibit the work of WCQN members. Each exhibition's theme has challenged my imagination and research skills.

www.michaelcummings.com

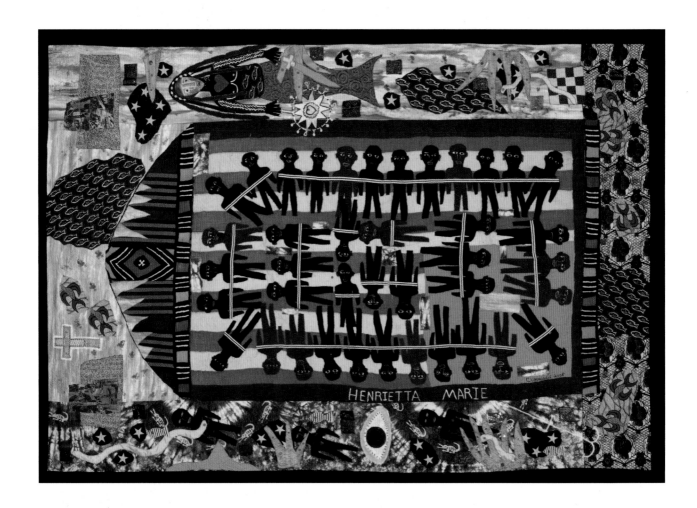

Slave Ship Henriette Marie. 2007. 120" x 156".
African prints, African mask (wood), cotton, blends, hand-painted cotton, metal, seashells, antique quilt block.
Photo: D. James Dee

OPPOSITE
President Obama Goes to India. 2015. 65" x 47".
Imported beaded work from India, satin, cotton, blends, gold lamé, textile paint, metal, hand painted cotton, trimmings from India.

African Jazz 10. 1990.
108" x 72".
Cotton, blends, rayon. zigzag machine stitched,
appliquéd, pieced border.
Photo: Dara Wells

Susan Else | SANTA CRUZ, CALIFORNIA, USA

I love color and pattern, but I rapidly become bored with the flat quilted surface. Applying that surface to three-dimensional figures gives me a structure for organizing the riot of pattern and color and keeps it focused on whatever story I am trying to tell. Though incredibly versatile, fabric is in some respects a primitive medium, so I feel that I have a single shot—the effective gesture—to tell my story.

I sometimes call my process "stealth art." The medium itself engages the viewer (it's so beautiful and safe), and then I can use that engagement to talk about some complex issues.

When Ponies Dream. 2013. 31" x 41" x 31".
Collaged and quilted cloth over armature, motorized with lights and audio. Machine collaged and quilted, hand-sewn assembly.
Photo: Marty McGillivray

Family has also been crucial in terms of my work. My facility with color comes from my painter father. My sense of figurative weight, balance, and gesture comes from my sculptor mother. The idea that one's narrative should resonate with people's lives comes from my author and filmmaker brother. The sheer joy of the medium (while keeping it real and not devolving into art-speak) comes from my sculptor sister-in-law. What a heritage!

I must add that my career would have been impossible without my enabling husband, who kept a roof over our heads while I was figuring it out, and who has done everything from my photography, website, and carpentry to serving as roadie and general "keeper of my sanity" since then.

One of the worst pieces of advice came early on in my career. An "expert" told me that I would have to "lose my beautiful surface" if I wanted to make it in the art (versus the textile) world. Ultimately, that made me dig my heels in, and I've been trying ever since (with varying degrees of success) to prove that it is possible to make significant art while maintaining the beauty and complexity of its surface.

www.susanelse.com

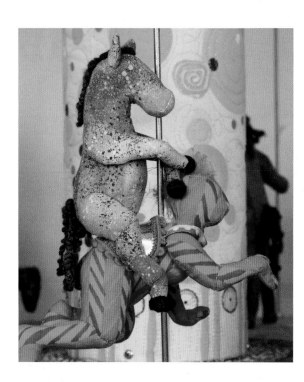

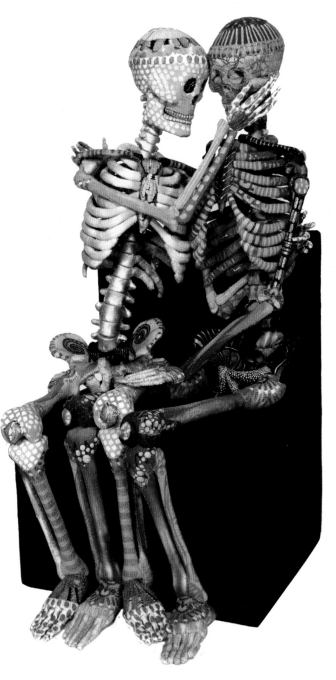

ABOVE *When Ponies Dream* (detail)

RIGHT
Forever Yours. 2010. 25" x 13" x 17".
Collaged and quilted cloth over armature, motorized with lights and audio. Machine collaged and quilted, hand-sewn assembly.
Collection: Sally Davey
Photo: Marty McGillivray

The Marbaum Quilt Collection was created by Marvin Fletcher and his wife, Hilary Morrow Fletcher, who was in charge of organizing the *Quilt National* exhibitions from 1983 through 2006. They named their collection after their two fathers. After Hilary died in 2006, Marvin continued building and sharing the collection, which he discusses below.

"Our first purchase was *Flowerseed Farm* by Holley Junker in 1985. The staff at the Dairy Barn Arts Center told me that Hilary liked it, and they suggested that I buy it as a gift for our twentieth wedding anniversary.

"We continued purchasing art quilts from the *Quilt National* exhibitions and during our travels. In the late 1980s we began to acquire more quilts but had no real place to display them in our house. Hilary thought it would be a good idea to expand our house and, in the process, create spaces to display our quilts.

"Hilary taught me that it was better for the quilts if they weren't continually on display but had a chance to 'rest' from the stress of hanging. I've continued to rotate them at least annually. When I do this, I always find new things to see. It is fun to see pieces I have not seen in person for years.

"I spend a great deal of my time looking at quilts: quilts offered on the SAQA website; in images submitted to *Quilt National*; at quilt shows I attend, such as at SJMQT (San Jose Museum of Quilts & Textiles) or *Visions* or IQF (International Quilt Festival). I note which ones appeal to me because of design and use of color. I also look at the size (can it fit in the space I have available?), whether I have a quilt by that artist (I tend to try to buy items from artists from whom I do not already have a quilt), and how much the quilt costs. The only real criterion is that I have to like the quilt.

"The majority of the Marbaum Collection was given in 2017 to the San Jose Museum of Quilts & Textiles, but I am continuing to collect. I want things to put up on my walls and be able to admire them all the time. I am amazed at how creative art quilters are, and I always look forward to seeing the creations of the incredible artists in this field."

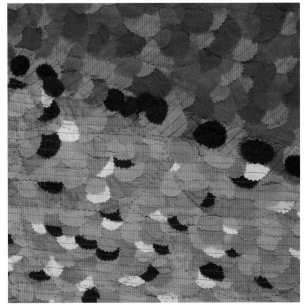

Holley Junker (d.)

USA
Flowerseed Farm. 1985–1986. 71" x 54".
Cotton. Hand and machine stitched.
The Marbaum Collection
Photo: Deidre Adams

BELOW *Flowerseed Farm* (detail).

Museum Collections

Museums in the United States had begun to acquire art quilts by the 1980s. Today more than eighty museums across the county have art quilts in their collections, 25 percent of which are dated after 2000. Not surprisingly, 75 percent of these works are in nine quilt museums, with nearly half of the total owned by the International Quilt Study Center & Museum at the University of Nebraska, Lincoln, and the National Quilt Museum in Paducah, Kentucky.

Both the American Folk Art Museum in New York City and the Smithsonian Institution have notable collections of art quilts, and several state museums own collections with a regional focus. Exhibitions of art quilts in museum venues have expanded tremendously during the twenty-first century, partly due to the efforts of Studio Art Quilt Associates and *Quilt National* (*QN*). During the past four years, SAQA has toured an average of twelve exhibitions internationally, and *Quilt National* organizes at least two groups of touring works from each *QN* competition.

Lena Vigna, curator of exhibitions at the Racine Art Museum, explains the popular appeal of this art form:

"New iterations of quilts extend a rich and fascinating history of making. Playing with design, composition, and objecthood, contemporary quilts offer new perspectives on a venerable tradition, blending something intimate and familiar with personal vision. . . . Because quilts have the potential to resonate beyond the wall and to operate metaphorically as well as aesthetically, they offer a dynamic and compelling approach" (email to the editor).

Gallery 2010–2017

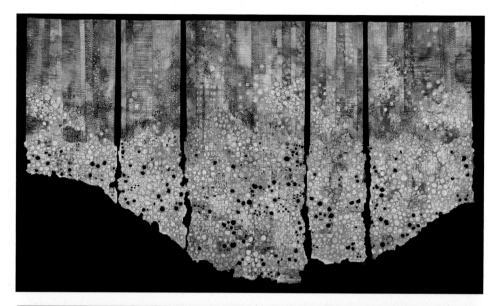

Deidre Adams

Littleton, Colorado, USA
disruption. 2014. 55" x 98".
Commercial cottons, acrylic paint, found papers. Layered and
stitched papers (from books, maps, newspapers, and other
sources) combined with stitched textile. Papers then randomly
peeled back through the various layers.

BELOW

Natalya Aikens

Pleasantville, New York, USA
Glass Bridge. 2013. 12" x 12".
Repurposed plastics, thread, acrylic paint, stretched
canvas. Collaged, thread sketched, hand stitched.
Collection: Kevan Rupp Lunney

Ludmila Aristova

Brooklyn, New York, USA
Illumination # 1. 2010. 34" x 45".
Silk, cotton, ribbons. Hand and machine pieced,
hand and machine quilted, hand painted, hand
pleated, tucks, individual prairie points.
Photo: D. James Dee

Brooke Atherton

Billings, Montana, USA
SpringField. 2012. 32" x 97".
Silk organza, paper maps, graphite, melted aluminum, glass,
found objects. Burned, dyed, rusted fabrics, layered, fused,
hand and machine stitched.
Collection: John M. Walsh III
Photo: Larry Hamel-Lambert, Gary J. Kirksey

BELOW

Alice Beasley

Oakland, California, USA
Entre Nous. 2010. 26" x 89".
Cotton fabric, thread. Raw-edge appliquéd.
Photo: Don Tuttle

Eliza Brewster

Honesdale, Pennsylvania, USA
Eye on the Prize. 2010. 24" x 21".
Cotton. Photo transferred, mono printed, hand quilted.
Photo: Sam Brewster

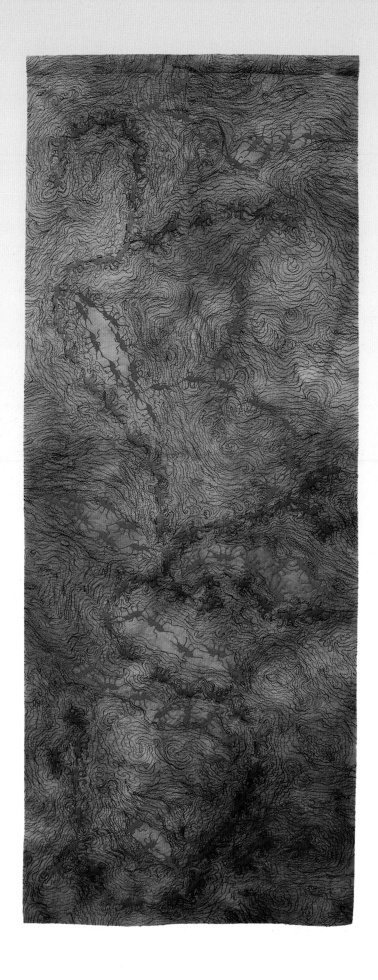

OPPOSITE

Jack Brockette

Dallas, Texas, USA
Traveling Red Ants. 2012. 49.5" x 16".
Hand-dyed silk organza. Machine quilted, embroidered.
Photo: Ann H. Brockette, PhD

Peggy Brown

Nashville, Indiana, USA
Alike but Not the Same III. 2015. 41" x 58".
Silk *habotai*, archival tissue paper, transparent
watercolor paint. Whole cloth with collage, hand
painted, machine quilted.

OPPOSITE

Susan Brubaker Knapp

Mooresville, North Carolina, USA
I See the Moon. 2012. 60" x 24".
Cotton, paint, acrylic ink. Whole-cloth painted,
free-motion machine quilted.
Collection: Quilts, Inc.

RIGHT

Betty Busby

Albuquerque, New Mexico, USA
Regeneration. 2014. 66" x 16" x 16".
Silk, mixed media. Hand and
machine stitched.

Maya Chaimovich

Ramat-Gan, Israel
A Source of Life in the Dead Sea.
2013. 61" x 70".
Recycled fabrics. Fused,
free-motion machine quilted.
Photo: Moti Chaimovich

Shin-hee Chin

McPherson, Kansas, USA
Chinmoku: Silence. 2012. 42" x 60".
Cotton, polyester, wool, recycled
fabric. Dyed, painted, fabric twisted,
blanket stitched, hand quilted.
Photo: Jim Turner

OPPOSITE

Jette Clover

Antwerp, Belgium
Metropolis 6. 2015. 41" x 40".
Cotton, linen, cheesecloth.
Painted, stamped, screen printed,
flour paste printed, collaged,
hand and machine quilted.
Photo: Pol Leemans

BELOW

Nancy Crasco

Brighton, Massachusetts, USA
Diatoms. 2010. Triptych: each
panel is 60" x 20".
Silk organza, gelatin prints on
mulberry paper, metallic thread.
Bojagi-inspired machine pieced,
hand and machine quilted.
Photo: Susan Byrne

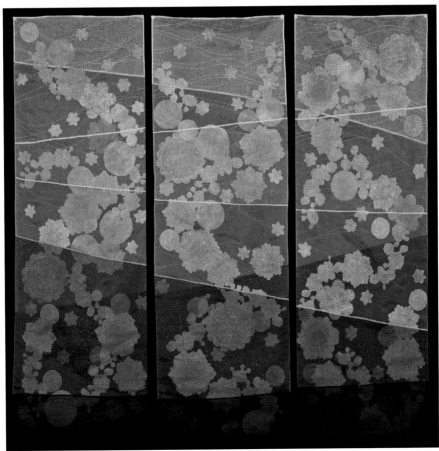

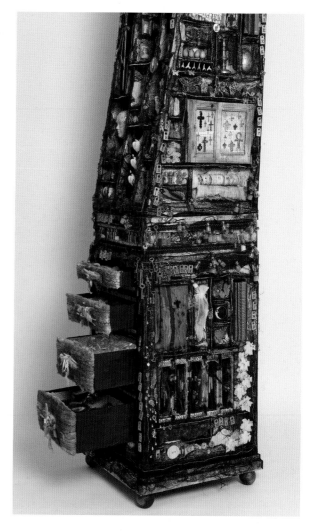

Kate Crossley

Oxford, United Kingdom
Box of Delights. 2011. 59" x 17" x 17".
Cabinet: foam board, card and papier
mâché overlaid with stitched and quilted
cotton, linen and silk. Objects: found,
altered, and made; embellished with
machine-embroidered leaves, vines,
charms, beads, butterflies, and more than
300 tiny bottles filled with herbs, spices,
beads and messages. The front has panels
of acid-etched fabric, hand stitched and
quilted. The front and sides are
embellished with handmade cords. Paper
and fabric mâché. Hand and machine
quilted and embroidered.
Collection: Carol Veillon
Photo: Keith Barnes

RIGHT *Box of Delights* (detail)

Carolyn Crump

Houston, Texas, USA
20 and Odd. 2012. 44" x 35" x 4".
Cotton, cotton cord, zipper, paint, dye, colored pencils,
wood, 3D paint, tulle. Appliquéd, fabric manipulated,
hand painted, printed, machine quilted.
Photo: Ash Wilson

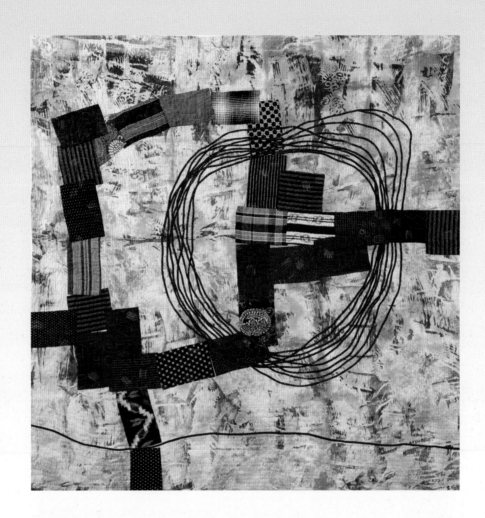

OPPOSITE

Joe Cunningham

San Francisco, California, USA
Patchwork Quilt 2012. 74" x 74".
Cotton. Machine pieced and appliquéd.

BELOW

Rosalie Dace

Durban, South Africa
Durban Dreams. 2008. 31" x 36".
Hand-dyed and commercial cottons, silk,
synthetics, beads. Machine pieced and
quilted, hand embellished with beads.
Private collection

Jennifer Day

Santa Fe, New Mexico, USA
Tibetan Treasure. 2014. 27" x 39".
Artist's photograph on fabric.
Digitally printed, intensely covered
in thread, free-motion quilted.

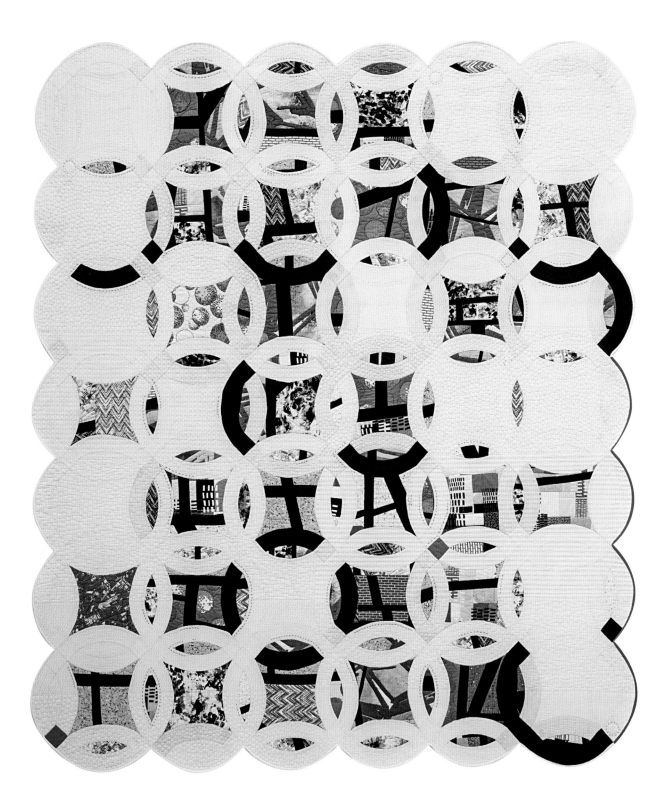

OPPOSITE

Sandra Townsend Donabed

Jupiter, Florida, USA
Evil Apples. 2012. 30" x 30".
Purchased hand-printed fabric, Marimekko found fabric, various cottons and vintage children's linens, toile, acrylic wash.
Hand and machine embroidered, quilted, inkjet-printed digital photographs.
Private collection

BELOW

Heather Dubreuil

Hudson, Quebec, Canada
Camden Town #2. 2014.
18" x 24".
Hand-dyed cotton. Fused, appliquéd, machine stitched.

Victoria Findlay Wolfe

New York, New York, USA
Double Edged Love. 2013. 77" x 66".
Cotton. Pieced, appliquéd, machine and hand quilted.
Collection: International Quilt Study Center & Museum, University of Nebraska–Lincoln
Photo: C&T Publishing

OPPOSITE

Dianne Firth

Canberra, Australian Capital Territory, Australia
Storm. 2012. 54.5" x 26".
Polyester net, viscose felt. Collaged, machine stitched, painted.
Collection: John M. Walsh III
Photo: Andrew Sikorski

Elena Folomeva

Saint Petersburg, Russia
Drawing Lessons. 2012. 53" x 39".
Cotton. Machine pieced, appliquéd, quilted, drawn.

Jayne Bentley Gaskins

Reston, Virginia, USA
Land of Cotton. 2015. 30" x 30".
Cotton broadcloth, inkjet ink. Digital photograph, appliquéd,
machine quilted, trapunto quilted.
Photo: Jayne Bentley Gaskins

Jacquie Gering

Kansas City, Missouri, USA
Bang You're Dead. 2013. 78" x 64".
Cotton. Machine pieced and quilted.
Photo: Gregory Case

BELOW

Patty Hawkins

Estes Park, Colorado, USA
Sunlit Canyon. 2012. 28" x 52.5".
Artist hand-dyed and marked fabrics, cotton,
silk. Deconstructed green printed, direct
appliquéd, machine quilted.
Collection: San Jose Museum of Quilts &
Textiles, The Marbaum Collection, Gift of
Marvin and Hilary Fletcher
Photo: Ken Sanville Photographic Services

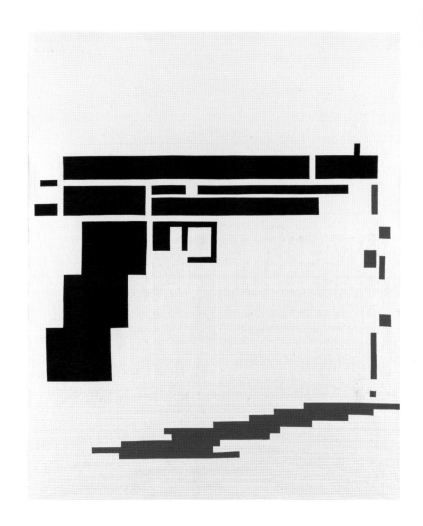

Luke Haynes

Kansas City, Missouri, USA
(The American Context #3)
American Gothic. 2012. 90" x 90".
Used textiles, wool batting, thread,
new fabric. Pieced, appliquéd.
Collection: Newark Museum
Photo: Howard Tu

OPPOSITE

Jenny Hearn

Johannesburg, Gauteng, South Africa
Wyeast (Volcano IV). 2012. 74" x 74".
Commercial and hand-dyed cotton and
silk, space-dyed embroidery cotton thread
and silk floss, tapestry yarn, thread-bound
metal washers, crocheted embellishments.
Machine pieced, embroidered and quilted,
hand embroidered.
Photo: Dion Cuyler

BELOW

Annie Helmericks-Louder

Warrensburg, Missouri, USA
No Room at the Table. 2010. 80" x 80".
Hand-dyed silks, manipulated
commercial fabrics. Hand and machine
pieced, hand quilted.
Photo: Gregory Case

Susan Hoffman

Germantown, New York, USA
Love Meditation. 2011. 96" x 93".
Cotton. Machine pieced,
hand quilted.
Photo: George Bouret

BELOW

Lisa Kijak

Laguna Hills, California, USA
Bridge Motel. 2011. 38" x 38".
Commercial cotton. Raw-edge
appliquéd.

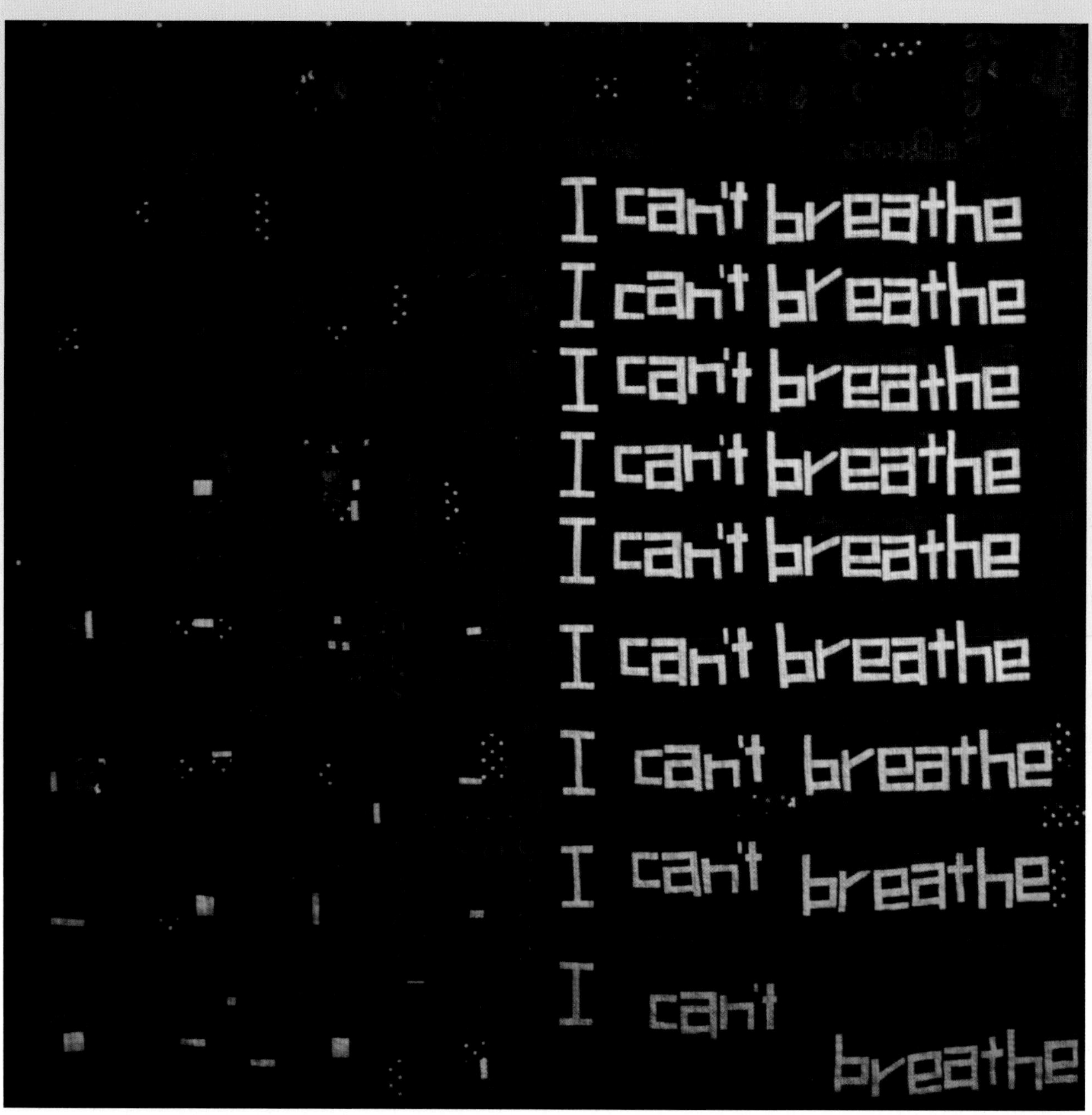
I can't breathe
I can't breathe
I can't breathe
I can't breathe
I can't breathe
I can't breathe
I can't breathe
I can't breathe
I can't breathe

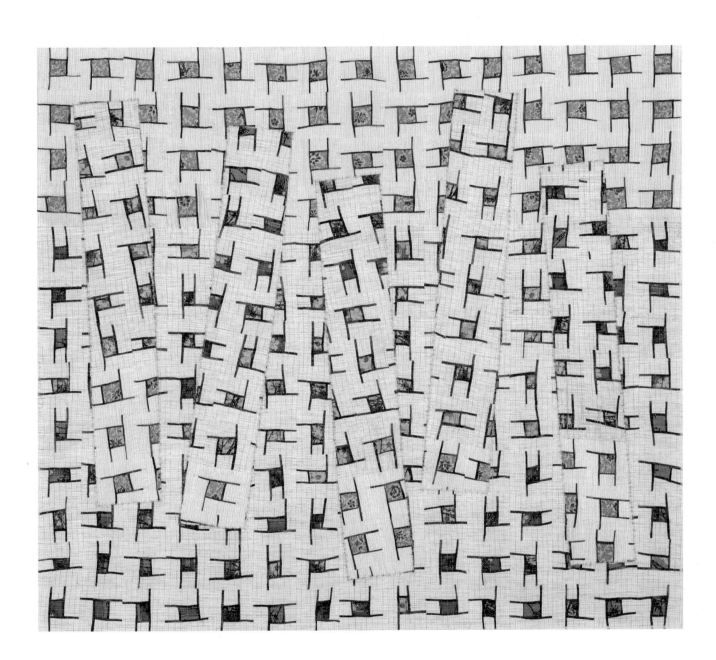

OPPOSITE

Chawne Kimber

Easton, Pennsylvania, USA
The One for Eric G. 2015. 78" x 78".
Cotton, hand-dyed perle cotton. Machine pieced, longarm machine quilted (by Pamela Cole), hand quilted (by Chawne Kimber).
Collection: Michigan State University Museum
Photo: Yvonne Fuchs

Harue Konishi

Nakano-ku, Tokyo, Japan
SYO #67. 2013. 47" x 54".
Silk, recycled kimono silk.
Machine pieced and quilted.

Brigitte Kopp

Kasel-Golzig, Germany
The Clock Is Ticking. 2016. 72" x 43".
Artist-painted and dyed silk, linen, cords. Stitched,
fused, appliquéd, inserted cords, tucked and pleated,
stuffed, hand and machine sewn, free-motion machine
quilted, hand embroidered and quilted.

Kristin La Flamme

Portland, Oregon, USA
Home Is Where the Army Sends Us. 2015.
38" x 17" x 16".
Mixed media.
Photo: Mark Frey

Gay E. Lasher

Denver, Colorado, USA
Abstraction II. 2010. 47" x 31.5".
Cotton, ink. Computer-altered photographic
elements printed on cotton, machine quilted.
Collection: San Jose Museum of Quilts &
Textiles, The Marbaum Collection, Gift of
Marvin and Hilary Fletcher
Photo: Deidre Adams

OPPOSITE

Susan Lenz

Columbia, South Carolina, USA
Spool Quilt. 2014. 56" x 28".
Repurposed plastic thread spools,
wire, metal rod, and waxed linen
thread. Hand stitched.
Photo: Susan Lenz

BELOW

Kathleen Loomis

Louisville, Kentucky, USA
Entropy. 2014. 71" x 85".
Commercial cottons. Machine
pieced and quilted.
Photo: George Plager

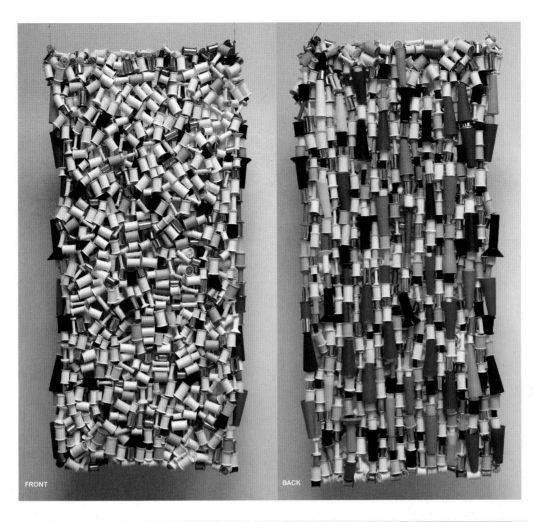

FRONT   BACK

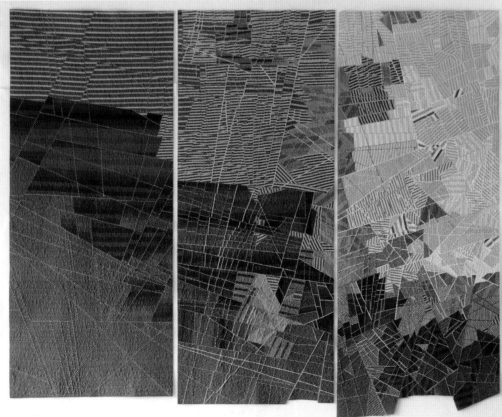

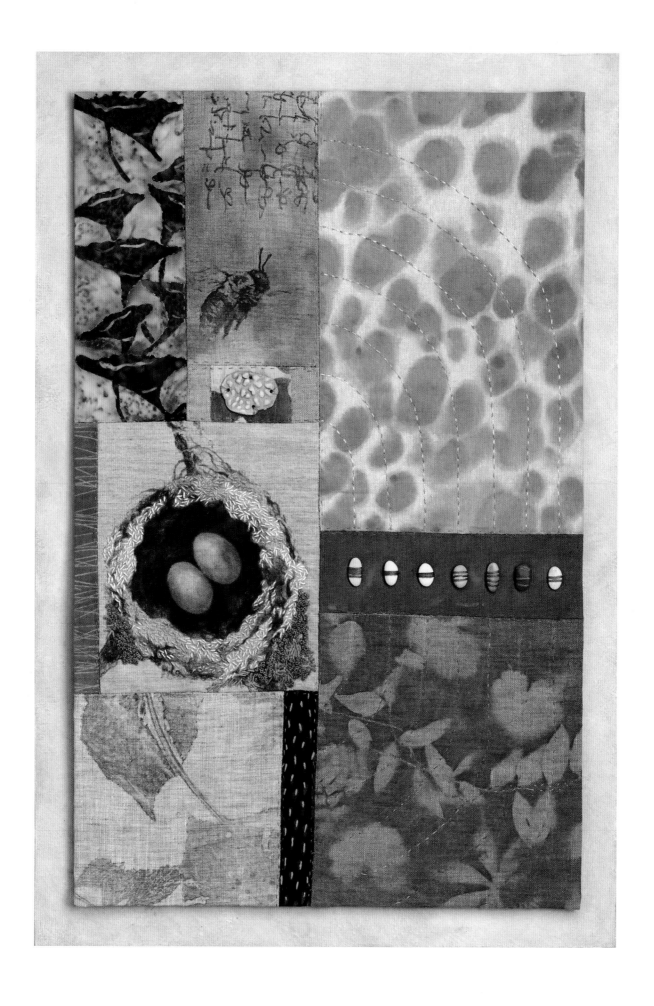

OPPOSITE

Sharon McCartney

Belchertown, Massachusetts, USA
Oasis. 2016. 19.5" x 12.5".
Cotton, linen, acrylic, stones, porcelain.
Hand stitched, embroidered, transferred,
sun-printed, painted.
Photo: John Polak Photography

Alicia Merrett

Wells, Somerset, United Kingdom
Port at Dusk Diptych. 2015. 54" x 56".
Hand-dyed cotton sateen fabrics. Freehand cut,
improvisationally pieced, appliquéd, fused,
machine stitched and quilted.

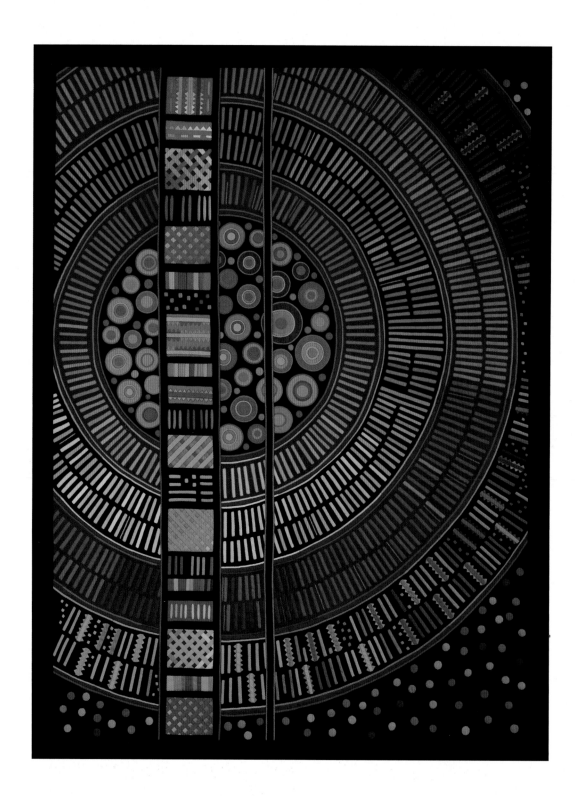

Fumiko Nakayama

Kyoto, Japan
Geometric. 2011. 45" x 34".
Cotton. Mola technique.

OPPOSITE

Pixeladies

Cameron Park, California, USA
American Still Life: The Weight of the Nation. 2012. 60" x 60".
Digitally printed cotton by artists using fiber-reactive dye, commercial cotton. Words and phrases cut from newspapers and magazines collaged on paper, then scanned and printed on fabric.
Photo: Glenn Marshall

BELOW

Wen Redmond

Strafford, New Hampshire, USA
Leaping Point. 2010. 32" x 51".
Inkjet-prepared cotton canvas, dyed pearl cotton, UV medium and paint. Digitally printed, stitched, hand-tied bookbinding method using dyed pearl cotton.
Collection: San Jose Museum of Quilts & Textiles, The Marbaum Collection, Gift of Marvin and Hilary Fletcher

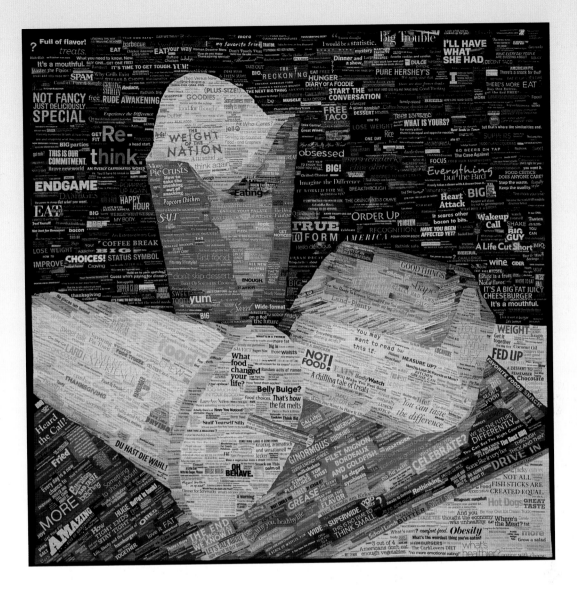

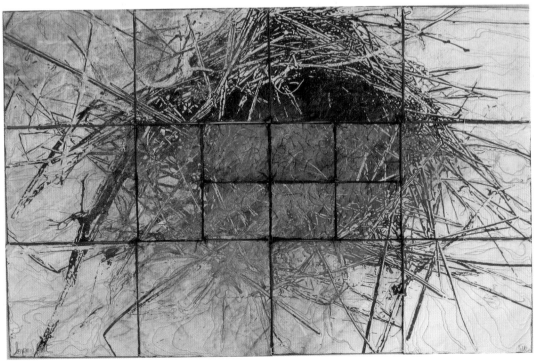

Toot Reid

Tacoma, Washington, USA
September 28, 2010–March 8, 2011. 2011.
63" x 98".
Cotton fabric, silk and metal fabric.
Machine pieced and appliquéd, hand quilted.
Photo: Ken Wagner

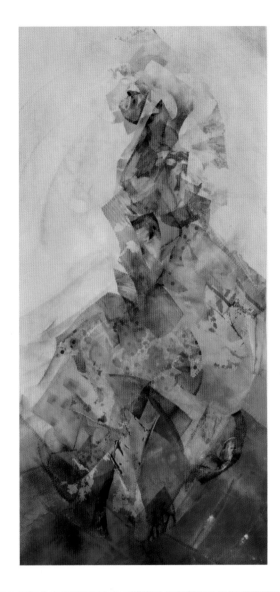

Emily Richardson

Philadelphia, Pennsylvania, USA
Into the Mist. 2015. 42" x 19".
Silk, acrylic paint. Hand stitched and
quilted.
Photo: Mark Garvin

Dinah Sargeant

Newhall, California, USA
Spirit Dogs Greet the Ghosts. 2014.
58" x 128".
Cotton, paint. Painted, hand and machine
appliquéd, machine quilted.
Photo: Bob Messina

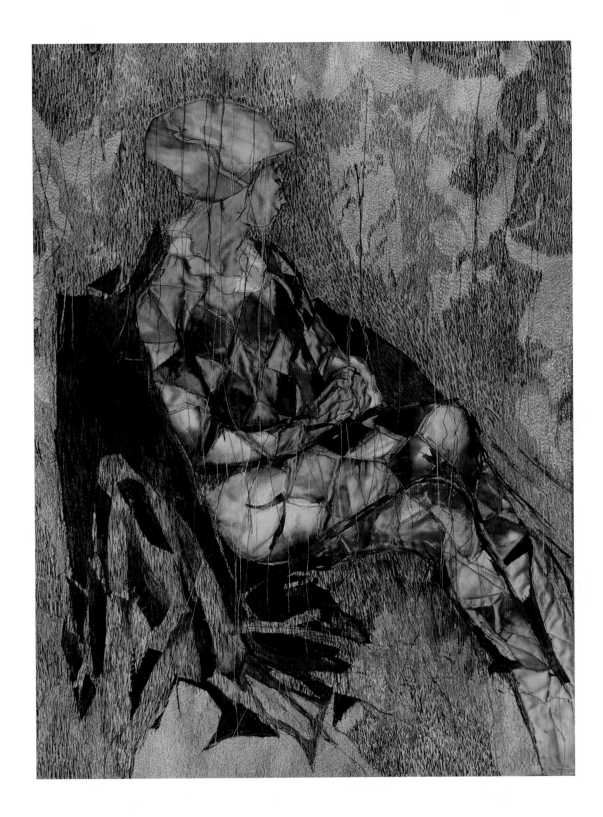

OPPOSITE

Alison Schwabe

Montevideo, Uruguay
Wheel of Time. 2016. 47" x 35.5".
Cotton, gold and metallic finish
leathers. Torn, fused, machine
appliquéd and quilted.
Photo: Eduardo Baldizan

Maria Shell

Anchorage, Alaska, USA
Wall of Sound. 2014. 52" x 52".
Vintage and modern cotton
textiles, hand-dyed fabric.
Improvisationally cut and pieced,
machine quilted.
Photo: Chris Arend

Francesca Sist

Fontanafredda, Italy
Arlecchino. 2010. 31.5" x 25".
Cotton, silk, wire. Machine
quilted.

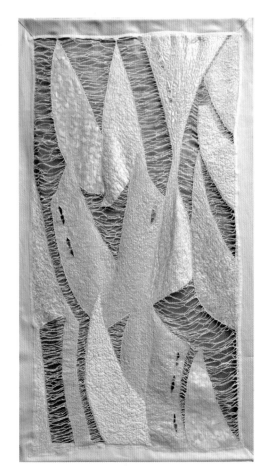

DETAIL

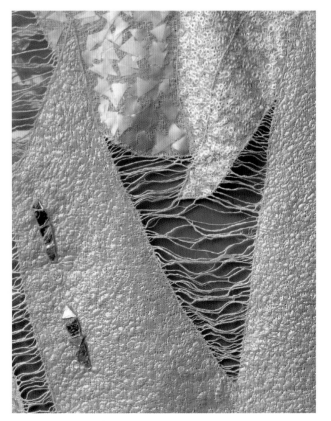

Mary Ruth Smith

Waco, Texas, USA
Face Off Together. 2011.
24" x 36".
Paper, silk organza,
embroidery floss. Paper
laminated, hand stitched.
Photo: Accurate Image,
Waco, Texas

BELOW

Marialuisa Sponga Archi (d.)

Italy
Bianco su Bianco—White Sails. 2010. 59" x 30".
Linen, polyester, PVC fabric, mirror, cellophane,
gauze, plastic, yarns. Assemblage with machine
embroidery.
Private collection

RIGHT *Bianco su Bianco—White Sails* (detail)

Tiziana Tateo

Vigevano (PV), Italy
Flowers and Champagne Streams. 2014.
55" x 37".
Hand-painted tissue paper, tulle, felt,
artificial silver metal leaf, silver paper,
vinyl. Hand embroidered on linen, metal
leaf laminated, free-motion machine
embroidered and quilted.

Kate Themel

Cheshire, Connecticut, USA
Stars Not Included. 2011. 25" x 31".
Hand-dyed and batik cotton. Raw-edged collage,
hand-guided machine stitched.

BELOW *Stars Not Included* (detail)

OPPOSITE

Judith Tomlinson Trager

Boulder, Colorado, USA
Quartet. 2016. 72" x 144".
Cotton, silk. Machine pieced and quilted,
direct appliquéd, silk-screened.
Collection: Patricia Habel and Joe Adams
Photo: Ken Sanville

BELOW

Jean Wells Keenan

Sisters, Oregon, USA
After the Rain. 2012. 51" x 41".
Cotton. Machine pieced and free-motion quilted.
Photo: Paige Vitek

RIGHT *After the Rain* (detail)

DETAIL

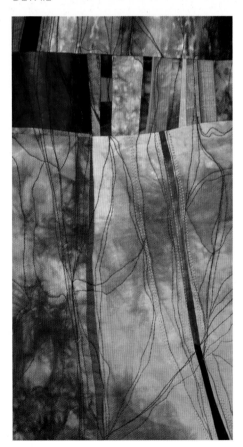

Grace Harbin Wever, PhD

Union Grove, Alabama, USA
Points of Departure. 2015.
72" x 34".
Hand-dyed cotton, batik, other
fabrics, art paper, encaustic wax,
charcoal pencil. Fused collage,
free-motion stitched.
Photo: Michael Arterburn Fine Art

Marianne R Williamson

Miami, Florida, USA
Cracks in My Composure. 2013.
66" x 51".
Hand ice-dyed silk and cotton,
paint, ink. Raw-edge appliquéd,
free-motion quilted.
Photo: Gregory Case Photography

BELOW

Hope Wilmarth

Spring, Texas, USA
Urban Cathedral. 2016. 45" x 44".
Cotton fabric. Machine pieced
and quilted.
Photo: Rick Wells

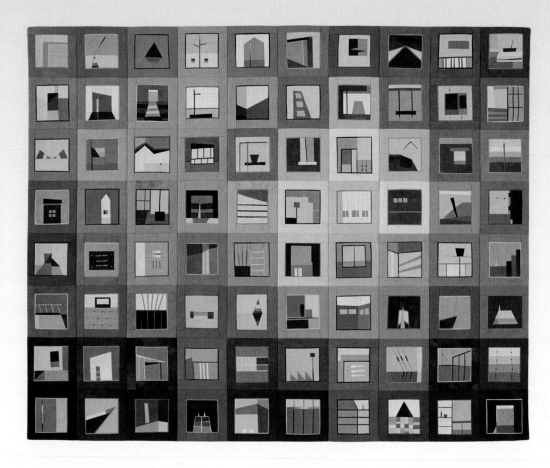

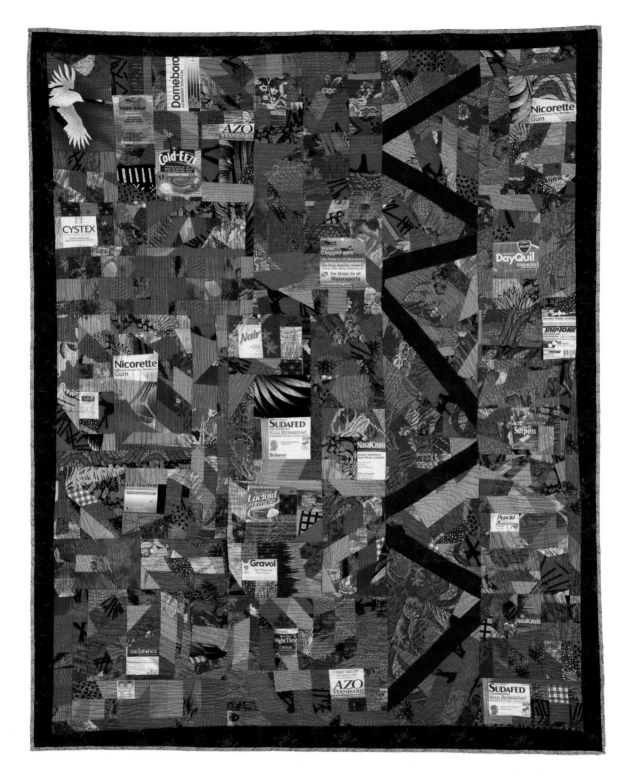

OPPOSITE

Erin Wilson

Brooklyn, New York, USA
Color Story: Roofline. 2015. 28" x 35".
Cotton, fiber-reactive dye. Hand dyed,
machine pieced, machine quilted.
Collection: Robert Wiener and Bill Norris
Photo: Black & Steil

BELOW

Martha Wolfe

Davis, California, USA
Waiting for Kelly. 2016. 40" x 48".
Linen, silk organza, abaca, lokta,
mulberry, and tissue papers, perle
cotton. Raw-edge appliquéd,
machine pieced and quilted,
hand embroidered.
Collection: Emily Murdoch &
Seth Duffey

Adrienne Yorinks

Palm Beach Gardens, Florida, USA
Over the Counter. 2011. 71" x 58".
Photo transfers, cotton, silk.
Machine pieced and quilted.
Photo: D. James Dee

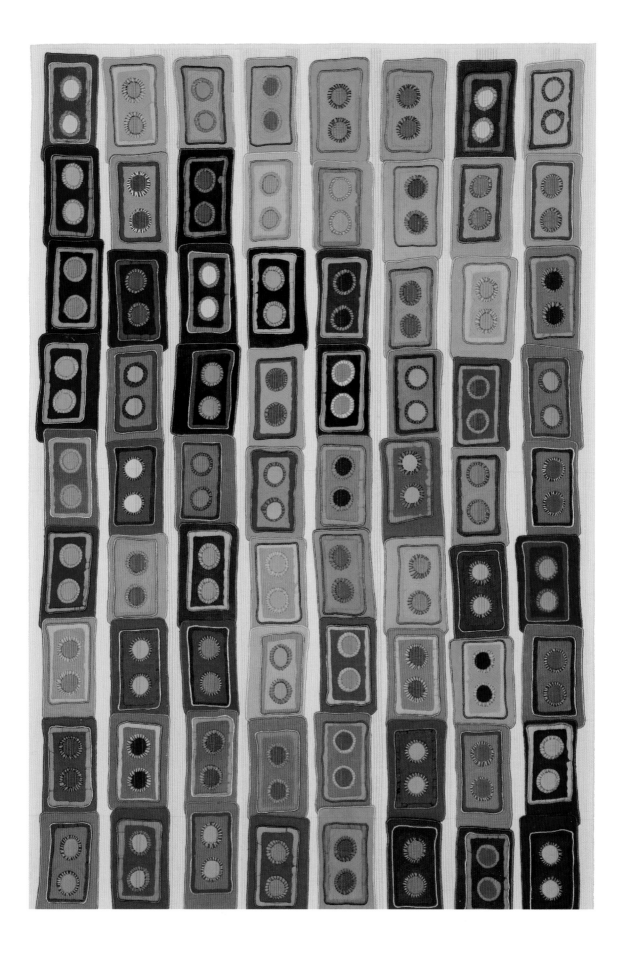

OPPOSITE

Kathy York

Austin, Texas, USA
High Rise. 2011. 50" x 33".
Artist hand-dyes and batiks, embroidery floss,
commercial cotton. Machine quilted, fused appliqué,
bleach discharge, overdyed, hand embroidered, satin
stitched, machine quilted.

Charlotte Ziebarth

Boulder, Colorado, USA
Liquid Sunset. 2014. 38" x 54".
Silk, cotton, pigment inks. Digital art
printed on silk, layered, fused, stitched.
Photo: Ken Sanville

Paula Kovarik | MEMPHIS, TENNESSEE, USA

I think that the turning point for me in terms of style was when I started drawing on a regular basis. I can't draw very well but I love to see how a point can travel to become line. I am inspired by textures in nature and pattern everywhere. Texture and line combining to tell stories never fail to entertain me.

I like the surprises—those times when the pathway diverges from my preconceived notions. It's like a little jolt of electricity that comes in the deep silence of contemplation.

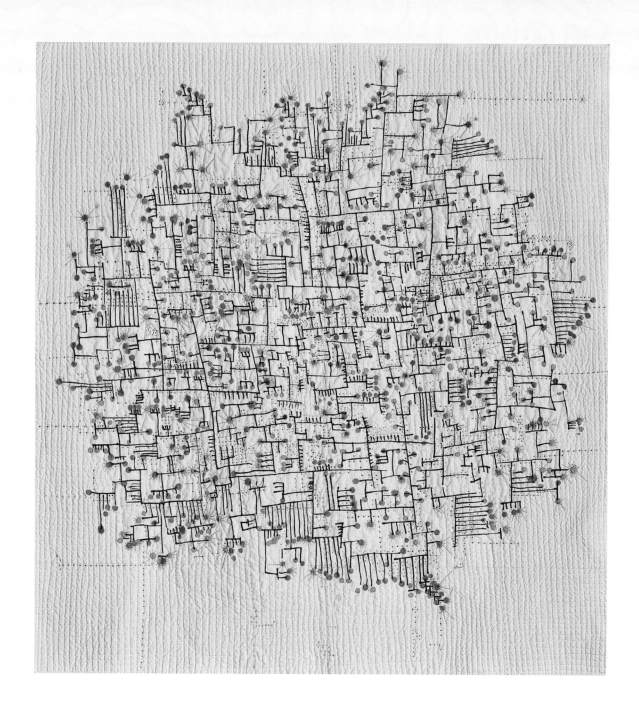

As time passes, my work has changed to reflect a subtle thoughtfulness that I feel informs the work. It's like a new way of listening. I'm less impatient. I'm willing to take the time for a piece to tell me what it needs.

My ideas come from various sources. I read; take pictures of shadows, patterns, and lines; and then read some more. Leaving my studio for walks or travel also brings inspiration.

My mother gave me the best piece of advice: "You create your own reality." She always said this to me when I was trying to make a decision. It has become my mantra.
www.paulakovarik.com

AHA! Moments. 2010. 57" x 54".
Hand-drawn, digitally printed cotton.
Free-motion machine stitched, hand stitched.
Photo: Allen Mims

Round and Round It Goes. 2013. 57" x 54".
Found cotton tablecloth. Free-motion machine stitched, hand stitched.
Photo: Allen Mims

John Lefelhocz | ATHENS, OHIO, USA

That catch phrase from the 1980s, "I love it when a plan comes together," sums up what I like best about the creative process involved in my work. The adrenaline kick that comes from the birth of a new idea and the gratification of a completed work on display keeps me going. Usually I have one really good question in mind for the basis of a new piece, and from there I work the idea and strive to surprise myself with something original.

I'm known as an artist who sometimes uses unconventional materials. My pieces incorporate multidimensional conceptual cross-referencing. The references are sometimes derived from the connotations associated

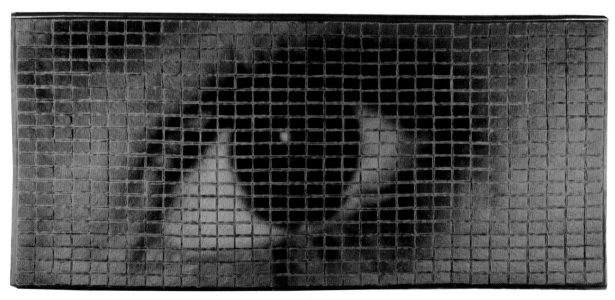

with the chosen materials and are frequently mixed together with the interplay of the work as viewed from afar and up close.

I started out as an artist who made quilts, and I think that my work has moved more toward the spectrum of a quilter who makes art. I didn't focus much on any quilt-specific cultural connectivity other than structure in those early works. It was nice to enter into the art quilt fold without too much influence or preconception on what I was supposed to be doing. I had ample elbow room to bang out all the details unfettered. My newest pieces possess more callback to traditional quilts. I'm incorporating more traditional materials, patterns, and styles, but I'm still trying to keep some of my outsider vibe by using unexpected approaches.

www.JuxtaPassion.com

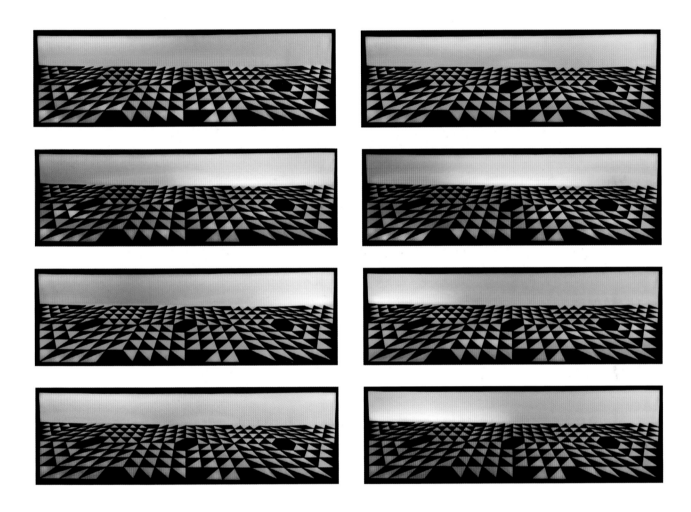

OPPOSITE

Money for Nothing. 1998. 33" x 73".
Sugar packets, nylon window screening, dental floss (mint flavored), green paper, and plastic flies.

BELOW *Money for Nothing* (reverse)

Light Waves. 2016. Each panel 21" x 69".
Upholstery fabric, fleece, thread, coroplast, fishing line, extruded aluminum angle, single-board micro controllers (Arduino), individually addressable RGB LED lights.

Mary Pal | ALMONTE, ONTARIO, CANADA

Unlike painting on canvas, where artists squeeze out color and immediately begin to paint, there are myriad methods and materials that I can call on to express my meaning in fiber. Color, texture, imagery, and sheen can be added, using a limitless variety of materials and techniques. My medium offers me endless choices and alternatives.

Like most fiber artists, I am both excited and challenged by the versatility of our medium. When a concept is forming in my mind, the thrill of the chase is on: how to express that concept—which fabrics, what techniques, which colors, what composition? With experimentation, I have honed my processes, especially my sculpting of cheesecloth, and adopted new tools

Leonard. 2017. 27" x 37".
Hand-dyed cheesecloth, cotton, silk organza. Inkjet-printed and hand-painted organza squares overlaid with cheesecloth sculpted with PVA adhesive, machine stitched.
Collection: Roberta Russell
Photo: Ray Pilon

OPPOSITE
Portrait. 2008. 12" x 12".
Cheesecloth, linen, acrylic paint. Sculpted with PVA adhesive, machine stitched.
Collection: Nysha Oren Nelson

that allow me to modify my techniques. Over time, and with countless hours in the studio, mastering techniques and creating work—some bad, some good—I gained confidence and a sense of freedom as my style developed.

It was only when my children were grown that I was able to turn my attention to art full-time. During my formative years in the 1960s and '70s, I was actively discouraged from considering the arts as a viable career option. As the world opened up for women and we had more choices, the opportunities in the business world compelled many women of my generation to seek paid employment in the workforce simply because we could.

But an engagement with art was always present, and I incorporated it into my life at every opportunity. I have to say it was my membership in Studio Art Quilt Associates later in life that encouraged me to call myself an artist.

My work ethic has been influenced so much by Twyla Tharp's book *The Creative Habit* that I would urge any aspiring artist to read it. But much of what she advises is summed up pithily by Chuck Close, who wrote, "Inspiration is for amateurs—the rest of us just show up and get to work."

www.marypaldesigns.com

Mirjam Pet-Jacobs | WAALRE, NETHERLANDS

I still remember the first two patches I stitched together and how I fell in love with quilting. After almost thirty years of trying out and learning all kinds of techniques, I have filtered out what suits me best. I prefer to keep it simple: "Less is more." The process is the only thing that really counts. Whatever comes out of it are the cherries on a cake, and if the cake should be burnt, I will have learned a great deal from the experience. It is important to me that the concept is present in several layers, often not visible at first sight. My work requires reflective observation to be fully understood.

I started the Mimi series in 2002 after having seen an exhibition of elongated wooden statues made by Aboriginal artists. Slowly my Mimi figures have disconnected from the Aboriginal world. Now they symbolize a person, many persons, society, or humanity. They have no arms to stress the fact that we are quite helpless in many situations.

I have opened my creative mind to adding photos and video to textiles (or even leaving out the textile part), making installations as well. It is my dream to make artwork in situ, site specific, and really monumental. *Passages* is an installation that shows all the people that join you during the path of your life. The two veils in the installation symbolize birth and death.

www.mirjampetjacobs.nl

OPPOSITE

Ancestral Shadows. 2002. 54" x 50".
Hand-painted and commercial cottons, silk, blends, organza, tulle, metal. Machine pieced, machine and hand appliquéd, machine and hand quilted, reverse embroidered, stamped.
Collection: Dr. H. Mauer
Photo: Peter Braatz

Passages. 2014. 79" x 59" x 91".
Tyvek, cotton, silk, plastic button cord stops, LED candle lights, tulle, aluminium frame.
Stitched, heat manipulated, screen printed.
Photo: Fotostudio Leemans

Susan Shie | WOOSTER, OHIO, USA

I'm interested in making uncorrected first-time images and words, which is hard to do in the intellectual world. I want my art to come straight out of my inner self, to stay open and innocent. To share my thinking and feelings. Freehand.

I love that both airbrush and airpen make a final mark the first time. Since 1994, I'd been using an airbrush to draw my big pieces and color them in, and in 2003 I added the airpen, using fabric paint, not ink, to write my stories on the paintings. My paintings are entirely made of first marks, not corrected. I also love working large, creating a complex composition and saying a lot in its writing. Switching to machine sewing

American Pie: 6 of Potholders (Coins) in the Kitchen Tarot. 2013. 60" x 90".
Whole-cloth painting with airbrush, small writing with airpen using fabric paint. Machine sewn.

OPPOSITE
Prayer for the Serpent Mound. 1993–1995. 73" x 62".
Hand- and airbrush-painted panels, Susan's clay angels, embroidery thread. Main painting cut apart and hand-sewn together again, after hand- and machine-quilting each panel. Machine sewn by James Acord.

in 2005 allowed me to make much larger, whole-cloth painted quilts, and made it easier for me to address very current events in my social commentary because I could make a piece so much faster.

When I was in college in 1979, Miriam Schapiro came to the College of Wooster twice, doing artist residencies in our very feminist art department. From my first talk with her, I decided to switch from painting on stretched canvas to painting on loose cloth and sewing it, as a conscious feminist action. What a radical move that was!

My mother, Marie Shie, was my role model. She loved making art but became a nurse. However, she always made sure that I had art supplies. An excellent seamstress, she taught me to sew. She was into ecology and the organic movement, a pacifist and a progressive freethinker.

My art is about what I think and believe, but I don't expect others to necessarily agree with me. I just want to witness the world from my point of view and share my reactions to it. I love seeing art that's made for that purpose—sharing our ideas, without having to agree. This attitude makes for more tolerance and understanding in the world, when we just share what's in our minds and hearts.

www.turtlemoon.com

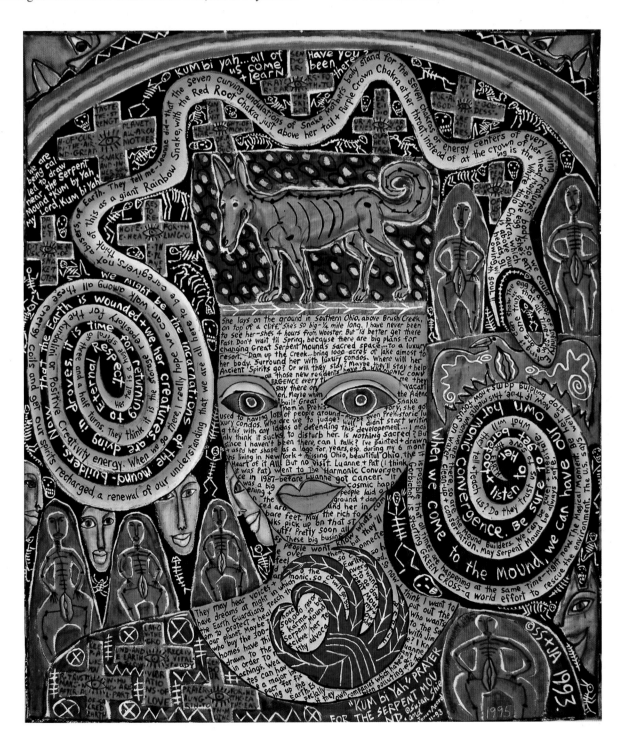

Tropical New York. 1988. 90" x 90".
Commercial fabrics, hand-painted whole-cloth panels, embroidery thread, various objects (sides have mussel shells attached). Hand painted and sewn, stuffed.

OPPOSITE

The Potluck / World: Card #21 in the Kitchen Tarot, aka Healing on Common Ground. 2008. 85" x 76".
Whole cloth painted with airbrush, small writing with airpen using fabric paint. Machine sewn.

Laura Wasilowski | ELGIN, ILLINOIS, USA

My personal style evolved by making a lot of artwork and honing art-making skills over the years. Stories of my home, family, friends, and places I've been are always in the background influencing my art. Also, my method of construction (fusing) lends itself to the organic shapes found in pictorial artwork and gives me the ability to develop designs rapidly.

Designing in an improvisational manner with fused fabrics makes me happy. Not only is it a challenge, but also the serendipity of creating art without a plan is thrilling and delightful. For me, creating artwork is play. It is a joyful experience that engages my mind and gives me hours of pleasure.

Over the years I've changed the size of the artwork I make. Compared to twenty years ago, my current work is smaller in scale and includes more hand embroidery. Smaller pieces allow me to design more work, and I enjoy the hand stitching that enhances these smaller pieces.

Many years ago an instructor told me that artwork comes before housework. It's a maxim I cherish every day.

www.artfabrik.com

OPPOSITE
Blue Book on Blue Chairs. 1995. 57" x 46".
Hand-dyed and printed cotton. Fused appliqué, machine quilted.

Pressing Matters. 2001. 51" x 41".
Hand-dyed cotton. Fused appliqué, machine quilted.

Seedpods #2. 2011. 22" x 32".
Hand-dyed cotton. Fused appliqué, hand
embroidered, machine quilted.

Studio Art Quilts: A Final Word

By Ulysses Dietz, Chief Curator and Curator of Decorative Arts,
the Newark Museum

I've been thinking about quilts for thirty-seven years now. In 1980, my inaugural year as Curator of Decorative Arts at Newark, I mounted my first quilt exhibition (which, in reviewing my files, I see was on crazy quilts). That year I also received my first gift of a quilt for the museum, an all-silk medallion quilt made in 1855 by a woman born in the late eighteenth century.

I won't pretend that the exhibition was any great shakes curatorially, but it got me looking at quilts; indeed, it got me looking at what I recognized as the first self-conscious "art" quilts produced by American makers.

The gift, a medallion quilt produced by Mrs. C. S. Conover of New York City for her grandson, immediately inspired me for two reasons: the amazing collection of largely pristine silk textiles of which it was composed, and the fact that it struck me as an intuitive work of art, every bit as powerful visually as any geometric abstraction I'd ever seen. It was eye dazzling, and while the stitching was nothing to write home about, the placement of color and the overall graphic quality of the quilt were extraordinary. This very first quilt to cross my path as a newborn curator gave me all the evidence I needed to begin my journey to understanding quilts as art. The crazy quilts, too, made me comprehend for the first time that the women (almost always women) who made them, while following some sort of vaguely accepted norm called "crazy quilt," were producing objects that were as distinctive as fingerprints and as much about art as any landscape or portrait done by a male artist at the same period.

Carol Watkins. *Passages II.* 1999. 68" x 39".
Photo: Ken Sanville

Another thing about my career in Newark that has been helpful to me in thinking through this art/craft/quilt conundrum is the fact that it was the Newark Museum that mounted the first museum exhibitions in America that looked at folk art and called it by that name. Folk art wasn't just "primitive" paintings and sculpture, but also needlework, coverlets, furniture, and quilts. Our Founding Director, John Cotton Dana, seems to have purchased the first quilts for the museum (in 1918 and 1919) not only because they were great examples of what would come to be known as folk art, but because they also looked like modern art. The strong graphic colors and simple geometry of these early-nineteenth-century quilts echoed graphic design coming out of Germany and Austria in the early 1900s. Mr. Dana was adamant about the idea that art is not just painting and sculpture, but *everything*. For him, the hand of the artist could be found in handicraft as well as in industrial design, and that was art that transcended mere paint and marble and bronze.

As far as I'm concerned, all quilts are art and have always been art, one way or another. Not all of them are good art—just as not all paintings and sculptures you see out in the world are good art. But thirty-seven years of looking at and thinking about quilts from four different centuries has me more convinced than ever that quilts were among the first fully artistic expressions of women in America, women who were bound by gender norms and educational limits. Other than the most basic one-piece woolen quilts, the very form of the quilt as it evolved by the early nineteenth century in the United States was, at best, quasi-functional. Women encouraged myths of frugality and using up scraps (myths often rooted in truth) in order to allow themselves the freedom to create things of beauty that incidentally served the very real purpose of warmth in a world with questionable domestic heating systems. There was no real functional point in creating the finely quilted and elaborately pieced quilts that flourished into the 1830s, much less the fancy album-type

To be quite honest, I think all craft people, and studio art quilts in particular, need to get past this need to be validated by people who think Damien Hirst is the answer to an important question. Someday, academic art historians will be trained with a big-picture perspective on what art is and has been throughout human history. But that day is not now. Art curators are still trained to focus on what they see as "art issues." The intellectual concerns of the Art World have little or nothing to do with what art actually is so much as reflecting ideas on artistic importance originally created by academic white men in the nineteenth century—the very men whose wives made quilts because they were allowed no other outlet for their artistic expression.

Pay no attention to the Art World.
You are all artists. Go. Make art.

quilts that became hugely popular from the 1840s through the 1870s. And we've already mentioned the crazy quilts, which weren't even properly quilted most of the time and existed as largely creative efforts at design and stitching in a time when women felt constant pressure to be domestic and useful and every inch the good housewife.

One of the main lines of curatorial thought in the folk art world today is to stop calling it folk art and just call it what it is: art. I would venture the same for the studio art quilt. Call it what it is, and forget what the Art World (the capital letters are ironic) thinks. A studio art quilt is an art quilt made in a studio. Where an art quilt made by a New Jersey farmer's wife in the 1860s is folk art, an art quilt made in a studio is automatically self-conscious of its "art-ness." A farmer's wife might have pretended she was making an elaborate album quilt because she and her husband (or her daughter and her fiancé) needed a warm cover on their bed. But the truth is, she was making a work of art according to what she knew and what skills she had. Quilters who make their quilts in studios know they're making art. They really don't need anyone else to tell them that. In fact, they don't need *me* to tell them that.

TOP LEFT
Noriko Endo. *Birds of a Feather Flock Together.* 2015. *(detail)*
Photo: Yuji Nomura

RIGHT
Leslie Gabriëlse. *Star.* 2000. *(detail)*
Collection: San Jose Museum of Quilts & Textiles
Gift of Penny Nii and Edward Feigenbaum
Photo: James Dewrance

Selected Bibliography

Atkins, Jacqueline M. *Quilting Transformed: Leaders in Contemporary Quilting in the United States—the 20th Century and Beyond.* Tokyo: Tadanobu SETO, 2007. (in Japanese and English)

Auther, Elissa. *String, Felt, Thread and the Hierarchy of Art and Craft in American Art, 1960–1980.* Minneapolis: University of Minnesota Press, 2009.

Bavor, Nancy. "The California Art Quilt Revolution." Master's thesis, University of Nebraska, 2011. http://digitalcommons.unl.edu/cehsdiss/98

Bavor, Nancy. "Common Threads: Nine California Art Quilt Pioneers." *Uncoverings* 33 (2012): 7–38.

Bere, Carol, ed. *The Art of the Quilt.* Morristown, NJ: Macculloch Hall Historical Museum, 1995.

Bernick, Susan E. "A Quilt Is an Art Object When It Stands Up Like a Man." In *Quilt Culture: Tracing the Pattern.* Edited by Cheryl B. Torsney and Judy Elsley, 134–150. Columbia: University of Missouri Press, 1994.

Chase, Pattie, with Mimi Dolbier. *The Contemporary Quilt: New American Quilts and Fabric Art.* Foreword by Radka Donnell. New York: E. P. Dutton, 1978.

Donnell, Radka. *Quilts as Women's Art: A Quilt Poetics.* North Vancouver, BC: Gallerie, 1990.

Farkas, Maxine, and Sandra Sider. *American Art Quits: Quilt 21/2000.* Exhibition catalogue with an introductory essay. Lowell, MA: Quilt 21 Press, 2000.

Hall-Patton, Colleen. "Jean Ray Laury in the 1960s: Foremother of a Quilt Revival." *Uncoverings 2005* (2005).

Ilse-Neuman, Ursula. Curator's statement for the exhibition *Art Quilts from the Collection of the Museum of Arts & Design*, at the American Textile History Museum, Lowell, MA, 2006.

James, Michael. "Beyond Tradition: The Art of the Studio Quilt." *American Craft* 45, no. 1 (February–March 1985): 16–22.

Kile, Michael, and Kiracofe, Roderick, eds. *The Quilt Digest 1–5.* San Francisco: Kiracofe and Kile, 1983.

Klaric, Arlette. *Contemporary Quilts USA.* Boston: Boston University Art Gallery, 1990.

Lenkowsky, Kate. *Contemporary Quilt Art: An Introduction and Guide.* Bloomington: Indiana University Press, 2008.

Leon, Eli. *Who'd a Thought It: Improvisation in African-American Quiltmaking.* San Francisco: San Francisco Craft and Folk Art Museum, 1987.

Lippard, Lucy. "Up, Down, and Across: A New Frame for New Quilts." In *The Artist and the Quilt.* Edited by Charlotte Robinson, 32–43. New York: Knopf, 1983.

Mazloomi, Carolyn. *Spirits of the Cloth: Contemporary African American Quilts.* Preface by Faith Ringgold. Foreword by Cuesta Benberry. New York: Clarkson Potter, 1998.

Mazloomi, Carolyn. *And Still We Rise: Race, Culture, and Visual Conversations.* Atglen, PA: Schiffer, 2015.

McMorris, Penny, and Michael Kile. *The Art Quilt.* San Francisco: Quilt Digest, 1984.

Packer, Barbara. *State of the Art Quilt: Contemporary Quilts for the Collector*. East Meadow, NY: Friends of Nassau City Recreation, 1985.

Peterson, Karin Elizabeth. "Discourse and Display: The Modern Eye, Entrepreneurship, and the Cultural Transformation of the Patchwork Quilt." *Sociological Perspectives* 46, no. 4 (Winter 2003): 461–490.

Pritchard, Gayle. *Uncommon Threads: Ohio's Art Quilt Revolution*. Athens: Ohio University Press, 2006.

Ramsey, Bets. "Art and Quilts, 1950–1970." *Uncoverings* 14 (1993): 9–39.

Reinstatler, Laura, and Smith, Kerry, eds. *Fine Art Quilts: Work by Artists of the Contemporary QuiltArt Association*. Bothell, WA: Fiber Studio Press, 1997.

Robinson, Sharon. *Contemporary Quilting*. Worcester, MA: Davis, 1982.

Seilman, Martha. *Masters: Art Quilts, Major Works by Leading Artists*. 2 vols. New York: Lark Books, 2008–2011.

Shaw, Robert. *The Art Quilt*. Southport, CT: Hugh Lauter Levin, 1997.

Shaw, Robert. *American Quilts: The Democratic Art, 1780–2007*. New York: Sterling, 2009.

Sider, Sandra. "Origins of American Art Quilts: Politics and Technology." In *Proceedings of the Textile History Forum 2007*. Edited by Jill Maney, 5–13. Cherry Valley, NY: Textile History Forum, 2007.

Sider, Sandra. *Pioneering Quilt Artists, 1960–1980: A New Direction in American Art*. New York: Photoart, 2010.

Steinbaum, Bernice. *The Definitive Contemporary American Quilt*. New York: Bernice Steinbaum Gallery, 1990.

Straus, Ludy. *Artist's Quilts: Quilts by Ten Contemporary Artists in Collaboration with Ludy Strauss*. Foreword by Jonathan Holstein. La Jolla, CA: La Jolla Museum of Contemporary Art, 1980.

Walker, Michelle. *Contemporary American Quilts*. London: Crafts Council, 1993.

INDEX

About the Authors

Nancy Bavor is currently the director of the San Jose Museum of Quilts & Textiles. She holds a bachelor's degree in art history from Northwestern University and a master's degree from the University of Nebraska–Lincoln, in the History of Textiles / Quilt Studies emphasis. Her thesis explored the origins and development of the art quilt in California ("The California Art Quilt Revolution," 2011). www.sjquiltmuseum.org

Lisa Ellis served as the president of Studio Art Quilt Associates from 2016 to 2018. A quilt artist, teacher, and lecturer, she is passionate about quilting and using quilts to make the world a better place. Lisa frequently lectures on healing quilts and inspires quilters to become involved in using their love of quilting to improve healthcare centers and hospitals. She has directed a number of projects for healing-related installations, including Walter Reed Army Medical Center, the University of Michigan, Auburn University, National Institutes of Health, and INOVA Fair Oaks Hospital. Ellis is also director of the nonprofit organization Sacred Threads. In 2010, she started her own company, Giving Back Technology, which provides information technology services to nonprofit museums, galleries, and other art organizations. Her website is www.ellisquilts.com.

Dr. Sandra Sider, a past president of Studio Art Quilt Associates and now curator for the Texas Quilt Museum and editor of *Art Quilt Quarterly*, has written about fiber and textile art for more than three decades. A studio quilt artist since the late 1970s, Sider focuses on photographic processes in her work, embellished with surface design techniques, including hand embroidery. Her art quilts have been acquired by several museums and corporate collections. She studied photography and printmaking at the School of Visual Arts (New York City) and Manhattan Graphics Center and has an MA in art history from the Institute of Fine Arts, New York University. Her website is www.sandrasider.com.

Martha Sielman is the executive director of Studio Art Quilt Associates, Inc. (SAQA), a nonprofit organization dedicated to advancing quilting as a fine-art medium. Sielman is the author of *Masters: Art Quilts, Major Works by Leading Artists*, Vols. 1 and 2 (New York: Lark Books, 2008–2011), *Art Quilt Portfolio: The Natural World* (New York: Lark Books, 2012), *Art Quilt Portfolio: People and Portraits* (New York: Lark Books, 2013), and *Art Quilts International: Abstracts and Geometrics* (Atglen, PA: Schiffer, 2016). Her website is www.marthasielman.com.

Left to right: Nancy Bavor, Photo: Clayton Bavor; Lisa Ellis;
Dr. Sandra Sider; and Martha Sielman, Photo: Bonnie McCaffery